Power-Glide
German Ultimate 2

Power-Glide
FOREIGN LANGUAGE
COURSES

Power-Glide German Ultimate 2
2004 Edition

Project Coordinator: James Blair

Development Manager: Dave Higginbotham

Editor: Heather Monson

Editorial Assistants: Jocelyn Spencer Rhynard, Debbie Haws, Erik D. Holley, Debi Rush, Robert Blair, Dell Blair, Matthias Kellmer, Adina Schröder, Sven Menson, Troy Cox

Translators: Matthias Kellmer, Sven Menson, Talita Osmond, Adina Schröder

Voice Talent: Dell Blair, Susan Farr, Thomas Glenn, Ingrid Kellmer, Matthias Kellmer, Andrew Mckee

Layout & Design: Erik D. Holley

Illustrators: Heather Monson, Apryl Robertson

Story Writers: Heather Monson, Kristen Knight

Musicians: Paul Anderson, Terrence Nicholson

Recording Engineers: Wade Chamberlain, Benjamin Blair

Power-Glide Language Courses, Inc.
1682 W 820 N, Provo, UT 84601

www.power-glide.com

Contents

NOTE

To track your progress through the course, place a ✓ in the ○ after you complete a semester, module, section, or activity. As a general guide, semesters take approximately 3 1/2 months to complete, modules take approximately 1 month, and sections take approximately 1 week. These times are just estimates—you're welcome to learn at your own pace!

Introduction

Using This Course

Welcome to Power-Glide Foreign Language Courses! You hold in your hands a very powerful and effective language learning tool. Power-Glide courses are designed so that individual students working alone can use them just as well as students in classrooms. However, before starting, we'd like to offer a few tips and explanations to help you get the most from your learning experience.

The course is divided into semesters, modules, sections, and activities. Each page has a tab denoting how it fits into the course structure, and students can use these tabs to navigate their way through the course.

Each semester has three modules. Each module has two or three sections, and each section begins with a page or two of adventure story, ends with a section quiz, and has several language activities in between.

Sections are followed by quizzes, and modules are followed by tests which we encourage students to use to solidify their mastery of the materials presented in the modules and sections. These quizzes and tests are very helpful for students seeking credit for their course work.

In this course, students will find a variety of different activities. These activities include Diglot Weave™ stories, counting and number activities, storytelling activities, activities designed to build conversational ability, audio-off activities for building reading comprehension, German-only activities for building listening comprehension, and much more. Word puzzles found at the beginning of some sections help the student to think and problem-solve German.

These different activity types accommodate different types of learning, and all are learner-tested and effective. Students will no doubt notice that each activity begins with a new picture. These pictures are drawn from German cultures and countries and are included for students' interest.

How to Use the Appendices

- Appendix A contains student answers for self quizzes, exercises, and section puzzles. Students using this appendix will receive immediate feedback on their work.

- Appendix B contains the Scope and Sequence for this course. This appendix outlines the specific language learning objectives for each section and is useful for students seeking credit or teachers looking to schedule curriculum.

- Appendix C is an index of marginalia, or information found in the margins throughout the course. In an effort to squeeze even more fun, useful information into this course, we have included cultural information on different German-speaking countries.

- Appendix D is a removable sheet designed for use by teachers or parents for grading purposes. Answers to module tests and section quizzes may be used by teachers to grade and track a student's progress through the course.

Students are encouraged to familiarize themselves with these appendices, as they can be valuable resources for finding information quickly.

Getting the Most Out of This Course

- Recognize the audio on and audio off symbols.
- Understand the text.
- Speak and write.

Audio Symbols

The audio-on and audio-off symbols, as mentioned previously, are highlighted bars like those below. Watch for them to know when to use your audio CDs.

When you see this bar, press play on your CD.

When you see this bar, press pause on your CD. Do not push stop. Pausing will allow you to continue the track where you left off, rather than at the beginning of the disc.

Understanding the Text

1. Look over the material and compare the German to the English.
2. Listen to the audio tracks while following the written text.
3. Listen to the audio tracks a couple of times without looking at the written text.
4. Use the pause button to stop the audio for a moment if you want more time to practice.

Speaking

1. Read the story or material out loud in chorus with the audio, and keep the meaning in mind.
2. Turn the audio off, read each sentence out loud in German, and then look away and repeat the same sentence without looking. Think of the meaning.
3. Now cover up the German, look at the first English sentence, and try to say it in German. Check to see if you did it right. Repeat this process for all the sentences in the activity.
4. Play the recording of the text, but pause the audio after each English sentence and say the German yourself.
5. Using notes of key words only, try to say the German sentences without using your activity book. It's okay to put the sentences into your own words, just keep them in German as much as possible.

Writing

To write, just follow the same directions for speaking, but write your sentences instead of speaking them.

Course Conventions

Objectives

Each activity has a shaded box letting learners know what they will learn during the activity.

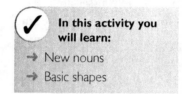

In this activity you will learn:
→ New nouns
→ Basic shapes

Sections also have objectives boxes. These section objectives are drawn from the activity objectives within the section. Appendix B contains a list of all the activity objectives for your convenience when reviewing for quizzes or tests.

Performance Challenges

While optional, students are encouraged to try performance challenges to fill out each activity and reinforce its content. Performance challenge boxes are located at the end of activities and look like this:

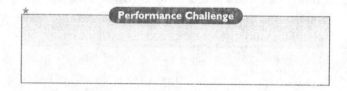

Performance Challenge

Not all activities have performance challenges and some have multiple challenges. Each performance challenge is labeled for use by an individual student or study group. If an activity has multiple performance challenges, the student may choose one or more to work on.

Audio Indicators

Some portions of this course have corresponding audio. The shaded audio boxes at the beginning of sections and selected activities indicate which audio disc and track to use. The sample audio box below indicates that disc 1, track 12 contains the audio for the given activity.

Recall the audio symbols described earlier.

You will use these bars together with the shaded audio box as you move through the course.

Here is a sample scenario for how to use the audio indicators:

- If an activity has audio, you will see the shaded audio box indicating which disc and track to use. In this example, we'll suppose that the audio box indicates disc 1, track 1.

- At the first audio-on bar you reach in the activity, insert audio disc 1 into your CD player and play track 1.

- When you reach the audio-off bar, press *pause*.

- The activity may or may not have more audio. If it does, you will see another audio-on bar. When you reach it, press *play*.

- When you reach another audio-off bar, press *pause* again.

- When you have finished your study session, press *stop* on your CD player.

Tracking Progress

The Table of Contents lists each semester, module, section, and activity in the course with a preceding checkmark circle. To track your progress through the course, place a ✓ in the ○ after you complete a semester, module, section, activity, semester test, module test, or section quiz. As a general guide, semesters take approximately 3 1/2 months to complete, modules take approximately 1 month, and sections take approximately 1 week. These times are just estimates—you're welcome to learn at your own pace!

The Power-Glide Difference

A Few of the Unique Features of Power-Glide

(And What They Mean To The Learner)

1. **Language specific.** Unlike most language training programs, Power-Glide courses are designed for speakers of specific languages, rather than the "one size fits all" approach. This takes advantage of what each language community knows and doesn't know, avoids wasted effort, and also allows special techniques to address language-specific problems.

2. **Based on up-to-date information/research on linguistics and learning methodology.** While the Power-Glide method is revolutionary, it is based on solid research and the most up-to-date information on the relevant disciplines.

3. **Involves learners in immediate use of the language in real situations.** Power-Glide courses avoid the drudgery of rote memorization of words and rules by immediately involving the learners in practical use of the language in real situations. This keeps interest, confidence, and motivation high.

4. **Uses adventure stories and activities.** From the beginning, the students are involved in an adventure story and activities that keep them engaged.

5. **Uses multiple methods of learning: music, stories, activities, and more.** People have different learning styles. By using various methods, music, stories, etc., everyone's style is addressed and learning is accelerated.

6. **Uses the Diglot Weave™ method.** Students start with familiar stories in their own language and gradually transition word by word, into the new language. The context provides the meaning and thus makes the learning an almost effortless, natural process.

7. **Takes learners from the known to the unknown along the easiest path.** While learning a foreign language can be challenging, it does not need to be brutal. The Power-Glide method guides the learners through the most productive and gentle paths.

8. **Uses memory devices and phonemic approximations.** Learning the right pronunciation and

remembering the words and phrases of another language are greatly facilitated by using memory devices and similar sounding words from the student's own language. This also reduces the "fear" of speaking the new language that many people experience.

9. **Doesn't require teachers.** One of the greatest advantages of Power-Glide courses is the fact that the teacher, parent, or facilitator doesn't need to know the language in order to assist the learner in the process. The one assisting also learns as an unexpected by-product of their teaching others.

10. **Many other linguistic strategies.** The variety of methods used increase motivation, retention, joy of learning, and desire to use the target language.

What People Are Saying About Power-Glide

Stephanie Heese, reviewer, *The Review Corner*:

"Speaking and thinking spontaneously in a foreign language is challenging, but is an important goal that is hard to achieve with traditional programs. In Power-Glide courses, emphasis is not on mechanics and rote learning. This course aims to teach children in a manner that simulates natural language acquisition."

Herbert Horne, linguist, former teacher for Wycliffe Bible Translators, and current homeschool co-op administrator:

"Thirty years ago, in Guatemala, I used Dr. Blair's materials and they were the best I had ever seen. Now that I could 'test' the materials with more than 40 students in various classes, I am even more convinced that they are the best language teaching materials in existence today."

Susan Moore, reviewer, *Editor's Choice*:

"Most curriculum developers seem to have forgotten what it was like to sit endlessly in a classroom listening and pretending to be interested in boring subject material, but not Dr. Blair."

Linda Rittner, Director, Pleasant Hill Academy:

"As one who designs educational programs for individual students in our school, I must tell you how impressed I have been with the Power-Glide material. I was able to examine the second year course material for our community college. Your course is more comprehensive!"

Anne Brodbeck, reviewer for Mary Pride's, *Practical Homeschooling*:

"Unlike other higher-priced courses, the approach does not contain repetitive drills, is not strictly hearsay, and does not promise subliminal learning. It is fast-paced and takes full concentration. The use of the full-sized textbook included with the [audio] makes it a more comprehensive course than others with twice the number of [audio CDs]."

Nancy Lande, author, *Homeschooling: A Patchwork of Days*:

"I really love the way that a concept is presented, used in various examples and then left for the student to take the next leap and apply key information in different ways. You can actually watch the light bulb flash brightly above your child's head! She gets it!"

Cafi Cohen, author, *And What about College? How Homeschooling Leads to Admissions to the Best Colleges and Universities*:

"I've been chipping away at Spanish for 20+ years and have purchased umpteen zillion programs. I was immediately impressed by how much conversational fluency I felt I gained in the two short hours of my flight home."

Semester 1

Module 1.1

Throughout this module we'll be learning about Berlin, Germany and Salzburg, Austria.

Keep these tips in mind as you progress through this module:

1. Read instructions carefully.

2. Repeat aloud all the German words you hear on the audio CDs.

3. Learn at your own pace.

4. Have fun with the activities and practice your new language skills with others.

5. Record yourself speaking German on tape so you can evaluate your own speaking progress.

N
Denmark
North Frisian Islands
Helgoland
Hamburg
Schwerin
Elbe River
Poland
Berlin
Netherlands
Harz Mountains
Düsseldorf
Cologne
Bonn
Germany
Liepzig
Weimar
Dresden
Belgium
Frankfurt
Luxembourg
Nuremberg
Czech Republic
Rhine River
Heidelberg
Danube River
Neuschwanstein
Stuttgart
France
Munich
Furtwangen
Bavaria
Salzburg
Vienna
Liechtenstein
Austria
Rust
Eisriesenwelt Caves
Bern
Lucerne
Innsbruck
Graz
Estavayer-le-Lac
Switzerland
Gurk
Schloss Oberhofen
Alps
Italy
Turin

A New Danger

It's pouring rain when you climb out of the old delivery truck, thank its driver, and rush across the street into your boss's Berlin office. You're glad you got out of the village of *Grünweise* before the worst of the storm broke. You hang your dripping overcoat in the entryway. You can't wait to finish this debriefing and get to your hotel for some real rest.

Unfortunately, as you enter the lobby, you notice that your boss's office is empty and dark. *"Sie ist in die Oper gegangen,"* the secretary explains. *"Sie möchte, dass Sie sich dort mit ihr treffen. Hier ist die Wegbeschreibung … und Ihre Eintrittskarte."* The secretary hands you a crisp, white envelope. You thank the secretary and slip back into your soggy overcoat. As you fight to get the wet fabric back over your clothes, you wonder what your boss is doing at the opera when she requested a late meeting with you.

Exhausted and annoyed, you walk back out into the glistening street where you catch a cab to the Berlin Opera House. You arrive during intermission and locate your boss in one of the boxes on the second level. Dripping wet and inappropriately dressed, you surreptitiously make your way past opera attendees milling around the lobby and up the stairs to your box seats. As you walk down the hallway, you see your boss through the glass window in the box door. You knock gently and let yourself in.

"Herzlich willkommen," she greets you warmly, "take a seat." She motions you to sit down next to her. Too tired to argue, you remove your rain-soaked coat and sit down.

The third seat in the box is occupied by one of your fellow secret agents. You and he have worked together before and nod to each other in greeting.

"I'm glad to see you two remember each other," your boss continues as you lean in. "As I was just telling Agent Spinne, you two will be working closely on this mission. I'm sorry to send you out again so soon, but this is important." You don't remember your boss ever looking quite so serious before. "This is perhaps the most crucial mission you, or any of us, will touch in our lifetimes, and I need my two best agents if we are going to be successful." She drops her voice to a whisper and says to you, "For this case, your code name will be Fliege."

"What's going on?" you ask.

"It's about the plague," says Spinne.

In this section you will:

- → Comprehend the meaning of a story.
- → Understand new vocabulary in a conversation or story.
- → Master object pronouns with finite and infinite verbs.
- → Test your knowledge of finite and infinite verbs.
- → Understand the story of "The Three Little Pigs" in German.
- → Understand new vocabulary in a conversation or story.
- → Understand and use small talk.

Disc 1   Track 1

"Plague?" you repeat.

"Of course, I'm sure the news hasn't reached a little village like *Grünweise* yet," your boss tells you, "but Spinne is right. One week ago, after you arrived in *Grünweise*, there was a bad outbreak back home. It hit eight major cities in 48 hours. You don't need me to tell you that indicates an organized attack. The plague is highly contagious and is spreading at a frightening rate."

"Is it deadly?" you ask. "What are the symptoms?"

"It starts with a simple head ache that turns into a fever, then…" your boss looks over at Spinne.

"Then what?" you prod.

"After about a week with a painful high fever, victims gradually slip into a coma and die." Your boss's face looks tired. You lean back in your chair, shocked at the news.

"Where did this come from?" you ask. "It doesn't sound like any disease I have heard of before."

You boss leans in closer, so as not to be heard. "Through our research, we've been able to determine that the plague is a variation of a disease that afflicted several of the *Habsburg* monarchs, as well as a number of the Bavarian royalty. It was known as the Red Starburst Plague, due to the strangely shaped sores it left on its victims' bodies."

"For centuries, the disease was rare—that's what the briefing said, anyway. It was mostly limited to royal families with a genetic susceptibility to it," Spinne interjects.

"Then we reached an age where we could manipulate the microorganism that caused the disease," your boss resumes. "Fliege, have you ever heard of a man named Franz Schuldig?"

You shake your head. "The name sounds familiar, but I can't place it."

"He's one of the world's foremost experts on microbiology," your boss explains. "For years, he put his knowledge and skills to great use. He developed very effective treatments for a dozen different diseases. He made a fortune. One year, he was even nominated for a Nobel Prize.

"Then his life took a grim turn. After a very messy ethical dispute at the firm where he worked, he left. Everyone assumed he'd gone into early retirement. We didn't learn how mistaken we were until one week ago, just after the plague outbreak hit the news, when leaders of most of the world's major governments received a letter from him. He proclaimed himself the rightful heir to the throne of Bavaria—"

"Bavaria?" Spinne interrupts.

"A part of Germany," your boss explains impatiently. "That should've been in your briefing, too, Spinne. Until the 1930s, it maintained a lot of autonomy and even had its own rulers. Have you ever heard of Mad King Ludwig?"

"Yes, of course," Spinne answers. "He had *Neuschwanstein* built, didn't he?"

"Along with other castles, yes," your boss continues. "He may himself have been a victim of this disease—his death remains very mysterious. Herr Schuldig is claiming descendency from that royal line and has proclaimed himself the rightful heir to the throne of Bavaria."

"He sounds crazy to me," says Spinne.

"Perhaps," your boss replies, "but dangerously so. In that letter, he claimed credit for the attack and told those leaders to whom he had written that if rule of Bavaria was not surrendered to him within one week, along with sufficient funds to establish a national army and treasury, he would strike down their nations until he and the re-established Bavaria were the only power remaining. If his demands were met, on the other hand, then he would make the cure available, and everyone—except those living in the area he wants to turn into Bavaria— could live happily ever after. He also wrote that if any attempts were made on his life, he had given other groups the wherewithal to make certain we were destroyed."

"I doubt our leaders took very kindly to that," you comment.

"Actually, none of them took it seriously at first," your boss answers ruefully. "Threats are nothing new, and horrible as it may sound, some groups will claim credit for things like this just for the media attention. We sent a team of operatives to 'retrieve' Herr Schuldig for questioning. They failed, and the very next day, just yesterday in fact, the plague broke out in eight previously unaffected cities. Now everyone believes that Herr Schuldig is capable of doing exactly as he threatened. However, no one is willing to negotiate with him after the awful things he has done, and even if someone were willing to negotiate, no one is having much luck finding him. As soon as he got wind of our capture attempt, he just vanished. We need that cure, though, and soon, or a lot of innocent people are going to die."

You nod and frown. This is not a good situation.

"That's not all," your boss continues. "We know now that Herr Schuldig hired other groups to help him. His own group doesn't yet have the numbers to cover all the nations he's threatened. One of these groups, code named Ungeschicklichkeit, accidentally released the plague on one of their own cells. So, they're pursuing the cure as well. They'll be a lot more ruthless in their pursuit, and you had better believe that if they get to it first, they won't be sharing with the rest of the world."

"Where did this plague come from?" you ask next.

"Shuldig found it on some royal artifacts from that time period, and through some creative manipulations developed a new and significantly more deadly strain of the virus," your boss explains.

"And more contagious," says Spinne. "Before Shuldig, the disease was limited to individuals with a particular genetic predisposition. This new strain, however, isn't picky, and can be caught by any one. All it takes is casual contact with the virus… touching the same cup, newspaper, or doorknob as an infected person."

"Wow," you say wearily, rubbing your forehead.

"It's spreading like wildfire," your boss continues. "People who have been exposed but aren't yet sick are fleeing the affected cities—and, in some cases, the entire country—as fast as they can. Quarantines aren't working. Even if there isn't another release of the plague, what's already there could bring all our major cities to their knees within the month and could decimate populations around the world within the year."

"How long does it take the disease to become terminal?" you ask.

"Three weeks," says Spinne grimly.

"We are running out of time," you murmur.

Your boss nods and frowns. "That's right. In time, doctors will be able to create an antidote, but it may be too late by then."

"You want us to find Schuldig's antidote," you guess.

"Exactly," your boss replies. The orchestra strikes up the first notes, and the lights dim—intermission is ending.

"You didn't know I loved opera did you?" your boss asks, shooting you a fleeting smile.

"No, I didn't," you whisper in response.

"Actually, this is not a performance simply for my pleasure," she answers, "we are here to find a clue."

Both you and Spider move your chairs in closer as your boss pulls a faded music score from her brief case. "Shuldig's operation isn't quite flawless. One of his employees has a conscience and has been concealing clues that lead to the antidote in each place he has visited. It couldn't be easy or obvious—interception would mean his death as well as his failure," your boss says as she straightens the papers on her knee.

"This secret informant seems to have a real passion for music," she continues. "This is an original score, very valuable. Yesterday, one of my contacts found it on top of the opera's archives. No one in their right mind would destroy it, but it wouldn't be an uncommon thing to find at many of the historical sites he and his employer seem to have visited. The first two pages have a message in invisible ink—some sort of riddle, I believe."

She hands the first two sheets of music to you. Notes are written in a bold, old-fashioned hand on both sides of each sheet. The heading at the top of the first page informs you that this is Wagner's "Flight of the Valkyries." She then hands you a small lighter in an elegant mother-of-pearl case. "Use this. Be careful not to singe the paper."

You hold the first page close to the light. As the light heats the paper, narrow, spidery handwriting appears beneath the notes. You read aloud, *"Unter der Erde und über dem Meer, hinter den sieben Schlössern, die alle geöffnet werden müssen, damit das Heilmittel nicht auf immer verloren geht. Silber in der Hand des Klavierstimmers; Holz versteckt sich hinter Vogelgesang, tief im Wald; Stein, mit bitterem Salz vermischt, ruht tief in der Erde; Feuer im Herzen des Löwen; Eis in den sich ständig wandelnden Höhlen, hoch über den Tälern; Gold vom Tisch des Königs; Eisen aus seiner Krone."*

You take the page away from the light, and the writing fades.

"Underground and over sea, behind the seven locks—each one must be opened, or the cure's forever lost. Silver in the tuner's hand; wood hides in birdsong, deep in the forest; stone, mixed with bitter salt, lies deep underground; fire in the lion's heart; ice in the shifting caves, high above the valleys; gold from the king's table; iron from his crown," you repeat in English. You shake your head. "That doesn't make much sense, and it doesn't explain what we're doing at the opera, either."

Your boss lifts a pair of opera glasses to look at the colorful performers on stage. "Check the next page, Fliege. I'll need to ask the stage manager to be certain, but I think this might be where his silver key is hidden."

You place the second sheet of paper close to the light, and a single line of text appears and darkens. *Wem gibt der kleine Junge die Blume?*

"I don't understand," you say, looking puzzled at your boss.

She smiles and hands you a book full of German activities. "Here you go. This is a great time to learn. You and Spinne don't have much time, so get to work. Decipher the clue in German, then retrieve the first key. You have no time to waste. There are thousands of lives depending on you."

Questions of a Small Child 4

✓ **In this activity you will:**

→ Comprehend the meaning of a story.

 Disc **1**   Track **2**

INSTRUCTIONS   Listen to and read the following dialogue.

English	German
Why do birds eat insects?	*Warum fressen Vögel Insekten?*
Because they like to eat them.	*Weil sie es mögen, sie zu fressen.*
Do I eat insects?	*Esse ich Insekten?*
No, you don't eat insects.	*Nein, du isst keine Insekten.*
You and Daddy, do you eat insects?	*Du und Vati, esst ihr Insekten?*
No, we don't eat insects.	*Nein, wir essen keine Insekten.*
Why?	*Warum?*
Well…because we are not birds.	*Hmm…weil wir keine Vögel sind.*

Performance Challenge

Individual 1   Write ten "Why" questions in German. Research the answers and share them with a friend or family member.

The Habsburgs, Part 1

The name Habsburg is derived from the Swiss Habichtsburg, referring to Hawk Castle in Switzerland. This was the seat of the Habsburg family during the 12th and 13th centuries.

1. ....

2. ....

3. ....

4. ....

5. ....

6. ....

7. ....

8. ....

9. ....

10. ....

Performance Challenge

Individual 2   Find a German-speaker in your town or city. Interview them using at least ten "Why" questions. Write an article or essay based on the information you collect from the interview.

Performance Challenge

Group 1   Choose a variety of Power-Glide Flash Cards and place them in a hat. Create teams and have them play twenty questions using the words from the hat.

Performance Challenge

Group 2   Organize a singing contest where learners must choose a song that contains at least three questions. Have them translate as many of the lyrics into German as they can. Next, have each student (or student group) perform their song.

The Lazy Son

ACTIVITY 2

 In this activity you will:

→ Understand new vocabulary in a conversation or story.

 Disc **I** Track **3**

INSTRUCTIONS Listen to this joke. Can you repeat it in German?

English	German
A son was complaining to his father.	*Ein Sohn beklagte sich bei seinem Vater.*
"I don't want to go to school."	*"Ich möchte nicht zur Schule gehen."*
The father said:	*Der Vater sagte:*
"Johnny, give me three reasons why you shouldn't go."	*"Johnny, gib mir drei Gründe, warum du nicht gehen sollst."*
The son responded:	*Der Sohn antwortete:*
"School is boring.	*"Schule ist langweilig.*
You have to work too much, and my teachers don't like me."	*Du musst zu viel arbeiten und meine Lehrer mögen mich nicht."*
"I understand your feelings, Johnny.	*"Ich verstehe deine Gefühle, Johnny.*
Sometimes I felt the same.	*Manchmal fühlte ich mich auch so.*
But let me give you three reasons why you should go anyway:	*Aber lass mich dir drei Gründe geben, warum du trotzdem gehen solltest:*
Some things we have to do, even if we don't feel like doing them.	*Manche Dinge müssen wir tun, selbst wenn wir uns nicht danach fühlen, sie zu tun.*
You are 47 years old.	*Du bist 47 Jahre alt.*
You're the principal!"	*Du bist der Schuldirektor!"*

Performance Challenge

Individual I　Take a walk around your block. On a piece of paper write the German names of fifteen activities you saw on your walk that could be described as "lazy."

....

....

....

....

....

....

....

....

....

....

....

Performance Challenge

Individual 2　Talk to a local school or pen pal agency about finding a German-speaking pen pal who is your age. In your first letter, ask them at least five questions about their school.

Performance Challenge

Group 1　Set up a pen pal program for your students (go through local school administration or a pen pal agency). Ask students to include a description about their school in the first letter and to ask at least five questions about the recipient's school.

Performance Challenge

Group 2　Set up stations throughout the room. At each station, place cards that list school-related items in German. Give the students a characteristic of the items they need to pick up at each station (e.g., things to write with, etc.).

Discovery of Grammar 12

 In this activity you will:

→ Master object pronouns with finite and infinite verbs.

INSTRUCTIONS   In this lesson you will learn about the infinitive—the base form or dictionary entry form of the verb—for the verbs *sollen* 'supposed to' and *wollen* 'want to.'

	English	German
1.	I can be here today.	*Ich <u>kann</u> heute hier <u>sein</u>.*
2.	You can have the money.	*Du <u>kannst</u> das Geld <u>haben</u>.*
3.	I must buy this book.	*Ich <u>muss</u> dieses Buch <u>kaufen</u>.*
4.	You must read it, you must study it.	*Du <u>musst</u> es <u>lesen</u>, du <u>musst</u> es <u>lernen</u>.*
5.	Hans can read and write Chinese.	*Hans <u>kann</u> Chinesisch <u>lesen</u> und <u>schrei-ben</u>.*
6.	One must work hard.	*Man <u>muss</u> hart <u>arbeiten</u>.*
7.	One should also play a bit.	*Man <u>muss</u> auch ein bisschen <u>spielen</u>.*
8.	You should eat wisely.	*Du <u>sollst</u> weise <u>essen</u>.*
9.	You must think clearly.	*Du <u>musst</u> klar <u>denken</u>.*
10.	You should learn this today.	*Du <u>sollst</u> das heute <u>lernen</u>.*
11.	You must learn to think clearly.	*Du <u>musst</u> lernen klar <u>zu</u> <u>denken</u>.*
12.	You've got to speak louder and more clearly.	*Du <u>musst</u> lauter und klarer <u>sprechen</u>.*
13.	I want to see and hear.	*Ich <u>will</u> besser <u>sehen</u> und <u>hören</u>.*
14.	Do you want to study now?	*<u>Willst</u> du jetzt <u>lernen</u>?*
15.	I cannot understand that.	*Ich <u>kann</u> das nicht <u>verstehen</u>.*

Commentary

The second underlined word in each of these sentences is in the infinitive form, which does not change. Dictionaries list verbs in their infinitive forms. The German infinitive always ends in *-n*, and except for the verb *sein*, the infinitive is always identical to the present tense plural form that you know (i.e. *wir haben*). In English, the particle "to" is often placed in front of the infinitive (i.e. "to go" or "to learn"). In German, the particle *"zu"* is used much the same way.

INSTRUCTIONS Write the meaning of these eleven high-frequency verbs. Check your answers in Appendix A, on page 389.

	Verb	Your Translation
1.	*kaufen*	
2.	*schreiben*	
3.	*arbeiten*	
4.	*spielen*	
5.	*verstehen*	
6.	*lesen*	
7.	*denken*	
8.	*lernen*	
9.	*sprechen*	
10.	*sehen*	
11.	*hören*	

Note the cognates among these: *lern-* with learn, *denk-* with think, *seh-* with see, *hör-* with hear, *schreib-* with scribe, and *arbeit-* with (believe it or not) robot. Can you come up with a memory aid for *lesen, kaufen, sprechen,* and *verstehen?*

Modal Auxiliary Verbs

The first underlined verb in each of the model strings is a modal auxiliary, parallel in form and function with English modal auxiliaries.

Study the present-tense conjugation of *können* (can, be able to), *müssen* (must, have to), *wollen* (want to, will), and *sollen* (should, shall) in the sentence frame "I ____ learn it."

Person	Singular	Plural	Singular or Plural
1st	*Ich kann es lernen*	*Wir können es lernen*	
2nd	*Du kannst es lernen*	*Ihr könnt es lernen*	*Sie können es lernen*
3rd	*Er / sie / es kann es lernen*	*Sie können es lernen*	

The Habsburgs, Part II

The Habsburg family was split into two groups, the Austrian Habsburgs and the Spanish Habsburgs. In 1700 the Spanish Habsburgs died out, followed by the Austrian Habsburgs in 1740. The extinction of both lines is attributed to extensive inter-marrying within the two families.

ACTIVITY 3

Person	Singular	Plural	Singular or Plural
1st	Ich <u>muss</u> es lernen	Wir <u>müssen</u> es lernen	
2nd	Du <u>musst</u> es lernen	Ihr <u>müsst</u> es lernen	Sie <u>müssen</u> es lernen
3rd	Er / sie / es <u>muss</u> es lernen	Sie <u>müssen</u> es lernen	
1st	Ich <u>will</u> es lernen	Wir <u>wollen</u> es lernen	
2nd	Du <u>willst</u> es lernen	Ihr <u>wollt</u> es lernen	Sie <u>wollen</u> es lernen
3rd	Er / sie / es <u>will</u> es lernen	Sie <u>wollen</u> es lernen	
1st	Ich <u>soll</u> es lernen	Wir <u>sollen</u> es lernen	
2nd	Du <u>sollst</u> es lernen	Ihr <u>sollt</u> es lernen	Sie <u>sollen</u> es lernen
3rd	Er / sie / es <u>soll</u> es lernen	Sie <u>sollen</u> es lernen	

Self Quiz

INSTRUCTIONS Read the English to get the meaning and then supply the missing words. Check your answers in Appendix A, on page 389.

> **NOTE**
>
> Remember from German I that the English word *you* has two forms: *du* (informal) and *sie* (formal). The word *You* (capital Y) refers to *sie*; while *you* refers to *du*.

	English	German
1.	I want to learn German.	Ich _____ Deutsch _____.
2.	We want to speak German well.	Wir _____ gutes Deutsch _____.
3.	Do You want to study German today?	_____ Sie heute Deutsch _____?
4.	Why must we speak louder?	Warum _____ wir lauter _____?
5.	Are they not able to hear us?	_____ sie uns nicht _____?
6.	Do you want to work or play?	_____ du _____ oder _____?
7.	Can You understand Chinese?	_____ Sie Chinesisch _____?
8.	Should you buy a car?	_____ du ein Auto _____?
9.	One must study and think hard.	Man _____ hart _____ und _____.
10.	They want to play with us now.	Sie _____ jetzt mit uns _____.

Performance Challenge

Individual 1   Write a song using all infinitive verbs. Perform the song or record it and share it with a friend or family-member. Rough out some ideas below.

....

....

....

....

....

....

....

Performance Challenge

Individual 2   Create a Diglot Weave™ using a piece of classic literature. Take a chapter of a book in English and translate all its modal auxiliary verbs into German. Read the chapter to a friend and see how many of the verbs they understand.

Performance Challenge

Group 1   Have students select either song-writing or poetry. Have them write a poem or song using only infinitives. Have them perform or read their work to the group.

Performance Challenge

Group 2   Split students into groups. Give each group ten Power-Glide Flash Cards. Using a stop watch, have them create as many sentences as they can with the flash cards, using modal auxiliary verbs.

Discovery of Grammar 12: Understanding

 In this activity you will:

→ Test your knowledge of finite and infinite verbs.

Self Quiz

INSTRUCTIONS   Translate the following sentences. Check your answers in Appendix A, on page 389.

1. I must study better.

   ....

2. They want to learn German with us.

   ....

3. Hans, you should read this book.

   ....

4. Mr. and Mrs. Schultz, You should buy a new car.

   ....

   ....

5. Can we buy a boat?

   ....

6. We can speak a bit faster. Is that better?

   ....

7. Hans, you must speak a bit louder.

   ....

8. Where do You want to work?

   ....

9. Can You work with us today?

....

10. Can you hear me now?

....

11. Who can write Chinese?

....

12. I can read Chinese, but I can't write it.

....

Scoring

INSTRUCTIONS Write the number of sentences you wrote correctly in the first score box. If you wrote three or more of the sentences incorrectly, review the material again. Then retake the test.

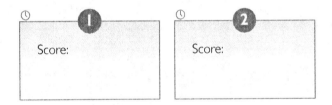

Score:

Score:

The Three Little Pigs

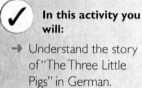

In this activity you will:

→ Understand the story of "The Three Little Pigs" in German.

INSTRUCTIONS Read this familiar story. Then cover the English and read the story again in German, working on your pronunciation.

English	German
There were once three pigs.	Es waren einmal drei Schweine.
Three little pigs.	Drei kleine Schweine.
They were brothers.	Sie waren Brüder.
But they were not the same.	Aber sie waren nicht gleich.
One day they were conversing.	Eines Tages unterhielten sie sich.
The three wanted to build themselves a house.	Die drei wollten sich ein Haus bauen.
As they were talking, they saw a man in a truck with a load of straw.	Während sie sich unterhielten, sahen sie einen Mann in einem Lastwagen mit einer Ladung Stroh.
"Let's build us a house of straw," said the first little pig.	"Lasst uns ein Haus aus Stroh bauen," sagte das erste kleine Schwein.
"No, we don't want a house of straw," said his brothers.	"Nein, wir möchten kein Haus aus Stroh," sagten seine Brüder.
"Well, then I am going to build it myself," said the first little pig.	"Na gut, dann werde ich es selbst bauen," sagte das erste kleine Schwein.
Then he went to talk with the man, and said to him:	Dann ging es hin, um mit dem Mann zu sprechen, und sagte ihm:
"Please, sir, sell me Your straw so that I can build my house with it."	"Bitte, mein Herr, verkaufen Sie mir Ihr Stroh, mit dem ich mein Haus bauen kann."
"Very well," said the man.	"Sehr gut," sagte der Mann.

English (cont.)	German
And he sold the straw to the first little pig, who rapidly built himself a house of straw.	Und er verkaufte das Stroh dem ersten kleinen Schwein, das sich schnell ein Strohhaus baute.
The second little pig saw a man in a truck with a load of sticks.	Das zweite kleine Schwein sah einen Mann in einem Lastwagen mit einer Ladung Zweige.
"You and me, let's build us a house of sticks," he said to the third little pig.	"Du und ich, lass uns ein Haus aus Zweige bauen," sagte es dem dritten kleinen Schwein.
"No, I don't want a house of sticks," said the third little pig.	"Nein, ich will kein Haus aus Zweige," sagte das dritte kleine Schwein.
"Well, then I am going to build it myself," said the second little pig.	"Na gut, denn werde ich es selbst bauen," sagte das zweite kleine Schwein.
Then he went to talk with the man, and he said to him:	Dann ging es hin, um mit dem Mann zu sprechen und es sagte ihm:
"Please, sir, sell me Your sticks so that I can build my house with them."	"Bitte, mein Herr, verkaufen Sie mir Ihre Zweige, mit denen ich mein Haus bauen kann."
"Very well," said the man.	"Sehr gut," sagte der Mann.
And he sold the sticks to the second little pig, who quickly built himself a house of sticks.	Und er verkaufte die Zweige dem zweiten kleinen Schwein, das sich schnell ein Zweighaus baute.
The third little pig didn't want a house of straw.	Das dritte Schwein wollte kein Strohhaus.
Nor did he want a house of sticks.	Noch wollte es kein Zweighaus.
But he saw a man in a truck with a load of bricks.	Aber es sah einen Mann in einem Lastwagen mit einer Ladung Ziegelsteine.
Then he decided to build a house of bricks.	Dann entschloss es sich ein Ziegelsteinhaus zu bauen.
He went to talk with the man.	Es ging hin, um mit dem Mann zu sprechen.
"Please, sir, sell me Your bricks so that I can build my house with them."	"Bitte, mein Herr, verkaufen Sie mir Ihre Ziegelsteine, mit denen ich mein Haus bauen kann."
"Very well," said the man.	"Sehr gut," sagte der Mann.

English *(cont.)*	German
And he sold the bricks to the third little pig, who quickly built himself a house of bricks.	*Und er verkaufte die Ziegelsteine dem dritten kleinen Schwein, das sich schnell ein Ziegelsteinhaus baute.*
Soon came a big, bad wolf.	*Bald kam ein großer, böser Wolf.*
He was hungry.	*Er war hungrig.*
And when he saw the house of straw with the first little pig inside, he knocked on the door and said:	*Und als er das Strohhaus, mit dem ersten kleinen Schwein darin sah, klopfte er an die Tür und sagte:*
"Little pig, little pig, let me in."	*"Kleines Schwein, kleines Schwein, lass mich herein."*
"No, you are the big, bad wolf; I won't let you come in here."	*"Nein! Du bist der große, böse Wolf; ich lasse dich nicht herein."*
"Then I'll huff and I'll puff until your house falls flat."	*"Dann werde ich blasen und pusten, bis dein Haus flach umfällt."*
And he huffed and he puffed until the house fell flat.	*Und er blies und pustete, bis das Haus flach umfiel.*
But the little pig went running to the house of the second pig.	*Aber das kleine Schwein rannte zu dem Haus des zweiten kleinen Schweines.*
The big, bad wolf couldn't catch him.	*Der große, böse Wolf konnte es nicht fangen.*
And the little pig escaped.	*Und das kleine Schwein entkam.*
Now the big, bad wolf was very angry, but he tried not to let it be seen how angry he was.	*Nun war der große, böse Wolf sehr zornig, aber er versuchte sich nicht anmerken zu lassen, wie zornig er war.*
He came to the house of the second little pig, the house of sticks, and said:	*Er kam zu dem Haus des zweiten kleinen Schweins, dem Zweighaus, und sagte:*
"Little pig, little pig, let me come in."	*"Kleines Schwein, kleines Schwein, lass mich herein."*
"No! You are the big, bad wolf; I won't let you in."	*"Nein! Du bist der große, böse Wolf; ich lasse dich nicht herein."*
"Then I'll huff and I'll puff until your house falls flat."	*"Dann werde ich blasen und pusten, bis dein Haus flach umfällt."*
And he huffed and he puffed until the house fell flat.	*Und er blies und pustete, bis das Haus flach umfiel.*

The Habsburgs, Part III

The Habsburg monarchs increased their ruling influence as they acquired several areas of land throughout central Europe. Leopold I, Joseph I, and Charles VI, of the Austrian Habsburgs, took over land in an area of the modern Czech Republic by driving the last Ottoman invaders out of Hungary.

English *(cont.)*	German
But the two little pigs went running to the house of bricks that belonged to their brother.	*Aber die zwei kleinen Schweine rannten zu dem Ziegelsteinhaus, das ihrem Bruder gehörte.*
The big, bad wolf was unable to catch them.	*Der große, böse Wolf war unfähig, sie zu fangen.*
And the little pigs escaped.	*Und die kleinen Schweine entkamen.*
Now indeed the big, bad wolf was really angry.	*Nun war der große, böse Wolf wirklich sehr zornig.*
And he was hungry.	*Und er war hungrig.*
But he tried not to let it be seen how angry he was.	*Aber er versuchte sich nicht anmerken zu lassen, wie zornig er war.*
He came to the house of the third little pig, the house of bricks, and said:	*Er kam zu dem Haus des dritten kleinen Schweins, das Ziegelsteinhaus, und sagte:*
"Little pig, little pig, let me in."	*"Kleines Schwein, kleines Schwein, lass mich herein."*
"No! You are the big, bad wolf; I won't let you in."	*"Nein! Du bist der große, böse Wolf; ich lasse dich nicht herein."*
"Then I'll huff and I'll puff until your house falls down."	*"Dann werde ich blasen und pusten, bis dein Haus flach umfällt."*
And he huffed and he puffed, and he puffed and he huffed, but he could not blow down the house of bricks.	*Und er blies und er pustete, und er pustete und er blies, aber er konnte das Ziegelsteinhaus nicht niederblasen.*
Finally the wolf went away, but very angry and very hungry.	*Schließlich ging der Wolf weg, aber sehr zornig und sehr hungrig.*
Then the first and the second little pigs said to the third little pig:	*Dann sagten das erste und das zweite kleine Schwein dem dritten kleinen Schwein:*
"Thanks, brother, for building a strong house."	*"Danke, Bruder, dass du ein stabiles Haus gebaut hast."*
And the three little pigs lived happily in the house of bricks for many years.	*Und die drei kleinen Schweinchen lebten viele Jahre glücklich in dem Ziegelsteinhaus.*
But the wolf died of hunger.	*Aber der Wolf starb vor Hunger.*
The poor wolf!	*Der arme Wolf!*

Performance Challenge

Individual   Write (and illustrate) a story about what happens to either the pigs or the wolf after the end of the story. Rough out some ideas below.

....

....

....

....

....

....

....

....

....

....

....

....

....

....

....

....

Performance Challenge

Group   Have students write a two-act play where the first act is the story of the three pigs and the second act is a new, additional story using the same characters. Have them perform it for each other, other students, or family and friends.

A Little Boy and a Flower

INSTRUCTIONS   Listen to and read this story. Recite the German text with the voice on the audio.

✓ **In this activity you will:**
→ Understand new vocabulary in a conversation or story.

Ein kleiner Junge fand eine schöne Blume.

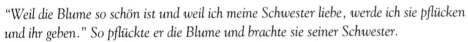

Disc **1**   Track **4**

"Weil die Blume so schön ist und weil ich meine Schwester liebe, werde ich sie pflücken und ihr geben." So pflückte er die Blume und brachte sie seiner Schwester.

"Hier," sagte er, "nimm dies! Die Blume ist von mir für dich. Sie bedeutet, dass ich dich liebe." Die Schwester nahm die Blume und sagte:

"Dann lieben wir einander. Danke, lieber Bruder." Die Schwester brachte die Blume ihrem Vater, gab sie ihm und sagte:

"Hier, nimm dies! Diese Blume ist für dich von mir. Sie bedeutet, dass ich dich liebe." Der Vater nahm die Blume und sagte:

"Dann lieben wir einander. Danke, liebe Tochter." Der Vater brachte die Blume seiner Frau, gab sie ihr und sagte:

"Hier, nimm dies! Diese Blume ist für dich von mir. Sie bedeutet, dass ich dich liebe." Die Frau nahm die Blume und sagte:

"Dann lieben wir einander. Danke, lieber Mann."

Performance Challenge

Individual 1   Visit a local nursery. Write down the names of your favorite flowers. When you get home, draw the flowers that you saw and rename them with your own descriptive German names.

Performance Challenge

Individual 2   Write a paragraph in German about five people you love and tell why you love them. Write each of them a letter describing five things you like about them. Teach them at least five German words in your letter. Rough out some ideas below.

....

....

....

....

....

....

....

....

....

....

....

....

Performance Challenge

Group 1   Show the students a flower painting by a German artist. Have them create a story about the painting or write an essay about why they think the artist made the choices he/she did.

Performance Challenge

Group 2   Have your students write valentines for each other or for another group of students using only German. Include *Strudel* or some other German pastry with the valentines.

A Small Child Answers the Phone

INSTRUCTIONS Listen to this conversation. Can you repeat it to someone else?

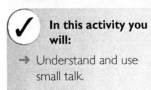

In this activity you will:
→ Understand and use small talk.

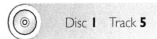

Disc **1** Track **5**

	English	German
(Whisper)	Hello.	Hallo.
(Caller)	Hello. Is your mother there?	Hallo. Ist deine Mutter da?
(Whisper)	Yes.	Ja.
(Caller)	May I talk with her?	Darf ich mit ihr sprechen?
(Whisper)	No.	Nein.
(Caller)	Why not?	Warum nicht?
(Whisper)	She's busy.	Sie ist beschäftigt.
(Caller)	Is your Father there?	Ist dein Vater da?
(Whisper)	Yes.	Ja.
(Caller)	May I talk with him?	Darf ich mit ihm sprechen?
(Whisper)	No.	Nein.
(Caller)	Why not?	Warum nicht?
(Whisper)	He's busy.	Er ist beschäftigt.
(Caller)	Well, is anyone else there?	Naja, ist jemand anders da?
(Whisper)	Yes.	Ja.
(Caller)	Who?	Wer?
(Whisper)	Hmm.	Hmm.
(Caller)	Who? Tell me!	Wer? Sag's mir!

	English (cont.)	German
(Whisper)	Some neighbors and some police.	*Einige Nachbarn und die Polizei.*
(Caller)	Oh, is there something wrong?	*Oh, stimmt da etwas nicht?*
(Whisper)	No.	*Nein.*
(Caller)	Well, could I talk with one of them?	*Nun, könnte ich mit jemandem von ihnen sprechen?*
(Whisper)	No.	*Nein.*
(Caller)	Why not?	*Warum nicht?*
(Whisper)	They're all busy.	*Sie sind alle beschäftigt.*
(Caller)	Well, what are they doing?	*Hmm, was machen sie denn?*
(Whisper)	They're looking for me.	*Sie suchen mich.*

Performance Challenge

Individual   Write a story about something you did as a small child. Use as much German as you can. Illustrate the story with at least two pictures when you are done and share it with a young child. Rough out some ideas below.

....

....

....

....

....

....

Performance Challenge

Group   Split students into pairs. Have them write their own phone "scenes" in German. Once complete, using real phones as props, have them act out their scenes for the group.

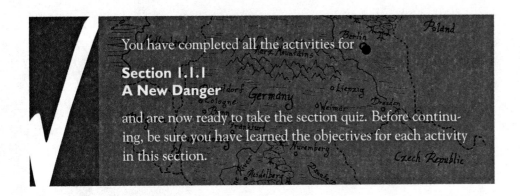

You have completed all the activities for

**Section 1.1.1
A New Danger**

and are now ready to take the section quiz. Before continuing, be sure you have learned the objectives for each activity in this section.

Section 1.1.1 Quiz

INSTRUCTIONS   Choose the correct response. Check your answers in Appendix D, on page 402.

1. In "The Lazy Son," which one of these was NOT stated as a reason why he should go to school?

   A. *Du bist 47 Jahre alt.*

   B. *Manche Dinge müssen wir tun, selbst wenn wir uns nicht danach fühlen, sie zu tun.*

   C. *Schule ist langweilig.*

   D. *Du bist der Schuldirektor.*

2. **"*Du musst lernen klar zu denken*" is correctly translated as:**

   A. You must think clearly.

   B. You never think clearly.

   C. You must learn this today

   D. You must learn to think clearly

3. **Who eats insects?**

   A. *Kinder*

   B. *Vögel*

   C. *Vati*

   D. *du*

4. **Which verb is in 2nd person plural form?**

   A. *könnt*

   B. *kann*

   C. *kannst*

   D. *können*

5. **Which verb is in 3rd person singular form?**

   A. *sollen*

   B. *sollt*

   C. *soll*

   D. *sollst*

6. **Where did the little pigs get the materials to build their houses?**

   A. *eine Schweine*

   B. *eine Blume*

   C. *eine Tochter*

   D. *ein Mann mit einen Lastwagen*

7. ***kaufen* means:**

   A. today

   B. think

   C. buy

   D. understand

8. ***arbeiten* means:**

   A. work

   B. eat

   C. speak

   D. must

9. **Infinitives usually end with the letter:**

   A. r

   B. e

   C. h

   D. n

10. **In "A Small Child Answers the Phone," why can't the child's mother come to the phone?**

    A. *Sie möchtet nicht.*

    B. *Sie ist beschäftigt.*

    C. *Sie ist nicht zu Hause.*

    D. *Sie hat ein stabiles Haus gebaut.*

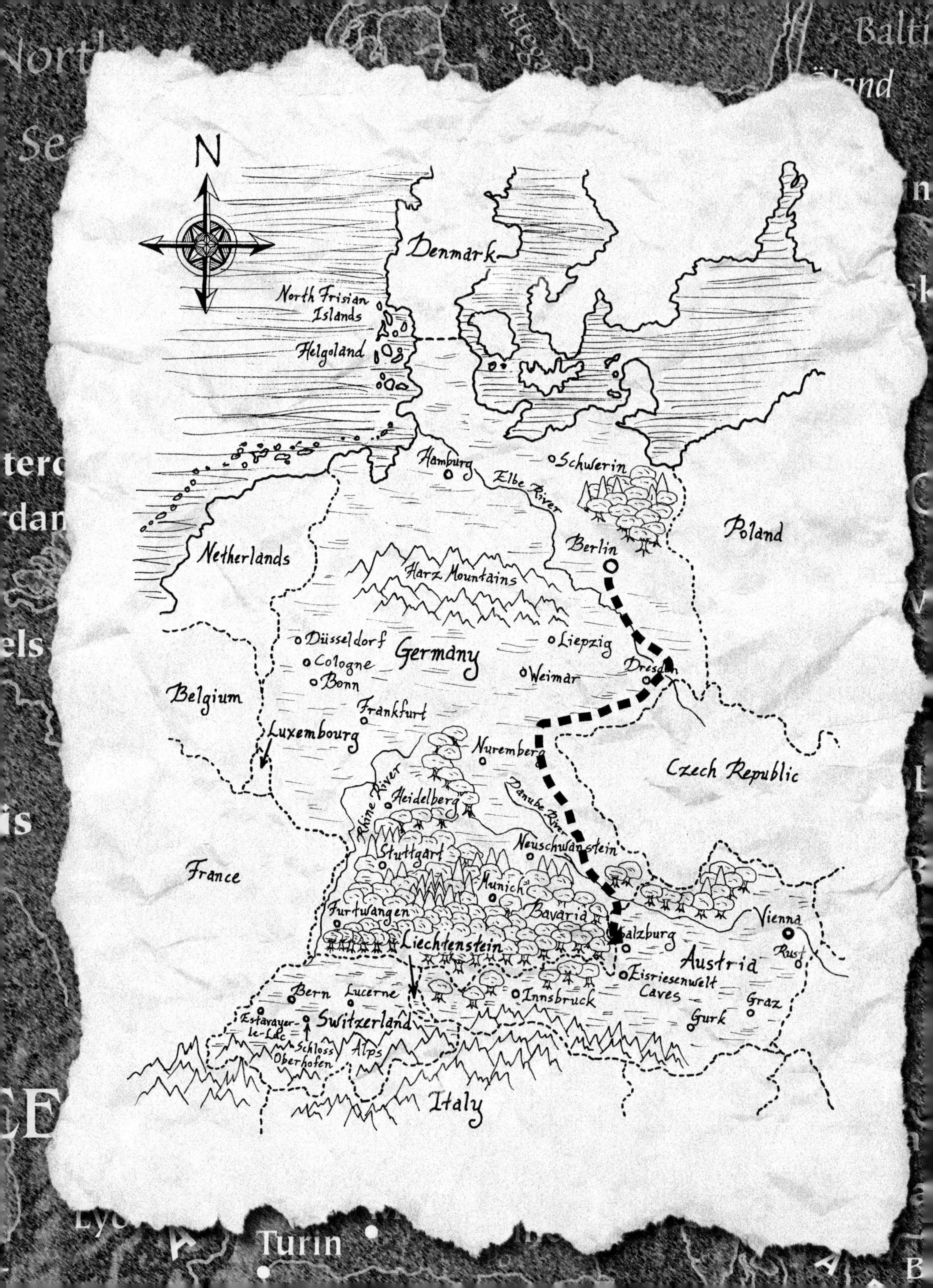

At the Opera

"I GOT IT!" shouts Spinne in the middle of the solo by a statuesque singer. The audience members in the boxes around you shush angrily.

"What is it?" asks your boss, whispering as quietly as she can.

"It's the sister of the boy in the story, 'A Little Boy and a Flower,'" Spinne comments.

Just then, an explosion of applause erupts throughout the hall.

The opera is over. The performers take their bows. As the house lights rise, you notice intricate carved relief around each layer of seating in the opera house. Flowers intermixed with ribbons, shells, and cherubs seem to drip from the ceiling. You wonder if the key is hidden somewhere in the carvings.

"Can I borrow your opera glasses?" you ask your boss.

"Sure, here you go," she responds as she offers them to you. You scan the relief work in the opera house to see if you can find any clues. After several minutes of searching, you lay the opera glasses down.

"See anything interesting?" Spinne asks.

"No. There has to be a faster way." You rub your eyes and check your watch, you realize that you haven't slept for a full 36 hours.

Your boss stands and gathers her belongings to leave. "Here, this might help," she says, handing the remainder of the sheet music to Spinne. "I was given this by the director of this opera. He is probably a good place to start."

"Great," you say. "What is his name?"

"You can check the playbill for his name. And, lucky for you… there he is." Your boss points to a man with a gray goatee standing in the wings of the theater, wearing a head-set and carrying a clipboard.

The three of you quickly move out of the box and down into the lobby. You wave goodbye to your boss as she wishes you good luck. By now there are only a few patrons left in the lobby, bundling up to face the sheets of rain. After finding the stage door, you quietly move back through a cramped hallway. The laughter and talking from the dressing room at the end of the hall covers the sound of your footsteps.

In this section you will:
→ Expand grammar skills.
→ Identify and describe objects.
→ Build fluency for dative case.
→ Recognize how much German you can comprehend, say, read, and write.
→ Comprehend the meaning of a story and use that knowledge to write your own story.
→ Understand the story of "The Three Billy Goats" in German.
→ Expand preposition skills.
→ Test your knowledge of prepositions.

 Disc 1 Track 6

Halfway down the hall, you turn and enter the wings of the stage where huge black velvet drapes soften the sound from the dressing rooms below.

"*Entschuldigung,*" you say to the gray-haired man, "*Sprechen Sie Englisch?*"

"Yes, I do," answers the man in coveralls. "Can I help you?"

Spinne steps forward, "We certainly hope so. We understand you are the director of this production."

"Yes," the man stands a little taller, "I am the director. Can I help you?"

"Yes," you respond. "We have been assigned to investigate the Red Starburst Plague, and we understand that you own the original score that you gave to our boss. She in turn passed the score on to us, and we are wondering what you can tell us about it." You hold up the sheet music. "Could you tell us where you got the music?"

"Actually," he replies, "it was a gift from a previous job with a marionette troupe in Salzburg, Austria."

"A marionette troupe?" asks Spinne.

"These are not your typical marionettes," answers the director. "The Salzburg Marionette Theater consists of life-sized puppets. The puppeteers stand on scaffolding behind an actual stage to manipulate the marionettes. It's quite remarkable."

"Interesting," you reply. "Who gave you the music?"

The director hesitates for a few seconds, looking at his feet. "Well," he answers, "this is a bit awkward. A young man who helped us with the puppet repairs for a few weeks last summer gave it to me. I asked him why, as we both knew it was valuable, and he just shook his head and said he hoped I'd never need to know. I thought it very odd but honored his request. He was a very decent fellow. The puppets he worked on are still in the marionette theater, I believe. Perhaps they can give you more information than I can."

"Great, thank you for your help," you say as you shake his hand.

"Don't thank me yet," he retorts, "you haven't met Gerta." The director furrows his brow and explains, "She's difficult."

"Difficult?" Spinne questions.

"Let's just say she doesn't take kindly to people who don't speak excellent German," answers the director. "Definitely brush up on your ability to ask her concise questions in German. Also, it might not hurt to prepare for a couple of evenings of volunteer work, if you want to get on her good side and be allowed backstage."

You and Spinne look knowingly at each other, thank the director, and quickly run to catch a cab. At the train station, you board a night train bound for Salzburg. As you settle into your seats, you notice a man with a diamond-shaped scar on his cheek intently watching you over his newspaper. You elbow Spinne and tip your head toward the man, but he is apparently absorbed in his newspaper. Spinne shrugs and returns to the task at hand—learning German.

Spinne opens the German book given to you by your boss. You turn to the second lesson and begin to brush up on your ability to ask questions. You want to be well-prepared for interviewing Gerta.

ACTIVITY

8

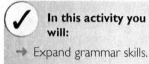

In this activity you will:

➔ Expand grammar skills.

From Word to Discourse 2

INSTRUCTIONS   Look over the words in the scatter chart, and then look over the sample sentences. Complete the rapid oral translation exercise after the sentences.

Scatter Chart

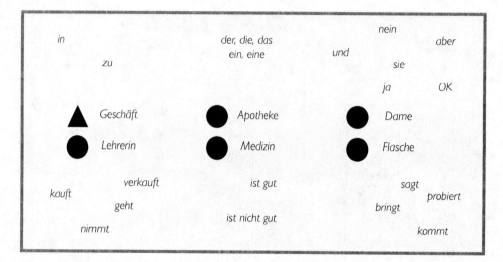

in	der, die, das		nein
	ein, eine	und	aber
zu			sie
			ja OK
▲ Geschäft	● Apotheke	● Dame	
● Lehrerin	● Medizin	● Flasche	
	verkauft	ist gut	sagt
kauft			probiert
	geht		bringt
		ist nicht gut	kommt
nimmt			

English Equivalent

in	the		no
	a / one	and	but
to (a place or person)			she
			yes OK
store	pharmacy	lady	
teacher (f)	medicine	bottle	
	buys	is good	says
sells			tries / tastes
	goes		brings
		is not good	comes
takes			

Sample Sentences

INSTRUCTIONS   Read through the following sentences.

English	German
1. a bottle	*eine Flasche*
2. a bottle of orange juice	*eine Flasche Orangensaft*
3. the bottle of lemonade	*die Flasche Limonade*
4. The bottle of orange juice is good.	*Die Flasche Orangensaft ist gut.*
5. The orange juice is good, but the lemonade is not good.	*Der Orangensaft ist gut, aber die Limonade ist nicht gut.*
6. goes to the store	*geht zu dem Geschäft*
7. A lady goes to the store.	*Eine Dame geht zu dem Geschäft.*
8. She goes to the store.	*Sie geht zu dem Geschäft.*
9. She buys a bottle of lemonade.	*Sie kauft eine Flasche Limonade.*
10. She takes the bottle to a teacher.	*Sie bringt die Flasche zu einer Lehrerin.*
11. The teacher goes to the pharmacy.	*Die Lehrerin geht zu der Apotheke.*
12. She buys a bottle of medicine.	*Sie kauft eine Flasche Medizin.*
13. She brings the medicine to the lady.	*Sie bringt die Flasche zu der Dame.*
14. The medicine is good.	*Die Medizin ist gut.*
15. This lemonade is not good.	*Die Limonade ist nicht gut.*
16. The teacher takes the bottle of lemonade to the store and says: "This lemonade is not good."	*Die Lehrerin bringt die Flasche Limonade zu dem Geschäft und sagt: "Die Limonade ist nicht gut."*
17. The lady in the store says: "The bottle is good."	*Die Dame in dem Geschäft sagt: "Die Flasche ist gut."*
18. The teacher says: "No, the lemonade is not good. The bottle is good, but the lemonade in the bottle is not good."	*Die Lehrerin sagt: "Nein, die Limonade ist nicht gut. Die Flasche ist gut, aber die Limonade in der Flasche ist nicht gut."*
19. The lady in the store says: "OK, the lemonade in the bottle is not good."	*Die Dame in dem Geschäft sagt: "OK, die Limonade in der Flasche ist nicht gut."*
20. The teacher says "OK" and buys a bottle of orange juice.	*Die Lehrerin sagt "OK" und kauft eine Flasche Orangensaft.*
21. She says: "The orange juice is good."	*Sie sagt: "Der Orangensaft ist gut."*

The Austro-Hungarian Empire, Part I

The Austro-Hungarian Empire covered a large area of 675,000 square kilometers. Among the fifty-one million people who lived in the Austro-Hungarian Empire, fifteen languages were spoken. The four main groups of people living in the Empire's boundaries were German, Hungarian, Slavic, and Italian.

Rapid Oral Translation Exercise

INSTRUCTIONS   For each sentence give the German equivalent.

1. a bottle
2. a bottle of orange juice
3. the bottle of lemonade
4. The bottle of orange juice is good.
5. The orange juice is good, but the lemonade is not good.
6. goes to the store
7. A lady goes to the store.
8. She goes to the store.
9. She buys a bottle of lemonade.
10. She takes the bottle to a teacher.
11. The teacher goes to the pharmacy.
12. She buys a bottle of medicine.
13. She brings the medicine to the lady.
14. The medicine is good.
15. This lemonade is not good.
16. The teacher takes the bottle of lemonade to the store and says: "This lemonade is not good."
17. The lady in the store says: "The bottle is good."
18. The teacher says: "No, the lemonade is not good. The bottle is good, but the lemonade in the bottle is not good."
19. The lady in the store says: "OK, the lemonade in the bottle is not good."
20. The teacher says "OK" and buys a bottle of orange juice.
21. She says: "The orange juice is good."

Challenge

INSTRUCTIONS   Compose 10 or more sentences using the words in the scatter chart and record them.

1. ....
2. ....
3. ....
4. ....
5. ....
6. ....

7. ....

8. ....

9. ....

10. ....

☆
Performance Challenge

Individual   Research the food exports from a German-speaking country. Find a specialty store that sells some of those food items and share them with a friend or family member. Teach them what you have learned about each item of food.

☆
Performance Challenge

Group   Split students into teams. Give each team cards with the words from the scatter chart written on them. Set a time limit. The team that creates the most correct sentences using the words provided wins.

Scatter Chart 5

INSTRUCTIONS This scatter chart combines the different genders you've learned so far. It focuses on the dative case and prepositions. You will learn how the German dative case and prepositions affect *der*, *die* and *das* nouns.

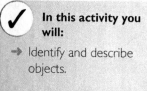

In this activity you will:

→ Identify and describe objects.

Scatter Chart

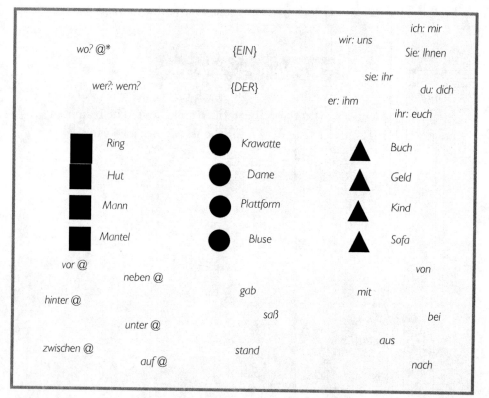

NOTE

* @ indicates "where at"—a place or location. See the observations in Activity 25 for a more thorough explanation.

ACTIVITY 9

English Equivalent

I: me

we: us

where at? {a} You: (to) You

she: her

who?: (to) whom? {the} you: (to) you

he: him

you guys: you guys

ring	tie	book
hat	lady	money
man	platform	child
coat	blouse	sofa

before @ from / of

beside @

behind @ gave with

under @ sat at / by

out of

between @ stood

on @ after / to

Performance Challenge

Individual Write a movie scene using all the words from the exercise twice. Get together with a friend and film the scene. Show the movie to your family or friends. Rough out some ideas below.

....

....

....

....

....

....

....

....

....

....

....

....

....

....

....

....

....

....

....

....

....

....

....

Performance Challenge

Group 1   Have your students create their own scatter charts and sentences using objects in the room.

Performance Challenge

Group 2   Split students into teams. Create a scavenger hunt using the objects from the scatter chart.

Scatter Chart 5: First Application

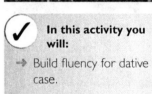

✓ In this activity you will:

→ Build fluency for dative case.

INSTRUCTIONS Examine the model strings below carefully. Then examine the right vs. wrong strings, trying to understand the principles used to create them. Translate the word strings from German to English and vice versa.

Model Strings

INSTRUCTIONS See the words you've learned being used in sentences. Study these examples and get a feel for how each word is used.

	English	German
1.	I gave a man a coat.	Ich gab <u>einem</u> Mann einen Mantel.
2.	I gave the man and the lady my rings.	Ich gab <u>dem</u> Mann und <u>der</u> Dame meine Ringe.
3.	The man gave you and me money.	Der Mann gab <u>dir</u> und <u>mir</u> Geld.
4.	The lady gave her and him money.	Die Dame gab <u>ihr</u> und <u>ihm</u> Geld.
5.	She also gave him a tie.	Sie gab <u>ihm</u> auch eine Krawatte.
6.	I gave a lady a blouse.	Ich gab <u>einer</u> Dame eine Bluse.
7.	Who gave the lady these rings?	Wer gab <u>der</u> Dame diese Ringe?
8.	To whom did the lady give money? Who did the lady give money to?	<u>Wem</u> gab die Dame Geld? <u>Wem</u> gab die Dame Geld?
9.	Who gave you this money, Hans?	Wer gab <u>dir</u> dieses Geld, Hans?
10.	Who gave you guys this money?	Wer gab <u>euch</u> dieses Geld?
11.	Do they have the money? I gave it to them.	Haben <u>sie</u> das Geld? Ich gab es <u>ihnen</u>.
12.	Do You have the money? I gave it to You.	Haben <u>Sie</u> das Geld? Ich gab es <u>Ihnen</u>.
13.	Do we have the money? He gave it to us.	Haben <u>wir</u> das Geld? Er gab es <u>uns</u>.

Right vs. Wrong Strings

INSTRUCTIONS Read through the English sentences and translate them without looking at the "Right" column. Then check your answers. Notice some common mistakes in the "Wrong" column. Did you make some of these mistakes?

		Right	Wrong
1.	He gave me the ring.	Er gab _mir_ den Ring.	*Er gab ich den Ring.
2.	He gave you the money.	Er gab _dir_ das Geld.	*Er gab du das Geld.
3.	He gave her a ring.	Er gab _ihr_ einen Ring.	*Er gab sie einen Ring.
4.	He gave him a hat.	Er gab _ihm_ einen Hut.	*Er gab er einen Hut.
5.	He gave the lady a coat.	Er gab _der_ Dame einen Mantel.	*Er gab dem Dame einen Mantel.
6.	He gave the man a hat.	Er gab _dem_ Mann einen Hut.	*Er gab der Mann einen Hut.
7.	He gave a man money.	Er gab _einem_ Mann Geld.	*Er gab ein Mann Geld.
8.	He gave a lady a book.	Er gab _einer_ Dame ein Buch.	*Er gab eine Dame ein Buch.
9.	You guys have money.	_Ihr_ habt Geld.	*Du haben Geld.
10.	Who gave you guys money?	Wer gab _euch_ Geld?	*Wer gab du Geld?
11.	Who did he give it to? To whom did he give it?	_Wem_ gab er es? _Wem_ gab er es?	*Wer gab er es?
12.	He gave it to us.	Er gab es _uns_.	*Er gab uns es.

The Dative Case

The sentence "Jane gave candy" identifies a giver (Jane), an action (gave) and the object given or acted upon by the giver (candy). The sentences "Jane gave John candy" identifies not only the object given, but also to whom Jane gave candy, who was the beneficiary of her action. The second object in such sentences is called the direct object; the first object in such sentences, designating the beneficiary of the action, the one to whom or for whom the action is directed, is called the indirect object. A word or phrase serving as an indirect object is said to be in the dative case. (Dative is a term from Latin meaning 'one being given or benefitted.')

In the following sentences the indirect object is underlined:

He built <u>us</u> a house. He bought <u>his wife</u> a present. They made <u>my son</u> an offer. She promised <u>me</u> a new bike. We sent <u>them</u> a letter. I ordered <u>our wealthy guest</u> a limousine. He offered <u>his friend</u> a job. We sent <u>you</u> a catalog.

Note that only a few verbs can take double objects.

Personal Pronouns: Nominative, Accusative, Dative

	Singular Nominative	Accusative	Dative
First Person	*ich*	*mich*	*mir*
Second Person	*du*	*dich*	*dir*
Third Person	*er*	*ihn*	*ihm*
	sie	*sie*	*ihr*
Question Words	*wer?*	*wen?*	*wem?*

	Plural Nominative	Accusative	Dative
First Person	*wir*	*uns*	*uns*
Second Person	*ihr*	*euch*	*euch*
Third Person	*sie*	*sie*	*ihnen*

	Singular or Plural Nominative	Accusative	Dative
First Person			
Second Person	*Sie*	*Sie*	*Ihnen*
Third Person			

Observations

INSTRUCTIONS Check to see if each of the following statements are true according to the chart above.

◯ First and second person singular pronouns have the same rhyming pattern in the accusative and dative cases.

◯ The dative case form of the third person singular pronouns *er* and *sie* almost match the sound of him and her.

◯ The dative case of the plural pronouns *wir* and *ihr* is the same as their accusative case form.

◯ The dative case of the plural pronouns *sie* and *Sie* is *ihnen*. (For second person it is capitalized—*Ihnen.*)

The Austro-Hungarian Empire, Part II

Austria and Hungary were united in 1867 by the *Ausgleich*, which is German for "settle" or "compromise." This Dual Monarchy satisfied Hungary's desire for increased independence and Austria's interest in a strong, centralized empire. The *Ausgleich* lasted for 50 years, but continual disputes between both halves of the empire resulted in its dissolution in 1918.

Model Strings

INSTRUCTIONS See the words you've learned being used in sentences. Study these examples and get a feel for how each word is used.

English	German
Who did he see there?	_Wen_ sah er da?
He saw him and her (the king and queen).	Er sah _ihn_ und _sie_ (_den_ König und _die_ Königin).
He saw them. And he saw (pointing) You.	Er sah _sie_. Und er sah _Sie_.
Who did he give it to?	_Wem_ gab er es?
He gave it to him and her (the king and queen).	Er gab es _ihm_ und _ihr_ (_dem_ König und _der_ Königin).
He gave it to them. And (pointing) to You.	Er gab es _ihnen_. Und _Ihnen_.

Review Chart of {DER}, {EIN}, and {DIES} in Nominative, Accusative, and Dative Case Singular

Nominative	Accusative	Dative
der Mann	_den_ Mann	_dem_ Mann
die Frau	_die_ Frau	_der_ Frau
das Kind	_das_ Kind	_dem_ Kind
ein Mann	ein_en_ Mann	ein_em_ Mann
ein_e_ Frau	ein_e_ Frau	ein_er_ Frau
ein Kind	ein Kind	ein_em_ Kind
dies_er_ Mann	dies_en_ Mann	dies_em_ Mann
dies_e_ Frau	dies_e_ Frau	dies_er_ Frau
dies_es_ Kind	dies_es_ Kind	dies_em_ Kind

Self Quiz

INSTRUCTIONS Read the English to get the meaning and then supply the missing suffix. Check your answers in Appendix A, on page 389.

	English	German
1.	Who did he give the hat to?	_____ gab er den Hut?
2.	He gave the hat to the lady.	Er gab den Hut _____ Dame.

English *(cont.)*	German
3. Who gave him the hat?	*Wer gab _____ den Hut?*
4. Who gave her the coat?	*Wer gab _____ den Mantel?*
5. Marie, did Hans give you this ring?	*Marie, gab Hans _____ diesen Ring?*
6. Did Hans give this lady this blouse?	*Gab Hans _____ Dame diese Bluse?*
7. Did he give this man this hat?	*Gab er _____ Mann diesen Hut?*
8. Did he give this money to you guys?	*Gab er _____ dieses Geld?*
9. Did he give the money to him or to her?	*Gab er das Geld _____ oder _____?*
10. Marie, did I give you this ring?	*Marie, gab ich _____ diesen Ring?*
11. Hans, did you give me this book?	*Hans, gabst du _____ dieses Buch?*

☆
Performance Challenge

Individual Read the sentences from this exercise out loud into a tape recorder. Next, practice your pronunciation using the audio from this exercise. Read the sentences into a tape recorder again and listen to the difference.

☆
Performance Challenge

Group Try a "Power Pronunciation" contest. Choose a few words from the Power-Glide Audio Flash Cards. Encourage students to see who can pronounce the words most fluently. Have the rest of the group vote who the "Power Pronouncer" is.

Scatter Chart 5: Understanding

✓ **In this activity you will:**

→ Recognize how much German you can comprehend, say, read, and write.

Self Quiz

INSTRUCTIONS Translate the following sentences. You may look back at the scatter chart only. Check your answers in Appendix A, on page 390.

1. He gave a man a coat.

....

2. He gave the man the coat.

....

3. He also gave him a hat.

....

4. He gave the child a cat.

....

5. He also gave her a hat.

....

6. He gave the lady a book.

....

7. He gave you and me money.

....

8. He gave my father a tie and my mother a ring.

....

9. He gave your daughter a blouse and your son a tie.

....

....

10. Who gave you guys money?

....

11. Hans, did Albert give you the money?

....

★ **Performance Challenge**

Individual   Using the sentences from the exercise, write a story in German. Once the story is complete, read it to a friend, teacher, or family member. Rough out some ideas below.

....

....

....

....

....

....

....

....

....

....

....

....

★ **Performance Challenge**

Group   Split the students into teams. Give each team a sentence from the activity. Have them create a story that both starts and ends with the assigned sentence. Have them read their stories aloud.

The Farmer and the Turnip

In this activity you will:

→ Comprehend the meaning of a story and use that knowledge to write your own story.

  Disc **1**   Track **7**

INSTRUCTIONS   Listen to and read the following story. Use some of this new vocabulary to create a story of your own.

🔊

English	German
Once upon a time there was a farmer.	*Es war einmal ein Bauer.*
The farmer planted some seeds,	*Der Bauer säte einige Samen,*
and he watered them,	*und er wässerte sie,*
and the sun shone,	*und die Sonne schien,*
and after a time, a tiny plant grew out.	*und nach einiger Zeit wuchs eine kleine Pflanze.*
And he watered it,	*Und er wässerte sie,*
and the sun shone,	*und die Sonne schien,*
and the little plant grew,	*und die kleine Pflanze wuchs,*
and he watered it,	*und er wässerte sie,*
and the sun shone,	*und die Sonne schien,*
and the little plant grew even more.	*und die kleine Pflanze wuchs immer mehr.*
And he watered it,	*Und er wässerte sie,*
and the sun shone,	*und die Sonne schien,*
and the little plant grew and grew.	*und die kleine Pflanze wuchs und wuchs.*
And one day the farmer said:	*Und eines Tages sagte der Bauer:*
"The plant is ripe."	*"Die Pflanze ist reif."*
So the farmer took hold of the plant,	*Der Bauer griff nach der Pflanze, und*
and tugged and tugged and tugged,	*zog und zog und zog,*

English *(cont.)*	German
but the plant didn't come out.	*aber die Pflanze kam nicht heraus.*
So the farmer called his wife:	*So rief der Bauer seine Frau:*
"Wife, come here, wife!"	*"Frau, komm her, Frau!"*
And so the wife came and took hold of the farmer,	*Seine Frau kam und hielt an dem Bauern fest,*
and the farmer grabbed the plant,	*und der Bauer griff nach der Pflanze,*
and they tugged and they tugged and they tugged,	*und sie zogen und zogen und zogen,*
but the plant didn't come out.	*aber die Pflanze kam nicht heraus.*
So the farmer called his daughter:	*So, rief der Bauer seine Tochter:*
"Daughter, come here, daughter!"	*"Tochter, komm her, Tochter!"*
And so the daughter came,	*Und die Tochter kam,*
and she grabbed onto the wife,	*und sie griff nach der Frau,*
and the wife grabbed onto the farmer,	*und die Frau griff nach dem Bauern,*
and the farmer grabbed the plant,	*und der Bauer griff nach der Pflanze,*
and they tugged and tugged and tugged,	*und sie zogen und zogen und zogen,*
but the plant didn't come out.	*aber die Pflanze kam nicht heraus.*
So they called the dog:	*So riefen sie den Hund:*
"Dog, come here, dog!"	*"Hund, komm her, Hund!"*
So the dog came, and the dog grabbed onto the daughter,	*Der Hund kam, und der Hund griff nach der Tochter,*
and the daughter grabbed onto the wife,	*und die Tochter griff nach der Frau,*
and the wife grabbed onto the farmer,	*und die Frau griff nach dem Bauern,*
and the farmer grabbed the plant,	*und der Bauer griff nach der Pflanze,*
and they tugged and tugged and tugged,	*und sie zogen und zogen und zogen,*
but the plant didn't come out.	*aber die Pflanze kam nicht heraus.*
So the farmer called the cat: "Cat, come here, cat!"	*So, rief der Bauer die Katze: "Katze, komm her, Katze!"*
So the cat came,	*Die Katze kam,*

English (cont.)	German
and the cat grabbed onto the dog,	und die Katze griff nach dem Hund,
and the dog grabbed onto the daughter,	und der Hund griff nach der Tochter,
and the daughter grabbed onto the wife,	und die Tochter griff nach der Frau,
and the wife grabbed onto the farmer,	und die Frau griff nach dem Bauern,
and the farmer grabbed the plant,	und der Bauer griff nach der Pflanze,
and they tugged and tugged and tugged,	und sie zogen und zogen und zogen,
but the plant didn't come out.	aber die Pflanze kam nicht heraus.
Then, at that moment, a little mouse came by and said:	Gerade in diesem Moment kam eine kleine Maus vorbei und sagte:
"What's going on here?"	"Was ist hier los?"
And the farmer explained to it that they were not able to get the plant out.	Und der Bauer erklärte ihr, dass sie nicht fähig waren die Pflanze herauszuziehen.
Then the mouse said: "I can help."	Dann sagte die Maus: "Ich kann helfen."
And they all laughed at him: "Ha-ha-ha.	Und sie alle lachten über ihn: "Ha-ha-ha.
You are so small. How are you going to help us?"	Du bist so klein. Wie willst du uns helfen?"
But the mouse convinced them.	Aber die Maus überzeugte sie.
And so the mouse grabbed onto the cat,	Und so griff die Maus nach der Katze,
and the cat grabbed onto the dog,	und die Katze griff nach dem Hund,
and the dog grabbed onto the daughter,	und der Hund griff nach der Tochter,
and the daughter grabbed onto the wife,	und die Tochter griff nach der Frau,
and the wife grabbed onto the farmer,	und die Frau griff nach dem Bauern,
and the farmer grabbed the plant,	und der Bauer griff nach der Pflanze,
and they tugged and tugged and tugged,	und sie zogen und zogen und zogen,

English *(cont.)*	German
and the plant came out.	*und die Pflanze kam heraus.*

Performance Challenge

Individual 1 Help neighbors or family members plant something in their garden. Ask them if you can label each kind of plant with its German name.

Performance Challenge

Individual 2 Choose three of your favorite plants (vegetables, flowers, trees) and create German seed packets for each. Include a drawing of the plant, how to care for it, and what the typical growing behavior of the plant is on each seed packet.

Performance Challenge

Group Split students into groups. Give each group a paragraph from the story. Ask them to write German lyrics to the tune of "Old Mac-Donald" to describe what happens in their paragraph. Have them teach their verse to the rest of the students.

The Three Billy Goats

In this activity you will:

→ Understand the story of "The Three Billy Goats" in German.

Disc **1**   Track **8**

INSTRUCTIONS   Listen to and read the following story. Work toward full comprehension.

English	German
There were once three goats that lived in the mountains.	*Es waren einmal drei Ziegen, die in den Bergen lebten.*
They were brothers.	*Sie waren Brüder.*
There was a big goat, a middle-sized goat, and a little goat.	*Da waren eine große Ziege, eine mittelgroße Ziege und eine kleine Ziege.*
The goats liked very much to eat green grass in the mountains.	*Die Ziegen fraßen sehr gerne grünes Gras in den Bergen.*
And they never went down to the valley.	*Und sie gingen nie hinab ins Tal.*
They never had crossed the bridge.	*Sie hatten nie die Brücke überquert.*
One day the small goat noticed that on the other side of the bridge there was a lot of green grass.	*Eines Tages bemerkte die kleine Ziege, dass es auf der anderen Seite der Brücke sehr viel grünes Gras gab.*
Then the small goat thought about crossing the bridge and descending to the valley to eat that green grass.	*Die kleine Ziege dachte dann darüber nach die Brücke zu überqueren und ins Tal hinabzusteigen, um das grüne Gras zu fressen.*
He didn't know that beneath the bridge there lived a very ugly and very fierce troll.	*Sie wusste nicht, dass unter der Brücke ein sehr hässlicher und grimmiger Kobold wohnte.*
Well, the little goat neared the bridge and began to cross it.	*Die kleine Ziege näherte sich der Brücke und begann sie zu überqueren.*
But when he was crossing the bridge, his footsteps sounded:	*Aber als sie die Brücke überquerte, klangen ihre Fußtritte:*

English (cont.)	German
TIP, TAP, TIP, TAP…	TIP, TAP, TIP, TAP…
Upon hearing the footsteps of the small goat, the troll jumped out of the water and yelled with a fierce voice:	Der Kobold hörte die Fußtritte der kleinen Ziege und sprang aus dem Wasser heraus und schrie mit grimmiger Stimme:
"Who is crossing my bridge?"	"Wer überquert da meine Brücke?"
"It's me, the little goat."	"Ich bin es, die kleine Ziege."
"And why do you come here?"	"Und warum kommst du hierher?"
"I am going to go down to the valley to eat the green grass over there."	"Ich gehe hinab zu dem Tal, um dort das grüne Gras zu fressen."
"Get off my bridge! If not, I will eat you."	"Verschwinde von meiner Brücke! Wenn nicht, werde ich dich fressen."
"Oh, please, don't eat me. I am very small.	"Oh, bitte friss mich nicht. Ich bin sehr klein.
Better wait until my brother passes by here.	Warte lieber bis mein Bruder hier vorbeikommt.
He is bigger and fatter than I am."	Er ist größer und fetter als ich."
"OK, then go ahead this time."	"Gut, dieses mal kannst du gehen."
A little later, the middle-sized goat saw that his little brother was happy eating green grass in the valley below.	Ein bisschen später, sah die mittelgroße Ziege, dass die kleine Ziege glücklich im Tal das grüne Gras fraß.
Now he also thought of crossing the bridge to go down into the valley where there was a lot of green grass.	Nun dachte auch sie darüber nach die Brücke zu überqueren und in das Tal hinabzugehen, wo es viel grünes Gras gab.
He neared the bridge and began to cross without knowing of the troll that lived below.	Sie näherte sich der Brücke und begann sie zu überqueren, ohne zu wissen, dass der Kobold darunter wohnte.
But when he went crossing the bridge his footsteps sounded:	Aber als sie die Brücke überquerte, klangen ihre Fußtritte:
TIP, TAP, TIP, TAP…	TIP, TAP, TIP, TAP…
Upon hearing the footsteps of the middle-sized goat on the bridge, the ugly troll jumped from the water and yelled with a fierce voice:	Der hässliche Kobold hörte die Schritte der mittelgroßen Ziege, sprang aus dem Wasser und schrie mit grimmiger Stimme:
"Who is crossing my bridge?"	"Wer überquert da meine Brücke?"
"I am, the middle-sized billy goat."	"Ich bin es, der mittelgroße Ziegenbock."

English *(cont.)*	German
"And why do you come here?"	*"Und warum kommst du hierher?"*
"I am going to go down to the valley to eat the green grass there with my brother."	*"Ich gehe hinab ins Tal, um dort mit meinem Bruder das grüne Gras zu fressen."*
"Get off my bridge! If not, I will eat you."	*"Verschwinde von meiner Brücke! Wenn nicht, werde ich dich fressen."*
"Oh, please, don't eat me. I am still very small.	*"Oh, bitte friss mich nicht. Ich bin noch sehr klein.*
Better wait until my big brother passes by here.	*Warte lieber bis mein großer Bruder hier vorbeikommt.*
He is bigger and fatter than I am."	*Er ist größer und fetter als ich."*
"OK, then, you can pass this time!"	*"Gut, dann darfst du sie dieses mal überqueren!"*
A little later the big billy goat saw that his little brothers were in the valley below happily eating green grass.	*Ein bisschen später sah der große Ziegenbock, dass seine kleinen Brüder glücklich in dem Tal grünes Gras frassen.*
Now he thought of crossing the bridge and going down to the valley to eat that grass.	*Nun dachte er darüber nach die Brücke zu überqueren und in das Tal hinabzugehen, um das Gras zu fressen.*
He neared the bridge and began to cross without knowing of the mean troll.	*Er näherte sich der Brücke und begann sie zu überqueren, ohne etwas über den gemeinen Kobold zu wissen.*
But as he is crossed the bridge, his footsteps were heard:	*Aber als er die Brücke überquerte, klangen seine Fußtritte:*
TOPE, TOPE, TOPE, TOPE,	*TOPE, TOPE, TOPE, TOPE,*
and the bridge rocked from such weight.	*und die Brücke schaukelte bei diesem Gewicht.*
Upon hearing the footsteps and feeling the bridge sway, the mean troll jumped from the water, and yelled with a fierce voice:	*Als der hässliche Kobold die Fußtritte hörte, und die Brücke schwingen spürte, sprang er aus dem Wasser und schrie mit grimmiger Stimme:*
"Who is crossing my bridge?"	*"Wer überquert da meine Brücke?"*
"I am, the big billy goat."	*"Ich bin es, der große Ziegenbock."*
"And why did you come here?"	*"Und warum bist du hierher gekommen?"*

English (cont.)	German
"I'm going to go down to the valley to eat some green grass there with my little brothers."	"Ich gehe hinab ins Tal, um dort mit meinen kleinen Brüdern grünes Gras zu fressen."
"Get off my bridge or I'll eat you."	"Verschwinde von meiner Brücke oder ich werde dich fressen!"
"Fine, then go ahead."	"Gut, dann mach schon."
The ugly troll moved up close, but the big billy goat lowered his head, and with his horns he gave a tremendous blow to the troll.	Der gemeine Kobold kam nah heran, aber der große Ziegenbock senkte seinen Kopf und gab dem Kobold einen schrecklichen Hieb mit seinen Hörnern.
The troll fell into the water and drowned.	Der Kobold fiel ins Wasser und ertrank.
And from that day onward, the mean troll hasn't bothered the billy goats.	Von diesem Tag an ärgerte der gemeine Kobold die Ziegenböcke nie wieder.
Now the billy goats can cross the bridge whenever they want, and they can eat the grass in the valley as well as in the mountains.	Jetzt können die Ziegenböcke die Brücke überqueren wann immer sie wollen, und sie können das Gras im Tal und in den Bergen fressen.

Performance Challenge

Individual   Research goat cheese and how it is used in Swiss or German cooking. Find a recipe that includes goat cheese and make it for your friends or family.

Performance Challenge

Group   Split the group into teams. Have them rewrite the story's ending, then act out their new endings. Have the students vote on the best ending and award the winning team with some goat cheese.

Scatter Chart 5: Second Application

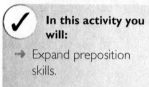

✓ In this activity you will:

→ Expand preposition skills.

INSTRUCTIONS Examine the model strings below very carefully. Then examine the right vs. wrong strings, trying to understand the principles used to create them. Translate the word strings from German to English and vice versa.

Model Strings

INSTRUCTIONS See the words you've learned being used in sentences. Study these examples and get a feel for how each word is used.

	English	German
1.	Where did the man stand?	*Wo stand der Mann?*
2.	He stood on the platform.	*Er stand auf der Plattform.*
3.	A lady stood beside the man.	*Eine Dame stand neben dem Mann.*
4.	A man stood behind the lady.	*Ein Mann stand hinter der Dame.*
5.	A child sat in front of the man.	*Ein Kind saß vor dem Mann.*
6.	A cat sat with her.	*Eine Katze saß bei ihr.*
7.	I sat between a child and a lady.	*Ich saß zwischen einem Kind und einer Dame.*
8.	Who did Hans stand in front of?	*Vor wem stand Hans?*

Right vs. Wrong Strings

INSTRUCTIONS   Read through the English sentences and translate them without looking at the "Right" column. Then check your answers. Notice some common mistakes in the "Wrong" column. Did you make some of these mistakes?

		Right	Wrong
1.	Where did Hans stand?	*Wo stand Hans?*	*Wer stand Hans?*
2.	He stood next to the man with the tie.	*Er stand neben <u>dem</u> Mann mit <u>der</u> Krawatte.*	*Er stand neben der Mann mit die Krawatte.*
3.	I sat by the king.	*Ich saß bei <u>dem</u> König.*	*Ich saß bei der König.*
4.	A child sat in front of me.	*Ein Kind saß vor <u>mir</u>.*	*Ein Kind saß vor mich.*
5.	Who stood in front of her?	*Wer stand vor <u>ihr</u>?*	*Wer stand vor sie.*
6.	Who stood behind you?	*Wer stand hinter <u>dir</u>?*	*Wer stand hinter dich.*
7.	He sat between you & me.	*Er saß zwischen <u>dir</u> und <u>mir</u>.*	*Er saß zwischen du und mich.*
8.	He sat next to you guys.	*Er saß neben <u>euch</u>.*	*Er saß neben du.*
9.	She sat between him and her.	*Sie saß zwischen <u>ihm</u> und <u>ihr</u>.*	*Sie saß zwischen er und sie.*
10.	Who lives at Your place?	*Wer wohnt bei <u>Ihnen</u>?*	*Wer wohnt bei Sie?*
11.	After me, please.	*Nach <u>mir</u>, bitte.*	*Nach mich, bitte.*
12.	For me or for you?	*Für <u>mich</u> oder für <u>dich</u>?*	*Für mir oder für dir?*
13.	From me to you.	*Von <u>mir</u> an <u>dich</u>.*	*Von mich zu dich.*

Prepositions that indicate where <u>at</u> govern the dative case: Where (at)? Behind the man, under the table, on the wall, between us, etc. (Prepositions that indicate where <u>to</u> govern the accusative, as you will soon see: Where (to)? Into the room, onto the table, up to the wall, etc.)

Self Quiz

INSTRUCTIONS   Read the English to get the meaning and then fill in the missing words in German. Check your answers in Appendix A, on page 390.

	English	German
1.	Where did Hans sit?	_____ saß Hans?
2.	He sat behind the lady.	Er saß ____ ____ ____.

The Austro-Hungarian Empire, Part III

The establishment of a Dual Monarchy divided the Habsburg Empire into two states, *Cisleithania* and *Transleithania*. Cisleithania was the Austrian half on one side of the *Leitha* River. It was made up of Bohemia, *Moravia*, Austrian Silesia, Slovenia, and Austrian Poland. The Hungarian half of the Empire was called Transleithania. It consisted of Hungary, Transylvania, Croatia, and part of the Dalmation coast. There was a division in the titles of those who ruled over each of these states. The Habsburg monarchs ruled as "Emperors of Austria" over *Cisleithania* and as "Kings of Hungary" over *Transleithania*.

English *(cont.)*	German
3. Did the lady sit in front of you, Trudy?	*Saß die Dame ____ ____, Trudi?*
4. Not in front of me, in front of my daughter.	*Nicht ____ ____, vor ____ ____.*
5. Who sat on the sofa between you guys?	*Wer saß____ ____ Sofa zwischen ____?*
6. Who sat with the man on the platform?	*Wer saß ____ ____ Mann ____ ____ Plattform?*

Performance Challenge

Individual   Research the Eurail system between Germany, Austria, and Switzerland. Make up your own mini adventure using the sentences from the exercise. Have your characters travel by train through these three countries. Rough out some ideas below.

....

....

....

....

....

....

....

....

....

....

Performance Challenge

Group   Assign a student to be the "Guesser." Without letting the Guesser know, assign another student to be the King/Queen. Have the Guesser ask questions to figure out who the King/Queen is. Once guessed, assign a new Guesser.

Scatter Chart 5: Understanding

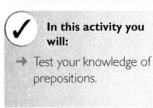

ACTIVITY 15

ACTIVITY 15

Self Quiz

INSTRUCTIONS Translate the following sentences. You may look back at the scatter chart only. Check your answers in Appendix A, on page 390.

✔ **In this activity you will:**
→ Test your knowledge of prepositions.

1. I sat next to the man who gave you the book.

....

2. Who sat next to the lady?

....

3. Hans sat next to you guys.

....

4. He sat on the sofa on the platform.

....

5. I sat beside the child, between the dog and the cat.

....

....

6. Who stood behind you guys?

....

7. In front of me sat a small child with a big book.

....

....

8. The lady who sat next to me gave you and him a tie.

....

....

ACTIVITY 15

Performance Challenge

Individual   Create a rhyming poem (in German) using sentences from the exercise. Once complete, share the poem with a friend, teacher, or family member. Rough out some ideas below.

....

....

....

....

....

....

....

....

....

....

....

....

....

....

....

Performance Challenge

Group   Form teams. Read an English sentence to the first student on each team, and have them translate their sentence into German. If they're correct, they sit down. If not, they stay standing. The team with all students sitting first wins.

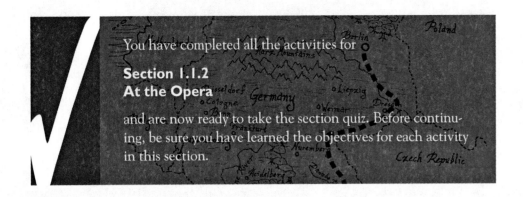

You have completed all the activities for

**Section 1.1.2
At the Opera**

and are now ready to take the section quiz. Before continuing, be sure you have learned the objectives for each activity in this section.

Section 1.1.2 Quiz

INSTRUCTIONS   Choose the correct response. Check your answers in Appendix D, on page 402.

1. *Sie geht zu dem Geschäft* **is correctly translated as:**
   A. She is going to the store.
   B. She is going shopping.
   C. She went to the store.
   D. A lady goes to the store.

2. **What is a *Mantel*?**
   A. a blouse
   B. a hat
   C. a coat
   D. a necktie

3. **In the sentence "Jane gave John candy," which word is identified as the direct object?**
   A. John
   B. Gave
   C. Jane
   D. candy

4. **How do you conjugate the verb *"haben"* in a sentence following the subject *"wir?"***
   A. *haben*
   B. *hat*
   C. *habe*
   D. *habt*

5. **What was the farmer's main problem in the story "The Farmer and the Turnip?"**

    A. *Kleine Pflanze wuchs.*

    B. *Seine Frau kam und hielt an dem Bauern fest.*

    C. *Der Bauer griff nach der Pflanze.*

    D. *Die Pflanze kam nicht heraus.*

6. **Who is the billy goats' enemy?**

    A. *Gras zu fressen*

    B. *der Kobold*

    C. *die Schritte*

    D. *die Ziege*

7. ***der Mann* is in the**

    A. nominative case

    B. accusative case

    C. dative case

    D. genitive case

8. **Which sentence is the correct translation of "He stood next to the man with the tie?"**

    A. *Er stand neben mit der Krawatte.*

    B. *Ein Mann stand neben dem mit der Krawatte.*

    C. *Er stand neben Krawatte mit der.*

    D. *Er stand neben dem Mann mit der Krawatte.*

9. **Which sentence is the correct translation of "He sat between you and me?"**

    A. *Er saß zwischen ihm und ihr.*

    B. *Sie saß zwischen ihm und ihr.*

    C. *Er saß zwischen dir und mir.*

    D. *Er saß neben euch.*

10. **The troll in the Three Billy Goats is very**

    A. *nett*

    B. *klein*

    C. *aufmerksam*

    D. *grimmig*

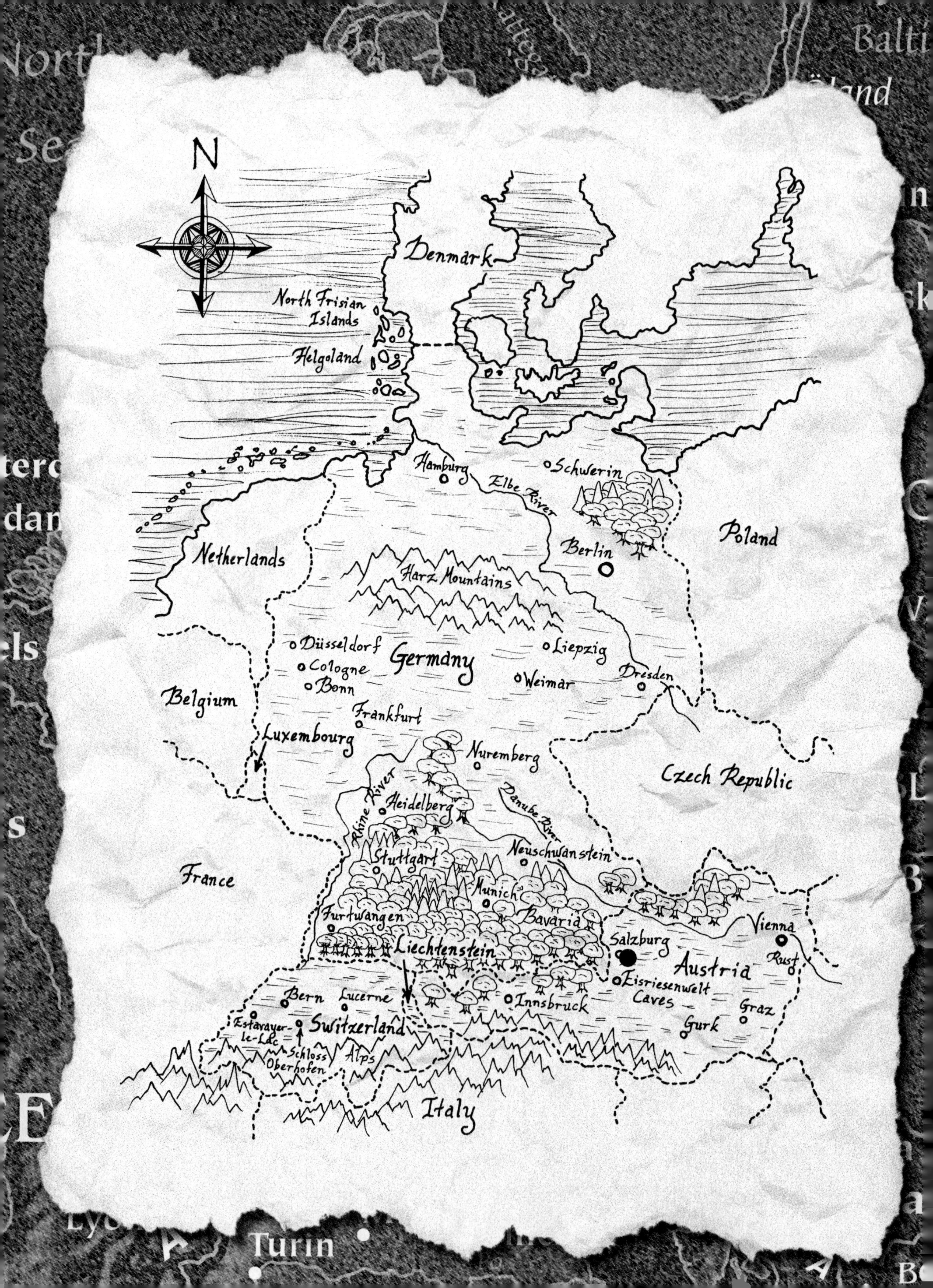

The Marionette Theater

Early the next morning, the train pulls into the station in Salzburg. The whistle wakes you out of a deep sleep that was too short for your liking. A touch of fog hovers around the rooftops of the city like a blanket. The streets are quiet, as only the earliest risers are out.

You and Spinne step off the train and reach for the map to the theater that the director gave you. Sure that the theater is not yet open, you and Spinne head for a coffee house for some breakfast and a chance to practice asking questions in German. You are relieved when the man with the scar does not follow you, but is warmly greeted and ushered into a car by a woman and a child.

As you sit down, your waitress asks if you would like something light or a full *Gabelfrühstück* ("fork breakfast"). You open your menu again and practice your German with the waitress.

After you have filled up on fruit and cheese, you and Spinne determine that the theater is too far to walk. As you emerge onto the now-bustling street, you see a shop that rents motor scooters. Rather than fight the morning rush hour in a cab, you each rent a scooter and helmet for the day.

The scooters are powerful for their size, and you and your partner zip out into traffic. Spinne, in front, navigates you out of rush hour traffic and through tiny side streets where you bounce along ancient cobblestone streets and around street vendors. After a few minutes, you notice a small blue car with darkened windows is following you through your circuitous route. Worried that you are being followed, you pull up next to Spinne and motion behind you. Spinne takes a quick look and nods. You decide to make yourselves more difficult to follow and look for places to lose the blue car.

At the next intersection, you motion for Spinne to follow you and pop the front wheel of your motor scooter up onto the sidewalk. Pedestrians scream and scatter at the sight of two oncoming scooters. The blue car follows, and you and Spinne increase your speed. The sidewalk empties into a town square where a beautiful cathedral stands guard. You and Spinne speed through the plaza, looking for ways through the supposed dead end. The blue car has now navigated the people and kiosks scattered throughout the plaza and is seconds from overtaking you.

In this section you will:

→ Learn family relationships.
→ Expand your comprehension toward complete understanding.
→ Expand comprehension, fluency, and use of past and present tense.
→ Build fluency for dative case.
→ Test your knowledge of the dative case.
→ Use more small talk on a formal level.

 Disc 1 Track 9

Suddenly, you spot a way out. To the right side of the cathedral is a gardener opening the wrought iron door of a narrow stone gate, barely wide enough to fit two people. You see a narrow walkway behind the gate and light from the street beyond it. Quickly, you motion for Spinne to follow you. You and Spinne speed up, and so does the blue car. Ducking down, you and Spinne move cleanly through the gate and walkway, then out onto the street. Just as you're safely merging into traffic, you hear screeching tires as the blue car slams on its breaks, then the crunch of metal against stone as it hits the opening of the stone gate.

After riding for a few minutes, making sure you are not being tailed, you and Spinne approach a majestic bridge. It's the bridge from your map! You speed over the old, elegant structure. Painters litter the sides of the road, each capturing their personal vision of the city.

Minutes later, you and Spinne pull to a stop in front of the Salzburg Opera House. You hide your scooters behind a hedge and go in through the service entrance.

As you enter the building, you hear someone yelling from a room at the end of the hallway. Cautiously approaching the source of the noise, you look into a cramped office and see a gray-haired woman, yelling at the top of her lungs at a small man with a green hat and a clip board. Next to the office, you peer into a large rehearsal hall filled with people playing games, chatting, and relaxing on the floor. A huge rack of life-sized marionettes lines one wall.

"I am sick and tired of this, Arnold!" the woman yells. "If you can't keep this troupe healthy, I will find someone who can!"

"Hallo," you venture.

"What do you want?" the woman barks.

"We are looking for Frau Berhold," Spider says.

"I am Frau Berhold. What do you want? I am busy here," the woman snaps.

"We need to ask you some questions about… this," you hold up the music score given to you by the theater director.

"I have no time to talk with you today!" she exclaims. "I have a two o'clock performance for the Salzburg Orphanage and I am two puppeteers short!"

"What are you performing?" you ask.

"Not that it is any of your business, but we are performing the classic 'The Farmer and the Turnip.'" Frau Berhold's voice still sounds cross, but her expression shows some interest.

You and Spinne look at each other and smile.

"Today is your lucky day," you say.

Frau Berhold crosses her arms and scowls. "Really. And why is that?"

"My friend and I both know the story you are performing," you say.

"*Wunderbar*, but how does that help me?" asks Frau Berhold.

"We also know puppeteering. We can help with your performer shortage," you say.

Frau Berhold looks skeptically at Arnold who shrugs and smiles. Frau Berhold looks back at you and Spinne, then reaches over to test your bicep muscle.

"Well… you seem strong enough. Life-sized marionettes are not like hand puppets, you know." Finally she throws down her arms in exasperation.

"I guess I have no other choice. You are hired." Frau Berhold reaches out to shake your hands. "There is no room for error here, though. These kids wait all year for this performance," she says. "Go with Arnold, he will get you a puppet and show you the ropes. Rehearsal starts again in 30 minutes." Frau Berhold moves quickly into the rehearsal hall then turns to say, "Oh, and work on your accent. I can tell you are foreign."

Spinne leans over to you, "Do we really have time for this?"

"We will have to make time," you say, "I don't know of any other way to get Frau Berhold's cooperation."

"Good point," says Spinne and you both follow Arnold to the rehearsal hall.

After an hour of practice with the puppets, you begin to feel comfortable with the movements and the story. You and Spinne spend a few minutes during a break practicing your accent when telling the story of "The Farmer and the Turnip."

The performance goes perfectly, and the children give the troupe a standing ovation. You and Spinne return to the opera house, where you help take the marionettes down into the storage room. Hundreds of intricately painted and costumed marionettes hang from racks. The rest of the performers clean and hang the puppets as you and Spinne walk through the racks, amazed at the beauty and craftsmanship around you.

Frau Berhold walks up behind you, "They are beautiful, aren't they?" she asks.

"Yes, they are," you agree.

"Some are one-of-a-kind and very valuable," she strokes the puppets lovingly as she passes each one.

"Which is your most valuable puppet?" you ask.

"Over here," Frau Berhold directs you towards the back of the storage room. "Here is our most valuable marionette," she lifts the arm of a puppet dressed to look like a craftsman of some kind. "He is a piano tuner, created by a famous Austrian sculptor. There is not another marionette like him in the world." Frau Berhold holds the puppet's hand for a moment, then places it back at his side and walks back up the row of puppets. A glint of silver catches your eye.

Looking more closely, you see that the puppet's carved hand is holding not a tuning fork, but an oddly-shaped, tarnished silver key.

"Spinne, look! Silver in the tuner's hand…" you whisper.

Spinne sees the key as well and struggles to pull it from the puppet's hand. "I can't get it out," said Spinne.

You turn to call for Frau Berhold and notice directly behind you matching boy and girl puppets. They catch your eye as they are much smaller than the rest of the puppets, child-sized rather than adult-sized. The boy holds a faded silk flower. Your eyes open wide as you see the pair.

"Spinne, I think we are in luck," you say and walk toward the puppet.

You examine both puppets and their costumes carefully. As you slide your hand under the suspenders of the boy, something under his costume shifts. The corner of a brown sheet of parchment appears in the neckline of his costume. You pull it out and gently open the folded paper. A huge smile crosses your face.

"What is it?" asks Spinne, still working to pry the key from the piano tuner's hand.

"Sheet music," you answer. "It's the next page of the 'Flight of the Valkyries.'" You gently fold the paper and tuck it into your shirt.

"What do you think you are doing?" Frau Berhold's biting voice startles you.

"Frau Berhold! We, uh…" you struggle to explain.

"You are thieves, is that what you were going to say?" She picks up her walkie-talkie, ready to call security.

"No, we are not thieves, but we are not tourists either. Let's sit down for a moment. We need your help."

You and Spinne and Frau Berhold find a private spot in the nearby furnace room. You reveal your intentions and the importance of both the music and the key. Frau Berhold listens intently, all the while scowling through her black-rimmed glasses.

"So, that is why we need your help," you finish, waiting for her response.

Frau Berhold looks you squarely in the eye, like an animal sizing up its prey. After a few awkward seconds, she stands and brushes off her skirt and even offers a bit of a smile.

"Well, why didn't you say so in the first place?" She walks toward the door. "I'd be happy to help."

You and Spider breathe a sigh of relief and follow the Frau to the piano tuner puppet where she reaches behind the elbow and flips a lever. The silver key drops neatly into her other hand. She offers it to you. "To tell you the truth, I'm not certain how that key got there. The puppet is supposed to have a proper tuning fork," she says.

You take the key and thank her. "We think we might have an idea," you reply with a grin.

"May I ask a favor in return?" she asks, looking at both you and Spinne.

"Absolutely, anything," you answer.

"I am still two performers short, and we have a performance in the morning for an important group of visitors. Would you both be kind enough to help us out again?"

You and Spinne exchange cautious glances but nod. "We would be happy to help," you answer.

"Good," she says. "The story we will be performing is, ironically, 'The Three Thieves.' Do you know it?"

"No, Frau Berhold, I am afraid we don't," you say, "but we'd be happy to learn it."

"Well, I suppose I can spare a little time to help you," she replies.

You and Spinne return to the rehearsal room with Frau Berhold where you spend the afternoon practicing for tomorrow's performance.

Questions of a Small Child 5

ACTIVITY 16

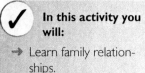

In this activity you will:

→ Learn family relationships.

Disc **1**   Track **10**

INSTRUCTIONS   Use this exercise to learn family relationships in German.

English	German
Do I have a nephew?	*Habe ich einen Neffen?*
Yes, Hans is your nephew.	*Ja, Hans ist dein Neffe.*
But what is a nephew?	*Aber was ist denn ein Neffe?*
Hans is the son of your brother, so he is your nephew.	*Hans ist der Sohn deines Bruders, und deshalb ist er dein Neffe.*
If you had a sister and she had a son, her son would also be your nephew.	*Wenn du eine Schwester hättest und sie einen Sohn hätte, würde ihr Sohn auch dein Neffe sein.*
So my nephew is the son of my brother or my sister?	*Also mein Neffe ist der Sohn meines Bruders oder meiner Schwester?*
Right.	*Richtig.*

Performance Challenge

Individual   Write a profile of your favorite relative. Include in the profile how you are related to this relative and some characteristics of your relative's personality. Rough out some ideas below.

....

....

....

....

....

....

....

....

....

....

....

....

....

....

....

....

....

....

....

....

....

....

Performance Challenge

Group   Have your students write riddles about family relations in both German and English. Create a riddle book to be shared with friends, family, and other students.

The Three Thieves

In this activity you will:

→ Expand your comprehension toward complete understanding.

Disc I   Track I I

INSTRUCTIONS   Listen to and read the following story.

English	German
There were once three thieves.	*Es waren einmal drei Räuber.*
One dark night they set about to rob the house of a rich man.	*In einer dunklen Nacht planten sie das Haus eines reichen Mannes auszurauben.*
The leader of the thieves said:	*Der Anführer der Räuber sagte:*
"I'll go first.	*"Ich gehe zuerst.*
You wait here for me, OK?"	*Ihr wartet hier auf mich, OK?"*
He crawled in through a window and began to grope his way across the dark room.	*Er kroch durch das Fenster und tastete sich seinen Weg durch den dunklen Raum.*
Suddenly he bumped into a chair and knocked it over.	*Plötzlich stieß er an einen Stuhl und kippte ihn um.*
The noise woke up the man.	*Das Geräusch weckte den Mann auf.*
He called out:	*Er rief:*
"Who's there?"	*"Wer ist da?"*
The thief answered:	*Der Räuber antwortete:*
"Meow!"	*"MIAU!"*
Thinking it was only a cat, the man went back to sleep.	*In dem Glauben, dass da nur eine Katze war, schlief der Mann wieder ein.*
The thief took some things and crawled outside through the window.	*Der Räuber nahm einige Dinge und kroch durch das Fenster nach draußen.*
His friends asked:	*Seine Freunde fragten:*
"How did it go?"	*"Wie ist es gelaufen?"*

English (cont.)	German
He told them:	Er erzählte ihnen:
"I accidentally knocked over a chair and woke up the man.	"Ich stolperte zufällig über einen Stuhl und weckte den Mann auf.
He called out:	Er rief:
'Who's there?'	'Wer ist da?'
I answered:	Ich antwortete:
'Meow!' and he thought it was only a cat."	'MIAU!' und er dachte, dass es nur eine Katze war."
The other thieves said:	Die anderen Räuber sagten:
"Man! That was close!"	"Mensch! Das war knapp!"
The second thief said:	Der zweite Räuber sagte:
"I'll be next, OK?"	"Ich bin der Nächste, OK?"
He crawled in through the window and began to grope his way across the dark room.	Er kroch durch das Fenster und tastete sich seinen Weg durch den dunklen Raum
Suddenly he bumped into the chair and knocked it over.	Plötzlich stieß er an einen Stuhl und kippte ihn um.
Again the noise woke up the man.	Das Geräusch weckte den Mann wieder auf.
He called out:	Er rief:
"Who's there?"	"Wer ist da?"
The thief answered:	Der Räuber antwortete:
"Meow!"	"MIAU!"
Thinking it was only a cat, the man went back to sleep.	In dem Glauben, dass da nur eine Katze war, schlief der Mann wieder ein.
The thief took some things and crawled back out the window.	Der Räuber nahm einige Dinge und kroch zurück durch das Fenster hinaus.
The leader of the thieves asked:	Der Anführer der Räuber fragte:
"How did it go?"	"Wie ist es gelaufen?"
He said:	Er sagte:
"The same thing that happened to you, happened to me.	"Mir ist das Gleiche passiert, wie dir.

Mozart's Home Town

Wolfgang Amadeus Mozart was born in Salzburg, Germany, on January 27, 1756. Mozart wrote 50 symphonies and 19 operas, amassing 626 compositions during his short lifetime. Today, thousands of visitors come to Salzburg to hear his masterpieces performed and to see the places where this great musician began his musical legacy.

English (cont.)	German
I accidentally knocked over a chair and woke up the man.	Ich stolperte aus Versehen über einen Stuhl und weckte den Mann auf.
He called out:	Er rief:
'Who's there?'	'Wer ist da?'
I said 'Meow' just like you did, and he went back to sleep."	Ich sagte 'MIAU' so wie du und er schlief wieder ein."
The third thief said:	Der dritte Räuber sagte:
"I'll be next, OK?"	"Ich bin der Nächste, OK?"
This thief wasn't very smart.	Dieser Räuber war nicht sehr intelligent.
He crawled in through the window and began to grope his way across the dark room.	Er kroch durch das Fenster und tastete sich seinen Weg durch den dunklen Raum.
Suddenly he bumped into the chair and knocked it over.	Plötzlich stieß er an einen Stuhl und kippte ihn um.
Of course the noise woke up the man.	Natürlich weckte das Geräusch den Mann auf.
He called out:	Er rief:
"Who's there?"	"Wer ist da?"
The thief replied:	Der Räuber antwortete:
"Another cat."	"Noch eine Katze."

Performance Challenge

Individual   Research the town of Gruyere, Switzerland. Find out why it would be difficult to steal anything big from the town today. Share what you learn with a friend.

Performance Challenge

Group   Split students into groups. Have each group work together to research a German, Swiss, or Austrian castle. Have them include information on dungeons and punishment for thieves in medieval times.

The Hunter and the Thief

INSTRUCTIONS   Read the following story. Focus on learning the past, present and future tenses in the German language.

English	German
In a minute, I'll tell you a story.	*In einer Minute werde ich euch eine Geschichte erzählen.*
Here's what my story is about:	*Hier ist, wovon die Geschichte handelt:*
In it a woman will prepare food.	*Eine Frau wird darin Speise vorbereiten.*
Here's the woman who will prepare the food.	*Hier ist die Frau, die die Speise vorbereiten wird.*
After this, a mouse will come and eat the food.	*Danach wird eine Maus kommen und die Speise fressen.*
Here's the mouse that will eat the food.	*Hier ist die Maus, die die Speise fressen wird.*
After this, a cat will come and catch the mouse.	*Danach wird eine Katze kommen und die Maus fangen.*
Here's the cat that will catch the mouse.	*Hier ist die Katze, die die Maus fangen wird.*
After this, a snake will come and swallow the cat.	*Danach wird eine Schlange kommen und die Katze verschlucken.*
Here's the snake that will swallow the cat.	*Hier ist die Schlange, die die Katze verschlucken wird.*
After this, an eagle will come and fall upon the snake.	*Danach wird ein Adler kommen und über die Schlange herfallen.*
Here's the eagle that will fall upon the snake.	*Hier ist der Adler, der über die Schlange herfallen wird.*
After this, a hunter will come and kill the eagle.	*Danach wird ein Jäger kommen und den Adler töten.*

✓ In this activity you will:

→ Expand comprehension, fluency, and use of past and present tense.

ACTIVITY 18

English (cont.)	German
Here's the hunter who will kill the eagle.	*Hier ist der Jäger, der den Adler töten wird.*
After this, a thief will come and steal the eagle.	*Danach wird ein Dieb kommen und den Adler stehlen.*
Here's the thief who will steal the eagle.	*Hier ist der Dieb, der den Adler stehlen wird.*
After this, a policeman will come and arrest the thief.	*Danach wird ein Polizist kommen und den Dieb verhaften.*
Here's the policeman who will arrest the thief.	*Hier ist der Polizist, der den Dieb verhaften wird.*
And the thief will go to jail.	*Und der Dieb wird ins Gefängnis kommen.*
Here's the thief that will go to jail.	*Hier ist der Dieb, der ins Gefängnis kommen wird.*
Poor woman!	*Arme Frau!*
Poor mouse!	*Arme Maus!*
Poor cat!	*Arme Katze!*
Poor snake!	*Arme Schlange!*
Poor eagle!	*Armer Adler!*
Poor hunter!	*Armer Jäger!*
And poor thief!	*Und armer Dieb!*

Performance Challenge

Individual Research zoos in a German-speaking country. Choose one and contact the zoo (by email or letter) to request a map, driving directions, a calendar of events, and additional information on the kinds of animals they house.

Performance Challenge

Group Organize a German Café. Bring foods from German-speaking countries. Have one group of students act as servers and the others act as patrons. Have them order, eat, and pay for their food all in German. Then have the groups trade roles.

Scatter Chart 5: Third Application

INSTRUCTIONS Examine the model strings below very carefully. Then examine the right vs. wrong strings, trying to understand the principles used to create them. Translate the word strings from German to English and vice versa.

 In this activity you will:

→ Build fluency for dative case.

Model Strings

INSTRUCTIONS See the words you've learned being used in sentences. Study these examples and get a feel for how each word is used.

English	German
1. She helps you, and I thank her.	Sie hilft <u>dir</u> und ich danke <u>ihr</u>.
2. They help the man and the lady.	Sie helfen <u>dem</u> Mann und <u>der</u> Dame.
3. He advises me, and I thank him.	Er rät <u>mir</u>, und ich danke <u>ihm</u>.
4. A man and a lady follow you guys.	Ein Mann und eine Dame folgen <u>euch</u>.
5. You follow this man and this lady.	Sie folgen <u>diesem</u> Mann und <u>dieser</u> Dame.
6. The servant serves his king and his queen.	Der Diener dient <u>seinem</u> König und <u>seiner</u> Königin.
7. I believe you; I don't believe her.	Ich glaube <u>dir</u>; <u>ihr</u> glaube ich nicht.
8. He asks, and she answers him.	Er spricht, und sie antwortet <u>ihm</u>.
9. Rita, how are you?	Rita, wie geht es <u>dir</u>? (Wie geht's <u>dir</u>?)
10. How are you guys?	Wie geht's <u>euch</u>?
11. How are You?	Wie geht's <u>Ihnen</u>?

Right vs. Wrong Strings

INSTRUCTIONS   Read through the English sentences and translate them without looking at the "Right" column. Then check your answers. Notice some common mistakes in the "Wrong" column. Did you make some of these mistakes?

		Right	Wrong
1.	I believe him.	*Ich glaube ihm.*	**Ich glaube ihn.*
2.	He follows me.	*Er folgt mir.*	**Er folgt mich.*
3.	She helps you.	*Sie hilft dir.*	**Sie hilft dich.*
4.	We serve her.	*Wir dienen ihr.*	**Wir dienen sie.*
5.	We thank you guys.	*Wir danken euch.*	**Wir danken du.*
6.	Do You want to answer me?	*Wollen Sie mir antworten?*	**Wollen Sie antworten mich?*
7.	What can You advise me?	*Was können Sie mir raten?*	**Was können Sie mich raten?*

Observations

• A few verbs require their direct object to be in the dative rather than the accusative case. Note the following examples:

Verb	English
dienen	to serve / give service to
danken	to thank / give thanks to
helfen	to help / give help to
antworten	to answer
glauben	to believe
folgen	to follow
raten	to advise

• In some idiomatic expressions such as *wie geht's dir* 'how goes it [with] you,' the pronoun is in the dative case.

INSTRUCTIONS   Write the meaning of these high-frequency verbs that take dative case object. Check your answers in Appendix A, on page 390.

	Verb	Your Translation
1.	*glauben*	....
2.	*folgen*	....

Verb (cont.)	Your Translation
3. *helfen*	
4. *dienen*	
5. *antworten*	
6. *raten*	

Learn these words. Note the cognates among these: *folgen* with follow, *helfen* with help.

Can you come up with a memory aid for *raten, glauben, dienen,* and *antworten*?

Self Quiz

INSTRUCTIONS   Translate the following sentences into German. Check your answers in Appendix A, on page 390.

1. Who believes me?

2. I believe You (Mr. Schmidt).

3. I want to help you, Hans.

4. Can you help us?

5. Who can help you guys?

6. Who should follow me?

7. Who should I follow?

8. You must follow this man, Hans.

9. One must serve one's father and mother.

10. Doesn't Hans believe me?

The Salzburg Festival

For five weeks each summer, the best operas, plays, and concerts are performed at the Salzburg Festival. This world famous festival has a reputation for maintaining the highest artistic standards and showcasing the most talented conductors, musicians, stage directors, actors, and singers. The prestige of the Salzburg Festival has made Salzburg "The Stage of the World," a cultural center for the arts.

Review of *du*, *ihr* and *Sie*: You will use *du* (with its other forms *dich* and *dir*) only in addressing a single individual. But it is not that simple, since *Sie* (and its other form *Ihnen*) are also used in addressing a single individual. You will use *ihr* (and its other form *euch*) only in addressing two or more individuals. But again it is not that simple, since *Sie* (and its other form *Ihnen*) is also used for that. So what rules does "German second person pronoun usage" follow? State your understanding of the rules.

Additional focus on prepositions that govern the dative case (*aus, nach, von, bei, zu*):

Model Strings

INSTRUCTIONS   See the words you've learned being used in sentences. Study these examples and get a feel for how each word is used.

English	German
1. He came out of this room.	*Er kam aus diesem Zimmer heraus.*
2. After You, sir.	*Nach Ihnen, mein Herr.*
3. She is from my city.	*Sie kommt aus meiner Stadt.*
4. He lives at my place.	*Er wohnt bei mir.*

Further Preparation

1. Review the model strings and the right vs. wrong strings. Be sure you can correctly translate each of them from German to English and from English to German.

2. With the scatter chart in front of you, spend several minutes creating a number of well-formed, meaningful statements.

Performance Challenge

Individual   Using the verbs from the Right vs. Wrong strings, write a scene that includes dialogue from an everyday situation (e.g., cashing a check, ordering food, asking for the time, etc.). Teach a friend at least three sentences from your scene. Rough out some ideas below.

....

....

....

....

....

....

....

....

....

....

....

....

....

....

....

....

....

....

Performance Challenge

Group   Split students into teams. Give two "speakers" several correct and incorrect sentences from the activity. Read the English sentence then have the "speakers" read their German versions. Having teams take turns guessing which is correct.

Scatter Chart 5: Understanding

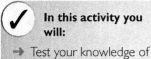

In this activity you will:

→ Test your knowledge of the dative case.

Self Quiz

INSTRUCTIONS   Translate the following sentences. You may look back at the scatter chart only. Check your answers in Appendix A, on page 390.

1. One must serve the king.

....

2. Hans, you should help this man.

....

3. I should follow You.

....

4. Who should follow me?

....

5. How can I help You (Mr. and Mrs. Schmidt)?

....

6. Hans, can you help me?

....

7. I don't want to answer you, Marie.

....

8. I don't believe you guys.

....

9. Doesn't Hans believe me?

....

10. Why should he believe You (Mr. Schmidt)?

....

Performance Challenge

Individual   Choose a job that you would like to have someday. Write a "Help Wanted" ad for such a job. The ad should include at least fifty German words. Rough out some ideas below.

....

....

....

....

....

....

....

....

....

....

....

....

....

....

Performance Challenge

Group   Have your students write "Help Wanted" ads in German for their dream occupation. Make sure that they use at least fifty German words in each ad.

ACTIVITY

21

In this activity you will:

➜ Use more small talk on a formal level.

Disc **1**   Track **12**

Conversation Snatches 9

INSTRUCTIONS   According to the dictionary, the definition of snatches is "A small amount; a bit or fragment: a snatch of dialogue." Listen to and read the following quick conversation snatches.

English	German
May I introduce myself? My name is Rudolf.	*Darf ich mich vorstellen? Ich heiße Rudolf.*
And my name is Olga.	*Und ich heiße Olga.*
Pardon, are You Miss Wagner?	*Verzeihung, sind Sie Fräulein Wagner?*
No, my name is Klara Schultz. And what is Your name?	*Nein, ich heiße Klara Schultz. Und wie heißen Sie?*
My name is Adolph Teller.	*Ich heiße Adolph Teller.*
Hmm, Adolph Teller, the painter.	*Hmm, Adolph Teller, der Mahler.*
Yes, that is right. How are You, Miss Wagner?	*Ja, das ist richtig. Wie geht es Ihnen, Fräulein Wagner?*
Please, Mr. Teller, my name is Schultz.	*Bitte, Herr Teller, ich heiße Schultz.*
Forgive me, Miss Schultz. I am sorry.	*Verzeihen Sie, Fräulein Schultz. Es tut mir leid.*
It's nothing. It's all right.	*Das macht nichts. Das ist schon gut.*
Well then, goodbye!	*Also, auf Wiedersehen!*
How's it going?	*Wie geht's?*
Pretty well, and with You?	*Ziemlich gut, und Ihnen?*
Erik is really on the ball.	*Erik ist wirklich auf Draht.*
I know.	*Ich weiß.*
What kind of machine is this?	*Was für eine Maschine ist das?*

Sites to See in Salzburg

Visitors come to the picturesque city of Salzburg to see where "The Sound of Music" was filmed. You can visit the place where Maria learned to be a nun, the Benedictine Convent on Nonnberg. You can also visit the *Felsenreitschule* where the von Trapp family performed together before fleeing their homeland. There are many other recognizable locations from this beloved movie that can be seen throughout Salzburg.

English *(cont.)*	German
This is a car and an airplane.	*Das ist ein Auto und ein Flugzeug.*
I'm interested in sports.	*Ich interessiere mich für Sport.*
Me too.	*Ich mich auch.*
We had to hurry.	*Wir mussten uns beeilen.*
We did too.	*Wir uns auch.*
May I go with you?	*Darf ich mit dir mitgehen?*
Fine.	*Aber gerne.*
Let's go to a movie tonight.	*Lass uns heute abend ins Kino gehen.*
A good idea!	*Eine gute Idee!*
I was sick yesterday.	*Ich war gestern krank.*
Terrible!	*Schrecklich!*
But today I feel better.	*Aber heute fühle ich mich wohler.*
Wonderful!	*Wunderbar!*

Performance Challenge

Individual   Find (or create) two puppets and assign them names. Write a scene for the puppets using as much German as you can. Perform the scene for a young child first in English, then in German. Rough out some ideas below.

....

....

....

....

....

....

....

....

ACTIVITY 21

Performance Challenge

Group   Break students into groups. Have them write a one-act puppet show using as many of the words in this conversation as possible. Have them create their own puppets and perform scenes for each other and perhaps a group of children.

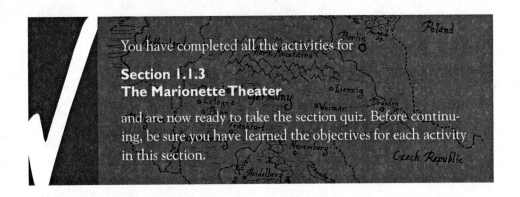

You have completed all the activities for
Section 1.1.3
The Marionette Theater
and are now ready to take the section quiz. Before continuing, be sure you have learned the objectives for each activity in this section.

Section 1.1.3 Quiz

INSTRUCTIONS   Choose the correct response. Check your answers in Appendix D, on page 402.

1. **What relation is your brother or sister's son to you?**
    A. *Schwester*
    B. *Sohn*
    C. *Neffen*
    D. *Nichts*

2. **What was the third thief's mistaken answer to the question *"Wer ist da?"* in "The Three Thieves?"**
    A. *Sie wissen es nicht.*
    B. *Miau.*
    C. *Sie sind nicht sehr intelligent.*
    D. *Noch eine Katze.*

3. **Who falls on the snake in the story "The Hunter and the Thief?"**
    A. *eine Frau*
    B. *ein Adler*
    C. *ein Dieb*
    D. *eine Schlange*

4. **What is the correct translation of "A man and a lady are following you guys?"**
    A. *Er rat mir, und ich danke ihm.*
    B. *Sie hilft dir und ich danke ihr.*
    C. *Ein Mann und eine Dame folgen euch.*
    D. *Ein Mann eine Dame neben euch.*

5. **glauben** means:
   A. to believe
   B. to serve
   C. to advise
   D. to help

6. **anworten** means:
   A. to listen
   B. to thank
   C. to answer
   D. to fight

7. **Which sport do Austrians most commonly play?**
   A. basketball
   B. cricket
   C. golf
   D. soccer

8. **In Conversation Snatches, which two machines were discussed?**
   A. *ein Auto und ein Flugzeug*
   B. *eine Serie und ein Bus*
   C. *ein Bus und ein Auto*
   D. *ein Fahrrad und eine Serie*

9. **Which of the following is not a method of transportation?**
   A. *Auto*
   B. *Flugzeug*
   C. *Schiff*
   D. *Mahlzeit*

10. **Which of the following is not a major composer who worked in Vienna?**
    A. Strauss
    B. Mozart
    C. Machiavelli
    D. Bach

You have completed all the sections for

Module 1.1

and are now ready to take the module test. Before continuing, be sure you have learned the objectives for each activity in this module.

Module 1.1 Test

INSTRUCTIONS   Choose the correct English translation of the German sentence. Check your answers in Appendix D, on page 401.

1. *Ich kann heute hier sein.*

    A. I can be here today.

    B. I was there today.

    C. I am here.

    D. I can't be there today.

2. *Du kannst das Geld haben.*

    A. They cannot have the gift.

    B. You can have the gift.

    C. You can have the money.

    D. I brought the money.

3. *Ich muss dieses Buch kaufen.*

    A. I cannot buy this box.

    B. I must go to the market.

    C. You must not do that.

    D. I must buy this book.

4. *Du musst es lesen.*

    A. You must learn this.

    B. They can go there.

    C. I was not aware.

    D. You must read it.

5. *Hans kann chinesisch lesen.*

    A. Hans can read Chinese.

    B. Let's go eat Chinese.

    C. Chinese is hard to read.

    D. Chinese is even harder to speak.

6. *Man muss hart arbeiten.*

    A. One should work diligently.

    B. One must work hard.

    C. I work hard.

    D. This is hard work.

7. *Man muss auch ein bisschen spielen.*

    A. You should play the piano.

    B. One can play at any time.

    C. They are playing over there.

    D. One must also play a little.

8. *Du solltest weise essen.*

    A. You should not eat quickly.

    B. You should come here to play.

    C. You should eat wisely.

    D. Let's eat out today.

9. *Du musst klar denken.*

    A. You must think clearly.

    B. Lawyers should think clearly.

    C. You should concentrate better.

    D. Clear the board.

10. *Du solltest das heute lernen.*

    A. They should go to town.

    B. You should learn that today.

    C. They can go tomorrow.

    D. You are wonderful.

11. *Du musst lernen klar zu denken.*

   A. You must learn this new principle.

   B. You should not learn that.

   C. You can go next week.

   D. You must learn to think clearly.

12. *Du musst lauter und klarer sprechen.*

   A. You must speak louder and clearer.

   B. You must speak more quickly.

   C. You must read more quietly.

   D. Your pronunciation is much clearer.

13. *Ich will besser sehen und hören.*

   A. I want to see you better.

   B. Do you hear that?

   C. I want to hear and see you better.

   D. I want to see and hear better.

14. *Willst du jetzt lernen?*

   A. What do you want to learn?

   B. How can you learn that?

   C. Do you want to learn now?

   D. Can you learn today?

15. *Ich kann das nicht verstehen.*

   A. I don't understand you.

   B. I don't understand that.

   C. We can't understand this principle.

   D. I understand everything fully.

INSTRUCTIONS True or False. The following sentences are translated correctly.

16. **I want to learn German. = *Ich muss Deutsch lernen.***

   A. True

   B. False

17. **We want to speak German well. = *Wir wollen gutes Deutsch sprechen.***

   A. True

   B. False

MODULE 1.1

18. Do you want to study German today? = *Wollen Sie heute Deutsch lernen?*
    A. True
    B. False

19. Why don't you want to read German? = *Wie kannst du Deutsch lesen?*
    A. True
    B. False

20. Is she able to see us now? = *Kann sie uns jetzt sehen?*
    A. True
    B. False

21. Why must we speak louder? = *Warum müssen wir klarer sprechen?*
    A. True
    B. False

22. Are they not able to hear us? = *Könnt ihr uns nicht hören?*
    A. True
    B. False

23. Do you want to work or to play? = *Willst du arbeiten oder essen?*
    A. True
    B. False

24. Are You able to understand Chinese? = *Können Sie Chinesisch verstehen?*
    A. True
    B. False

25. Should you buy a car? = *Sollst du ein Auto verkaufen?*
    A. True
    B. False

Module 1.2

Throughout this module we'll be learning about Salzburg, Austria, the Black Forest in Germany, and Innsbruck, Austria.

Keep these tips in mind as you progress through this module:

1. Read instructions carefully.
2. Repeat aloud all the German words you hear on the audio CDs.
3. Learn at your own pace.
4. Have fun with the activities and practice your new language skills with others.
5. Record yourself speaking German on tape so you can evaluate your own speaking progress.

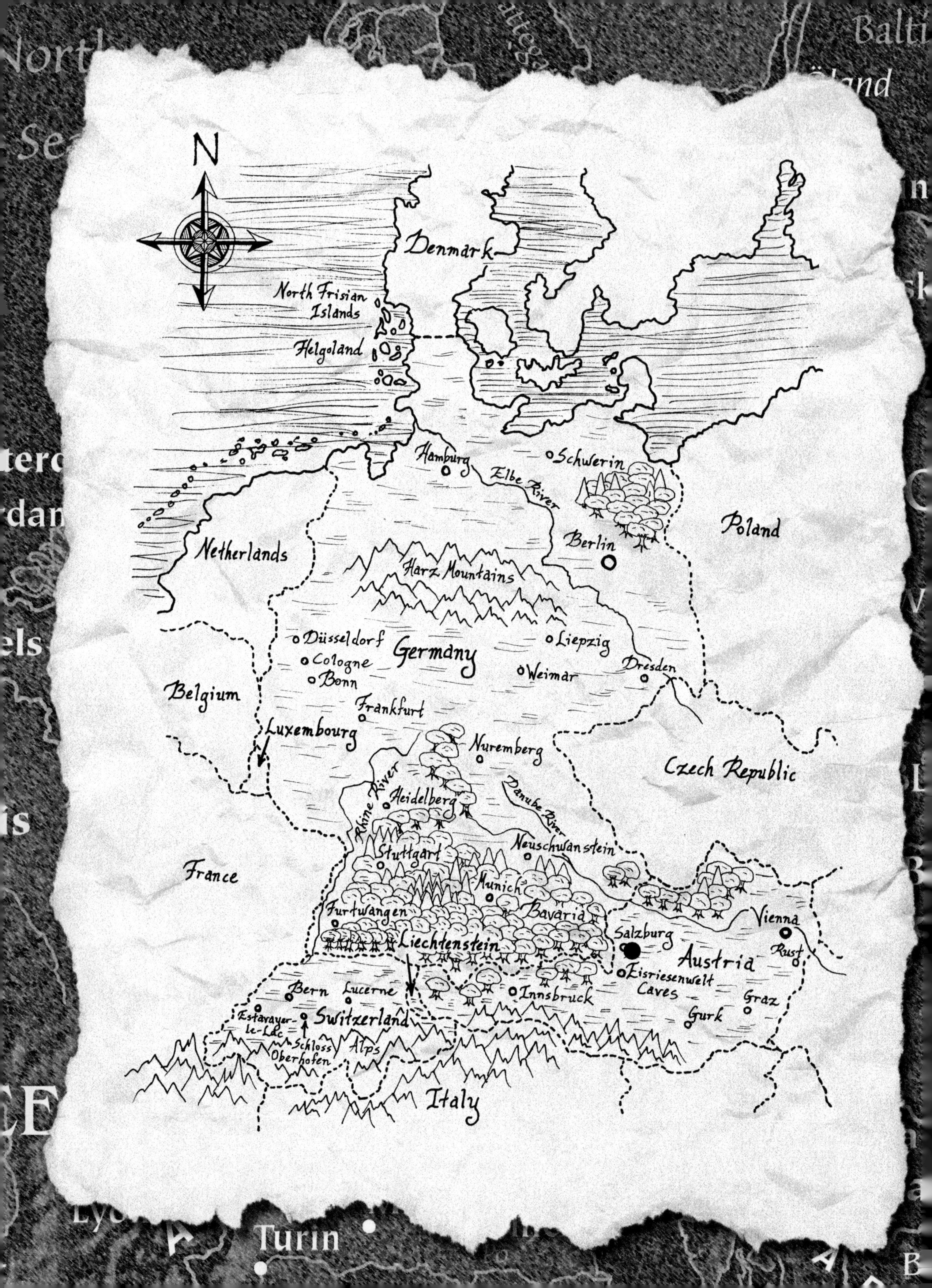

Hidden in Birdsong

"Well, that went well," you say as you and Spinne gather your things after the performance. After saying good bye to Frau Berhold and the troupe, you retrieve your scooters from their hiding place.

You and Spinne ride for a few minutes along the river, then find a café where you can decide what to do next. Thick hot chocolate and flaky strudel give you energy, and you review the riddle. *"Unter der Erde und über dem Meer, hinter den sieben Schlössern, die alle geöffnet werden müssen, damit das Heilmittel nicht auf immer verloren geht. Silber in der Hand des Klavierstimmers; Holz versteckt sich hinter Vogelgesang, tief im Wald; Stein, mit bitterem Salz vermischt, ruht tief in der Erde; Feuer im Herzen des Löwen; Eis in den sich ständig wandelnden Höhlen, hoch über den Tälern; Gold vom Tisch des Königs; Eisen aus seiner Krone."*

"So," says Spinne, "the next key will be found hidden in birdsong, deep in the forest. Which forest?"

"Well, let's take a look at the map," you say, unfolding the map onto the café table. Dozens of forests stare back at you from the map of Europe. You both breathe out, concerned about the time and the number of possible places to search.

Your waitress walks up and you decide to take a shot.

"Excuse me, may I ask you a question?" you say to the waitress. "If you were going to visit a forest, which one would you pick?"

"There is really only one forest to visit," says your waitress as she refills your hot chocolate.

"Really?" asked Spinne. "Which one?"

"The Black Forest, of course," she answers.

"The Black Forest," you and Spinne exclaim together. "Of course! *Vielen Dank.*" You pull out the sheet of music you found on the boy puppet and hold it over the small candle on your table. The heat from the candle shines through, and you breathe out slowly as the spidery lines of the invisible ink form into words.

In this section you will:

→ Recognize how much German you can comprehend, say, read, and write.

→ Understand new vocabulary in a conversation or story.

→ Learn how to use the accusative case, dative case, and motion verbs.

→ Practice the use of prepositional compounds.

→ Practice the use of motion verbs.

→ Master new vocabulary.

→ Follow a *Geschichte* with full comprehension.

→ Follow a conversation and understand its meaning.

 Disc **2**   Track **1**

"What does this one say?" Spinne asks.

You wait a few more seconds for the words to become clear and read the clue. "What days do the fishermen talk?"

"What does that mean?" Spinne queries.

"I have no idea," you answer. "But we need to get moving. Let's head toward the Black Forest and hope that the rest becomes clear later."

You quickly pay the waitress for your snack and start up your motor scooters. Driving through the streets of Salzburg, you take several side streets to make sure you are not being followed. You and Spinne return your scooters and walk to the train station just as a large black train is pulling in. The station is crowded, and you have to wait in line to get your tickets to the Black Forest.

As you stand in line, a rack of books catches your eye. One on the Black Forest looks particularly informative, and you purchase it. You start thumbing through the book to find any information you can on wood that could hide bird song. Through page after page, you look for anything you can find on wild birds, song birds, bird-watching, or national birds, but nothing seems to fit the clue.

"Spinne, any ideas on what this clue means?" you ask, handing over the book.

"Hmm, let's see…" Spinne starts flipping through the book. "What about wood-peckers? Do they have woodpeckers in the Black Forest?"

"I don't know," you reply. The line is moving very slowly. "Do you see a train schedule posted anywhere, Spinne? I hope we won't end up missing the train."

Spinne looks around. He doesn't spot a schedule, but he does point out an over-sized cuckoo clock on the wall. As you both look at the clock, it strikes twelve o'clock. As the clock strikes, four doors open in the front of it. Through the first dance a man and woman, through the second a set of bears, through the third a lumberjack chopping with a silver axe. Through the fourth and final door come a series of cuckoos: green, yellow, and blue all chirping for a total of twelve times.

"Wow, that cuckoo clock is incredible," says Spinne.

"Spinne! That's it!" you say excitedly.

"What is?" asks Spinne, now shuffling up to the ticket window.

"Cuckoo clocks! Maybe that is the 'wood that hides in birdsong,'" you answer. "Look for something about cuckoo clocks in the Black Forest."

Spinne quickly thumbs through the book as you stall the clerk at the ticket window.

"It looks like there is a cuckoo clock factory in the Black Forest," says Spinne.

"*Wo ist sie?*" you ask.

"*Sie liegt in der Nähe von Furtwangen,*" says the clerk at the desk.

"Ausgezeichnet. Dann hätten wir gerne zwei Fahrscheine nach Furtwangen," you say and pull the train fare out of your wallet.

You and Spinne race to the train platform. You reach the train just before its doors close, and it lurches into motion as the two of you find your seats. You and Spinne review your clues on your way to the Black Forest. For good measure, you do some studying as well—you don't want to be caught unprepared at the factory.

The Crocodile

ACTIVITY 22

In this activity you will:

→ Recognize how much German you can comprehend, say, read, and write.

Disc **2** Track **2**

INSTRUCTIONS Listen to and read the following story. Circle all the vocabulary words you already know.

English	German
A pale, nervous man came into the office of a psychiatrist who was his personal friend.	*Ein blasser, nervöser Mann kam in die Praxis eines Psychiaters, der sein persönlicher Freund war.*
The doctor said:	*Der Doktor sagte:*
"Fritz, my friend, I see that you are under great stress.	*"Fritz, mein Freund, ich sehe, dass du unter großem Stress leidest.*
Tell me what your problem is!"	*Sag mir, wo dein Problem liegt!"*
"Oh doctor, please help me.	*"Ach Doktor, bitte hilf mir.*
I am extremely frightened."	*Ich bin sehr verängstigt."*
"What is it that frightens you?"	*"Was ängstigt dich?"*
"There's a crocodile under my bed."	*"Es gibt ein Krokodil unter meinem Bett."*
"A crocodile under your bed?"	*"Ein Krokodil unter deinem Bett?"*
"Yes, there's a one-meter-long crocodile under my bed.	*"Ja, es gibt ein ein Meter langes Krokodil unter meinem Bett.*
I'm afraid it's going to eat me."	*Ich habe Angst, dass es mich fressen wird."*
"Don't worry, Fritz," said the doctor.	*"Sei nicht beunruhigt, Fritz," sagte der Doktor.*
"It's only an illusion.	*"Es ist nur eine Einbildung.*
I have many patients who have a similar problem.	*Ich habe viele Patienten, die ein ähnliches Problem haben.*
It's really nothing serious.	*Es ist wirklich nichts ernsthaftes.*
I have some pills that will cure your ailment in a short time.	*Ich habe Tabletten, die dein Leiden in kurzer Zeit heilen werden.*

English (cont.)	German
Here, take three of these little pills three times a day: in the morning, at noon, and at night before going to bed.	Hier, nimm drei von diesen kleinen Tabletten dreimal pro Tag: morgens, mittags und abends bevor du schlafen gehst.
I can assure you, you'll soon be well again.	Ich kann dir versichern, dass es dir bald wieder besser gehen wird.
Come back and see me in three weeks, will you?"	Komm' in drei Wochen zurück, um mich zu sehe OK?"
"Thank you doctor, thank you very much."	"Danke Doktor, vielen Dank."
In three weeks the man came again to the office.	Der Mann kam nach drei Wochen wieder in die Praxis.
He was even paler and thinner than before.	Er war sogar noch blasser und dünner als vorher.
He said:	Er sagte:
"Oh doctor, I still have the same problem.	"Oh Doktor, ich habe immer noch das gleiche Problem.
And it's getting worse and worse.	Und es wird schlimmer und schlimmer.
The crocodile is still under my bed, only now it is one-and-a-half meters long.	Das Krokodil ist immer noch unter meinem Bett, aber jetzt ist es eineinhalb Meter lang.
I'm sure it's going to eat me.	Ich bin mir sicher, dass es mich fressen wird.
Oh, what will I do?	Ach, was werde ich bloß tun?
You've got to help me."	Du musst mir helfen!"
"Have you taken the pills three times a day as I prescribed?"	"Hast du die Tabletten eingenommen dreimal pro Tag, wie ich es dir verschrieben habe?"
"Yes, yes, of course.	"Ja, ja, natürlich.
In the morning, at noon, and at night before going to bed."	Morgens, mittags und abends bevor ich ins Bett gehe."
"Well then, I'll give you these new pills.	"Gut, dann gebe ich dir diese neuen Tabletten.
They are more powerful than the others.	Diese sind wirkungsvoller als die anderen.

The Black Forest, Part I

The Black Forest region, 'Schwarzwald,' is known for its dense woods, tasty cherry cakes, and traditional cuckoo clocks. In earlier times, the forest was impenetrable and dark; thus it was named the Black Forest. There are many tales about this fascinating ancient forest.

English (cont.)	German
Take six of them, three times a day: six in the morning, six at noon, and six at night before going to bed.	Nimm sechs davon, dreimal pro Tag: sechs morgens, sechs mittags und sechs abends bevor du schlafen gehst.
I can assure you, you'll be well again.	Ich kann dir versichern, dass es dir bald wieder besser gehen wird.
Come back and see me in six weeks, will you?"	Komm' in sechs Wochen zurück, um mich zu sehen."
"Thank you, doctor, thank you very much."	"Danke, Doktor, vielen Dank."
In six weeks the man came again to the office.	Nach sechs Wochen kam der Mann wieder in die Praxis.
He was even thinner, paler, and more nervous than before.	Er war noch dünner, blasser und nervöser als vorher.
He said:	Er sagte:
"Oh doctor, I still have the same problem.	"Ach Doktor, ich habe immer noch das gleiche Problem.
And it's getting worse.	Und es wird schlimmer.
The crocodile is still under my bed, only now it is two meters long.	Das Krokodil ist immer noch unter meinem Bett, aber jetzt ist es zwei Meter lang.
I know it's going to eat me.	Ich weiß, dass es mich fressen wird.
What shall I do?	Was soll ich tun?
You've got to help me."	Du musst mir helfen!"
"Have you taken the six pills three times a day as I prescribed?"	"Hast du die sechs Tabletten eingenommen, dreimal pro Tag, wie ich es dir verschrieben habe?"
"Yes, yes, of course.	"Ja, ja, natürlich.
Six in the morning, six at noon, and six at night before going to bed."	Sechs morgens, sechs mittags und sechs abends bevor ich schlafen gehe."
"Well then, I'll give you these new pills.	"Gut, dann gebe ich dir diese neuen Tabletten.
They are extremely powerful.	Diese sind sehr stark.

English (cont.)	German
I want you to take nine of them three times a day: nine in the morning, nine at noon, and nine at night before going to bed.	*Ich möchte, dass du neun davon nimmst, dreimal pro Tag: neun morgens, neun mittags und neun abends bevor du schlafen gehst.*
I can assure you you'll be well again.	*Ich kann dir versichern, dass es dir bald besser gehen wird.*
Come back and see me in nine weeks, will you?"	*Komm' in neun Wochen zurück, um mich zu sehen, OK?"*
Nine weeks went by, but the man didn't come.	*Neun Wochen gingen vorbei, aber der Mann kam nicht.*
Ten weeks, eleven weeks, twelve weeks.	*Zehn Wochen, elf Wochen, zwölf Wochen.*
At the end of the twelfth week, the doctor by chance was walking along a street, and he passed the house of his sick friend.	*Am Ende der zwölften Woche ging der Doktor zufällig eine Straße entlang und kam am Haus seines kranken Freundes vorbei.*
He decided to stop and call on him.	*Er entschied sich anzuhalten und nach ihm zu sehen.*
He knocked on the door.	*Er klopfte an die Tür.*
His friend's wife answered the door.	*Die Frau seines Freundes öffnete die Tür.*
She was crying.	*Sie weinte.*
"Good evening, Mrs. Schmidt!	*"Guten Abend, Frau Schmidt!*
I came to see how Fritz is doing."	*Ich kam, um zu sehen, wie es Fritz geht."*
"Oh doctor, haven't You heard?"	*"Ach Doktor, haben Sie nicht gehört?"*
"What?"	*"Was?"*
"Fritz is dead."	*"Fritz ist tot."*
"Dead?"	*"Tot?"*
"Yes, he was eaten by the crocodile."	*"Ja, er wurde von dem Krokodil gefressen."*

ACTIVITY 22

Performance Challenge

Individual   Take one of the occurrences in this story and change it completely. Finish writing the ending with the new plot point.

....

....

....

....

....

....

....

....

....

....

....

....

....

....

Performance Challenge

Group   Have students write jokes in German using a doctor and a crocodile for characters. Have them read the jokes for each other and any other students.

The Man Who Will Be Our King

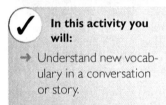

INSTRUCTIONS Listen to and read this vocabulary-building story.

English	German
Here is a tent.	*Hier ist ein Zelt.*
Here is a cave.	*Hier ist eine Höhle.*
Here is a hut.	*Hier ist eine Hütte.*
Here is a house.	*Hier ist ein Haus.*
Here is a mansion.	*Hier ist eine Villa.*
Here is a castle.	*Hier ist ein Schloss.*
Here is a palace.	*Hier ist ein Palast.*
Here is a famous man.	*Hier ist ein berühmter Mann.*
The man was born in this tent.	*Der Mann wurde in diesem Zelt geboren.*
When he was five, his family moved from the tent to the nearby cave.	*Als er fünf war, zog seine Familie aus dem Zelt in die nahegelegene Höhle.*
When he was eight, his family moved from the cave to the nearby hut.	*Als er acht war, zog seine Familie aus der Höhle in die nahegelegene Hütte.*
When he was twelve, his family moved from the hut to the nearby house.	*Als er zwölf war, zog seine Familie aus der Hütte in das nahegelegene Haus.*
When he was eighteen, his family moved from the house to the nearby mansion.	*Als er achtzehn war, zog seine Familie aus dem Haus in eine nahegelegene Villa.*
When he was twenty, his family moved from the mansion to the nearby castle.	*Als er zwanzig war, zog seine Familie aus der Villa in das nahegelegene Schloss.*
Now he lives in this castle.	*Nun lebt er in dem Schloss.*

ACTIVITY 23

ACTIVITY 23

✓ **In this activity you will:**
→ Understand new vocabulary in a conversation or story.

◎ Disc **2** Track **3**

The Black Forest, Part II

Olden times are remembered and revered in the Black Forest. Visitors to the Black Forest are taken back to a time when raftsmen transported huge Black Forest trees all the way to Holland, when glass blowing was a popular trade, when men worked in deep mine shafts, and when it was common for people to live in castles. Historic steam engines still chug up the hills and through the valleys of the Black Forest as they did a hundred years ago. The oldest restaurant in all of Germany is, of course, located in the Black Forest.

English (cont.)	German
When he is thirty, he will live in this nearby palace.	Wenn er dreißig ist, wird er in dem nahegelegenen Palast wohnen.
For five years, he lived with his family in a tent.	Er lebte mit seiner Familie fünf Jahre lang in einem Zelt.
For three years, he lived with his family in a cave.	Er lebte mit seiner Familie drei Jahre lang in einer Höhle.
For four years, he lived with his family in a hut.	Er lebte mit seiner Familie vier Jahre lang in einer Hütte.
For six years, he lived with his family in a house.	Er lebte mit seiner Familie sechs Jahre lang in einem Haus.
For two years, he lived with his family in a mansion.	Er lebte mit seiner Familie zwei Jahre lang in einer Villa.
Now he lives with his family in this castle.	Nun lebt er mit seiner Familie in diesem Schloss.
And when he is thirty, he'll live in this palace.	Und wenn er dreißig ist, wird er in diesem Palast leben.
For this man will be our king!	Denn dieser Mann wird unser König sein!

Performance Challenge

Individual　　Research three German, Swiss, or Austrian castles. Write a one-page report on each castle. Include a picture and share what you have learned with a friend. Rough out some ideas below.

....

....

....

....

....

....

....

....

....

....

....

....

....

....

....

....

....

....

....

....

....

....

....

....

....

Performance Challenge

Group   Find several photographs of famous German, Swiss, or Austrian castles, mansions, or houses (e.g. the home of Mozart in Austria). Have each student choose a dwelling to research. Then have them write about the dwelling.

Scatter Chart 6

 In this activity you will:

→ Learn how to use the accusative case, dative case, and motion verbs.

This scatter chart combines the different genders you've learned so far. It focuses on additional important grammatical dimensions in German: the dative case, the accusative case and verbs of motion.

Scatter Chart

	hierher ^	ich: mich-mir
wo? @		wir: uns-uns
	dorthin ^	sie: sie-ihr
wer?: wen?-wem?		er: ihn-ihm
wohin ^*?	da- / dar-	du: dich-dir
		ihr: euch-euch
zwischen @ ^	■ Mann	
unter @ ^	● Dame	von
auf @ ^	▲ Sofa	mit
über @ ^		bei
hinter @ ^	▲ Kind	
vor @ ^		aus
	● Plattform	
in @ ^ neben @ ^		nach

fliegen: flog, geflogen	gehen: ging, gegangen	stellen ^: stellte, gestellt
essen: aß, gegessen	kommen: kam, gekommen	legen ^: legte, gelegt
singen: sang, gesungen	rennen: rannte, gerannt	steigen: stieg, gestiegen
tanzen: tanzte, getanzt	kriechen: kroch, gekrochen	setzen ^: setzte, gesetzt

NOTE

* ^ indicates movement. See the observations in Activity 25 for further explanation.

English Equivalent

I: me

(to) here ^

where (at)? @

we: us

(to) there ^

she: her

who?: whom?

h e: him

(preposition + it)

where (to)? ^

you: you

you (all): you (all)

man

between @ ^

from / of

lady

under @ ^

with

sofa

on @ ^

at / by

under @ ^

child

behind @ ^

out of

platform

before @ ^

after / to

in @ ^   beside @ ^

to fly: flew, flown	to go: went, gone	to stand ^: stood, stood
to eat: ate, eaten	to come: came, come	to lay ^: laid, laid
to sing: sang, sung	to run: ran, run	to climb: climbed, climbed
to dance: danced, danced	to crawl: crawled, crawled	to put ^: put, put

Performance Challenge

Individual   Write the German words from the scatter chart on index cards. See how many new sentences you can create using the words on the cards.

Performance Challenge

Group   Write the German words from the scatter chart on slips of paper and place them inside balloons. Blow up the balloons. Have the students pop the balloons. If they correctly translate the word inside, they receive a point.

ACTIVITY 25

Scatter Chart 6: First Application

 In this activity you will:

→ Practice the use of prepositional compounds.

INSTRUCTIONS Examine the model strings below very carefully. Then examine the right vs. wrong strings, trying to understand the principles used to create them. Translate the word strings from German to English and vice versa.

Model Strings

INSTRUCTIONS You've learned the words. Now see them used in sentences. Study these examples and get a feel for how each word is used.

	English	German
1.	I went onto the platform, and now I'm singing on the platform.	*Ich bin auf die Plattform gegangen, und jetzt singe ich auf der Plattform.*
2.	The dog crawled behind the sofa, and now it is sleeping behind the sofa.	*Der Hund ist hinter das Sofa gekrochen, und jetzt schläft er hinter dem Sofa.*
3.	Ruth ran behind the tree, and now she's standing behind the tree.	*Ruth ist hinter den Baum gerannt, und jetzt steht sie hinter dem Baum.*
4.	Hans came into the room, and now he is eating in the room.	*Hans ist in das Zimmer gekommen, und jetzt isst er in dem Zimmer.*
5.	We climbed onto the table, and now we're dancing on the table.	*Wir sind auf den Tisch gestiegen, und jetzt tanzen wir auf dem Tisch.*
6.	He slept here; I slept there.	*Er hat hier geschlafen; ich habe dort geschlafen.*
7.	He came here yesterday; I went there today.	*Er ist gestern hierher gekommen; ich bin heute dorthin gegangen.*
8.	Who climbed onto the table?	*Wer ist auf den Tisch gestiegen?*
9.	Who crawled under it?	*Wer ist darunter gekrochen?*
10.	Who crawled over the sofa?	*Wer ist über das Sofa gekrochen?*

English (cont.)	German
11. Did Hans crawl over it?	*Ist Hans darüber gekrochen?*
12. Has he crawled behind it?	*Ist er dahinter gekrochen?*

Right vs. Wrong Strings

INSTRUCTIONS Read through the English sentences and translate them without looking at the "Right" column. Then check your answers. Notice some common mistakes in the "Wrong" column. Did you make some of these mistakes?

		Right	Wrong
1.	Who stands here?	*Wer steht hier?*	**Wer steht hierher?*
2.	Who is singing there?	*Wer singt dort?*	**Wer singt dorthin?*
3.	He came onto the platform.	*Er kam auf die Plattform.*	**Er kam auf der Platt-form.*
		Er ist auf die Plattform gekommen.	**Er ist auf der Plattform gekommen.*
4.	He went into the room.	*Er ging in das Zimmer.*	**Er ging in dem Zimmer.*
		Er ist in das Zimmer gegangen.	**Er hat in das Zimmer gegangen.*
5.	He ate in this room.	*Er hat in diesem Zimmer gegessen?*	**Er ist in diesem Zimmer gegessen?*
6.	Who slept behind the sofa?	*Wer schlief hinter dem Sofa?*	**Wer schlief hinter den Sofa?*
7.	Who climbed onto the table?	*Wer stieg auf den Tisch?*	**Wer stieg auf der Tisch?*
8.	Who was dancing in front of the house?	*Wer tanzte vor dem Haus?*	**Wer tanzte vor das Haus?*

Observations

- In modern English, we say "come here, stand here; go there, stand there." But in Shakespeare's day the wording would have been "come hither, stand here; go thither, stand there." "Hither" and "thither" indicated movement, crossing a line from one place to a new destination, whereas "here" and "there" indicated location or position. The Shakespearean English "hither" and "thither" corresponds to German *hin* and *her*.

- A similar distinction between "where at" and "where to" was made in Shakespeare's day. If you had said: "They danced behind a curtain," it would be ambiguous as to whether the dancing was done behind the curtain or whether, while dancing, the dancers crossed the line marked by the curtain. If you

The City of Clocks

Furtwangen, "The City of Clocks," is home to the largest collection of clocks in all of Germany. The German Clock Museum located in Furtwangen boasts more than 4,000 clocks, some of which are over 150 years old. There are renaissance clocks, sand clocks, music clocks, and, of course, cuckoo clocks as well as many other clocks included in this large collection of German clocks.

meant to express that the dancers crossed the line and reached an area behind the curtain, in German you would use the preposition *hinter* with the accusative case: *sie tanzten hinter* <u>*den*</u> *Vorhang*. If you meant to express that the dancers were dancing at a location behind the curtain, in German you would use the preposition *hinter* with the dative case: *sie tanzten hinter* <u>*dem*</u> *Vorhang*. The accusative case marks "where to"; the dative case marks "where at."

• These German prepositional compounds match those of English:

German	English
dahinter	behind it
davor	in front of it
darüber	over it
darauf	on it
dazwischen	between them

• Note that *da* is used before prepositions beginning with a consonant, and *dar* before prepositions beginning with a vowel.

Self Quiz

INSTRUCTIONS   Fill in the missing blanks. Check your answers in Appendix A, on page 390.

English	German
1. Who is dancing there?	*Wer tanzt* ____?
2. When did Marie go there?	*Wann ist Marie* ____ *gegangen?*
3. Does Hans sleep on the sofa?	*Schläft Hans auf* ____ *Sofa?*
4. Does Kitty sleep behind it?	*Schläft Kitty* ____?
5. Who sleeps in front of it?	*Wer schläft* ____?
6. Who sleeps on it?	*Wer schläft* ____?

Performance Challenge

Individual   Choose a mountain range in a German-speaking country (e.g. Swiss Alps). Write a story about climbing one of the mountains and use as many of the words from this activity as possible. Rough out some ideas below.

....

....

....

....

....

....

....

....

....

....

....

....

....

....

....

....

....

....

....

Performance Challenge

Group   The Swiss Alp horns are very long wooden horns used for communicating across the Alps. Have your students create and decorate a long horn from cardboard. Have them use as much German as possible.

Scatter Chart 6: Second Application

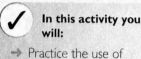

In this activity you will:

→ Practice the use of motion verbs.

INSTRUCTIONS Examine the model strings below very carefully. Then examine the right vs. wrong strings, trying to understand the principles used to create them. Translate the word strings from German to English and vice versa.

Model Strings

INSTRUCTIONS See the words you've learned being used in sentences. Study these examples and get a feel for how each word is used.

	English	German
1.	A glass is standing on the table.	*Ein Glas steht auf dem Tisch.*
2.	Who put the glass on the table?	*Wer hat das Glas auf den Tisch gestellt?*
3.	My blouse is lying on the bed.	*Meine Bluse liegt auf dem Bett.*
4.	Who laid my blouse on the bed?	*Wer hat meine Bluse auf das Bett gelegt?*
5.	Why is the green vase between the black vase and the white book?	*Warum steht die grüne Vase zwischen der schwarzen Vase und dem weißen Buch?*
6.	I placed it between the black vase and the white book.	*Ich habe sie zwischen die schwarze Vase und das weiße Buch gestellt.*
7.	Put the child on the table.	*Setzen Sie das Kind auf den Tisch.*
8.	Who hung this picture on this wall?	*Wer hat dieses Bild an diese Wand gehängt?*

Right vs. Wrong Strings

INSTRUCTIONS   Read through the English sentences and translate them without looking at the "Right" column. Then check your answers. Notice some common mistakes in the "Wrong" column. Did you make some of these mistakes?

	Right	Wrong
1. He stood it (the vase) on the table.	*Er stellte sie auf den Tisch.*	**Er stellte sie auf dem Tisch.*
	Er hat sie auf den Tisch gestellt.	**Er ist sie auf den Tisch gestellt.*
2. He laid it (the book) on the bed.	*Er legte es auf das Bett.*	**Er lag es auf dem Bett.*
	Er hat es auf das Bett gelegt.	**Er ist es auf das Bett gelegt.*
3. He laid it (the ball) in the room.	*Er legte ihn in das Zimmer.*	**Er setzte ihn in dem Zimmer.*
	Er hat ihn in das Zimmer gelegt.	**Er ist ihn in den Zimmer gesetzt.*
4. He hung it (the picture) on the wall.	*Er hing es an die Wand.*	**Er hing es auf das Wand.*
	Er hat es an die Wand gehängt.	**Er hat es auf das Wand gehängt.*

Furtwangen's Clock School

More than a century ago, Furtwangen was the center of clock making in the Black Forest. Clocks produced in this town were known for their high quality and beauty. The first clock making school was established in Furtwangen by the Grand Duke of Baden in 1850. Students were instructed in the art of clock making so that the high quality and beauty of clocks could be maintained and even improved. The school grew and evolved through the years until it became what it is today, a university of applied sciences.

Observations

- The verbs *stellen: stellte, gestellt; liegen: legte, gelegt; setzen: setzte, gesetzt;* and *hängen: hing, gehängt* have to do with activities that result in something being moved to a place, not with activities taking place in a given location. Therefore, the place of destination is in the accusative case, not the dative.

- Note once more that the auxiliary that goes with these four verbs and all other (except motion) verbs is *haben*. For example, "*ich habe das Buch hingestellt*." The auxiliary that goes with motion verbs is *sein*.

Performance Challenge

Individual   Paint or draw a still life using all the nouns in this activity. Name the artwork in German and include a short story about the picture. Rough out some ideas below.

....

....

....

....

....

....

....

....

....

....

....

....

....

....

....

....

....

....

....

★

Performance Challenge

Group   Find a DVD with German language and German subtitles. Give
each student a flag and a list of words to watch/listen for. As students see
the object or hear the word spoken in the film, have them raise their flag

Chatter at a Royal Ball 4

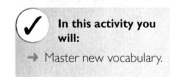

Getting Ready for Conversation

INSTRUCTIONS   Learn these words and the pictographs that go with them. Then practice these conversations.

In this activity you will:

→ Master new vocabulary.

Disc **2**   Track **4**

Pictograph	English	German
🐕	the dog	*der Hund*
🐈	the cat	*die Katze*
👓	it seems so	*es scheint so*
👎	worse than	*schlechter als*
❗	of course	*natürlich*
💡	imagine that	*stellen Sie sich das vor*
(-)	oh gee	*na so was*
👥	together	*zusammen*
♀⌀☺	she does not like ____	*sie ____ nicht gern*

125

Pictograph (cont.)	English	German
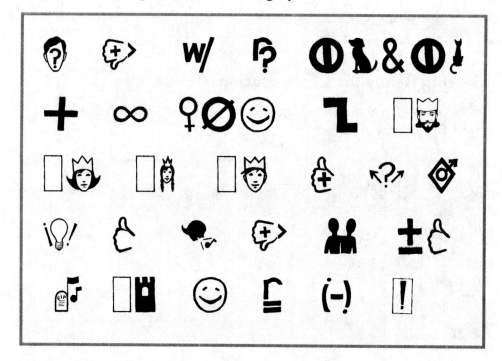	a dog and a cat	*ein Hund und eine Katze*

Self Quiz on Recognition of the Pictographs

Checklist

INSTRUCTIONS   Practice reading, writing and saying the following phrases until you feel comfortable with them. Check off phrases you are comfortable with.

Checklist		
○ welche	○ natürlich	○ es scheint so
○ auch	○ gut	○ er / sie ___ nicht gern
○ die Prinzessin	○ immer	○ besser als
○ stellen Sie sich	○ der Prinz	○ trommeln
○ das vor	○ zusammen	○ der Turm
○ mit	○ Trauerlieder	○ aber
○ wer	○ singen	○ warum
○ der König	○ schlechter als	○ weil

Checklist

○ ein Hund und eine Katze   ○ die Königin   ○ Na so was!

○ mehr oder weniger gut

Conversation

◀))

English	German
••: Polo and Misti sing also. They sing with the king and the queen in the tower.	Polo und Misti singen auch. Sie singen mit dem König und der Königin in dem Turm.
•: Polo and Misti?	Polo und Misti?
••: The cat and the dog.	Die Katze und der Hund.
•: A king and a queen with a dog and a cat. And they sing together?	Ein König und eine Königin mit einem Hund und einer Katze. Und sie singen zusammen?
••: It seems so.	Es scheint so.
•: And the princess?	Und die Prinzessin?
••: The princess doesn't sing.	Die Prinzessin singt nicht.
•: Why not?	Warum nicht?
••: Because she doesn't like to sing. She doesn't sing well. She sings worse than the dog.	Weil sie nicht gerne singt. Sie singt nicht gut. Sie singt schlechter als der Hund.
•: But better than the cat!	Aber besser als die Katze!
••: Of course. Imagine that!	Natürlich. Stellen Sie sich das vor!

◀▶

Go back and listen to this conversation several times. Focus on the new vocabulary.

Task 1

INSTRUCTIONS   Use your hands as puppets and dramatize the dialogue, looking only at the German. Visualize the situation and get into the spirit of the conversation. Aim for a flowing German quality. Then go on to the next task.

Furtwangen or Fuhrtwangen?

The name of the town, Furtwangen, is clearly missing an "h" since the German word for clock is "uhr." If any town should have the word "clock" in its name, it should be this town. Clocks and clock making have been an important part of Furtwangen for much of its history.

Task 2

INSTRUCTIONS Do the same as in Task 1, but now look only at the pictographic representation of the dialogue. Throw yourself into this performance. Bring thought down in German without thinking in English. Aim for high-quality performance.

Pictographic Representation of the Same Dialogue

INSTRUCTIONS Make sure you understand the new vocabulary in this activity.

Pictographic Representation (cont.)

! ¡Ω! !

(-)!

⭐ **Performance Challenge**

Individual   Choose a member of any German-speaking royal family. Research his or her life and reign. Create a family tree, then write up a short biography. Include at least three specific stories from his or her life. Rough out some ideas below.

....

....

....

....

....

....

....

....

....

....

....

....

⭐ **Performance Challenge**

Group   Split students into groups. Give each group a children's book in English. Have students create a Diglot Weave™ using their story. Have students share their stories with the class.

The Silent Fisherman

In this activity you will:

→ Follow a *Geschichte* with full comprehension.

Disc **2**   Track **5**

Clock Street

Furtwangen has a Clock Street that runs right through the center of the town. On Clock Street you can find clocks of every kind. There are sundials, salt clocks, and a whole lot of cuckoo clocks because they are the specialty of the region. Time really does fly when you're having fun in this city!

INSTRUCTIONS   Listen to and read this story. Learn new words about fishing and weather in German.

English	German
Early one Saturday morning a fisherman and his son went out fishing.	*An einem frühen Samstagmorgen gingen ein Fischer und sein Sohn fischen.*
Because fishermen don't like to talk a lot, the men in our story were as quiet as fish.	*Weil Fischer nicht gerne viel sprechen, sind die Männer in unserer Geschichte ruhig wie Fische.*
Not until noon, when clouds appeared on the horizon, did the son say to the father:	*Erst am Mittag, als Wolken am Himmel auftauchten, sagte der Sohn zum Vater:*
"Looks like it's going to rain."	*"Es sieht so aus, als wenn es regnen wird."*
The father looked up for a moment and nodded to the son, but he didn't say a word.	*Der Vater schaute einen Moment nach oben und nickte seinem Sohn zu, aber sagte kein Wort.*
The day went by like that.	*So ging der Tag vorbei.*
On Sunday they took a rest.	*Am Sonntag ruhten sie sich aus.*
But as usual, they said nothing to each other.	*Aber wie immer, sprachen sie nicht miteinander.*
On Monday they went fishing again.	*Am Montag gingen sie wieder fischen.*
But they were still in silence.	*Aber sie waren immer noch still.*
Tuesday, Wednesday, Thursday, Friday—all passed in the same way.	*Dienstag, Mittwoch, Donnerstag, Freitag—alle Tage vergingen wie die anderen Tage.*

English (cont.)	German
It was only on Friday evening when it was raining hard, the father wiped his forehead with his hand and said:	*Erst am Freitagabend, als es sehr stark regnete, wischte der Vater sich die Stirn mit seiner Hand und sagte:*
"You're right."	*"Du hast recht."*

Performance Challenge

Individual 1   Visit a local aquarium or fish hatchery. Research the names of fish, in German, before you go. As you see each fish, teach the names you know to a friend or family member.

Performance Challenge

Individual 2   Rent a DVD about fish that has German language and/or subtitles. Watch the movie (or set of scenes) once in English, then in English with German subtitles, then only in German. See how much you can understand and learn.

Performance Challenge

Group 1   Plan a field trip to a local aquarium or fish hatchery and prepare a German list of fish or items that can be found there. Then split the students into teams and give each team a list. Have them go on a scavenger hunt to find each item.

Performance Challenge

Group 2   Using a few sets of Power-Glide Flash Cards, have your students play "Go Fish" all in German.

Questions of a Small Child 6

✓ In this activity you will:

→ Follow a conversation and understand its meaning.

 Disc **2** Track **6**

INSTRUCTIONS Listen to and read this conversation.

English	German
Do I have a niece?	*Habe ich eine Nichte?*
Yes, Trudy is your niece.	*Ja, Trudy ist deine Nichte.*
What is a niece then?	*Was ist denn eine Nichte?*
Trudy is the daughter of your sister, so she is your niece.	*Trudy ist die Tochter deiner Schwester, deshalb ist sie deine Nichte.*
If you had a brother and he had a daughter, his daughter would also be your niece.	*Wenn du einen Bruder hättest und er eine Tochter hätte, würde seine Tochter auch deine Nichte sein.*
So my niece is the daughter of my brother or my sister?	*Also, meine Nichte ist die Tochter meines Bruders oder meiner Schwester?*
Right!	*Richtig!*

Performance Challenge

Individual   Ask fifty people a question in German this week. See how many you can get to respond correctly by using gestures or context to convey the meaning.

Performance Challenge

Group   Have your students choose a famous German-speaking person in history. Have them write a short synopsis of that person's life in German.

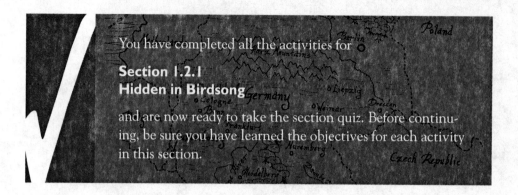

You have completed all the activities for

**Section 1.2.1
Hidden in Birdsong**

and are now ready to take the section quiz. Before continuing, be sure you have learned the objectives for each activity in this section.

Section 1.2.1 Quiz

INSTRUCTIONS   Choose the correct response. Check your answers in Appendix D, on page 402.

1. **In "The Crocodile," which of the following is NOT a reason why the man is pale and nervous?**

    A. *Ein Krokodil liegt unter seinem Bett.*

    B. *Er hat Angst, dass es ihn fressen wird.*

    C. *Es ist wirklich nichts ernsthaftes.*

    D. *Das Krokodil ist zwei Meter lang.*

2. **Which of the following is NOT a place where people live?**

    A. *Haus*

    B. *Zelt*

    C. *Wohnung*

    D. *Kamin*

3. **One of these words is not like the others...which word does not belong?**

    A. *Dame*

    B. *hinter*

    C. *unter*

    D. *neben*

4. **How do you translate the phrase "in front of?"**

    A. *darauf*

    B. *dazwischen*

    C. *dahinter*

    D. *davor*

5. **Which of the following sentences is incorrect?**

   A. *Er lag es auf dem Bett.*

   B. *Er ist sie auf den Tisch gestellt.*

   C. *Er hing es an die Wand.*

   D. *Er stellte es auf den Tisch.*

6. **Which of the following is NOT a characteristic of the princess' singing?**

   A. *Sie singt besser als die Katze.*

   B. *Sie singt in dem Turm.*

   C. *Sie singt nicht gern.*

   D. *Sie singt schlechter als der Hund.*

7. **What did the father finally say in "The Silent Fishermen?"**

   A. *Es sieht so aus, das es regnen wird.*

   B. *Nicht gerne viel sprechen.*

   C. *Du hast recht.*

   D. *Aber sie waren immer noch still.*

8. **Who is Polo in "Chatter at a Royal Ball?"**

   A. *die Prinzessin*

   B. *die Katze*

   C. *der Hund*

   D. *der Fisch*

9. **Which of the following questions does NOT deal with relationships?**

   A. *Du hast eine gute Erinnerung.*

   B. *Meine Nichte ist die Tochter meines Bruders oder meiner Schwester?*

   C. *Habe ich eine Nichte?*

   D. *Was ist denn eine Nichte?*

10. **The German word *hin* corresponds to which Shakespearean word?**

    A. thither

    B. hence

    C. hie

    D. hither

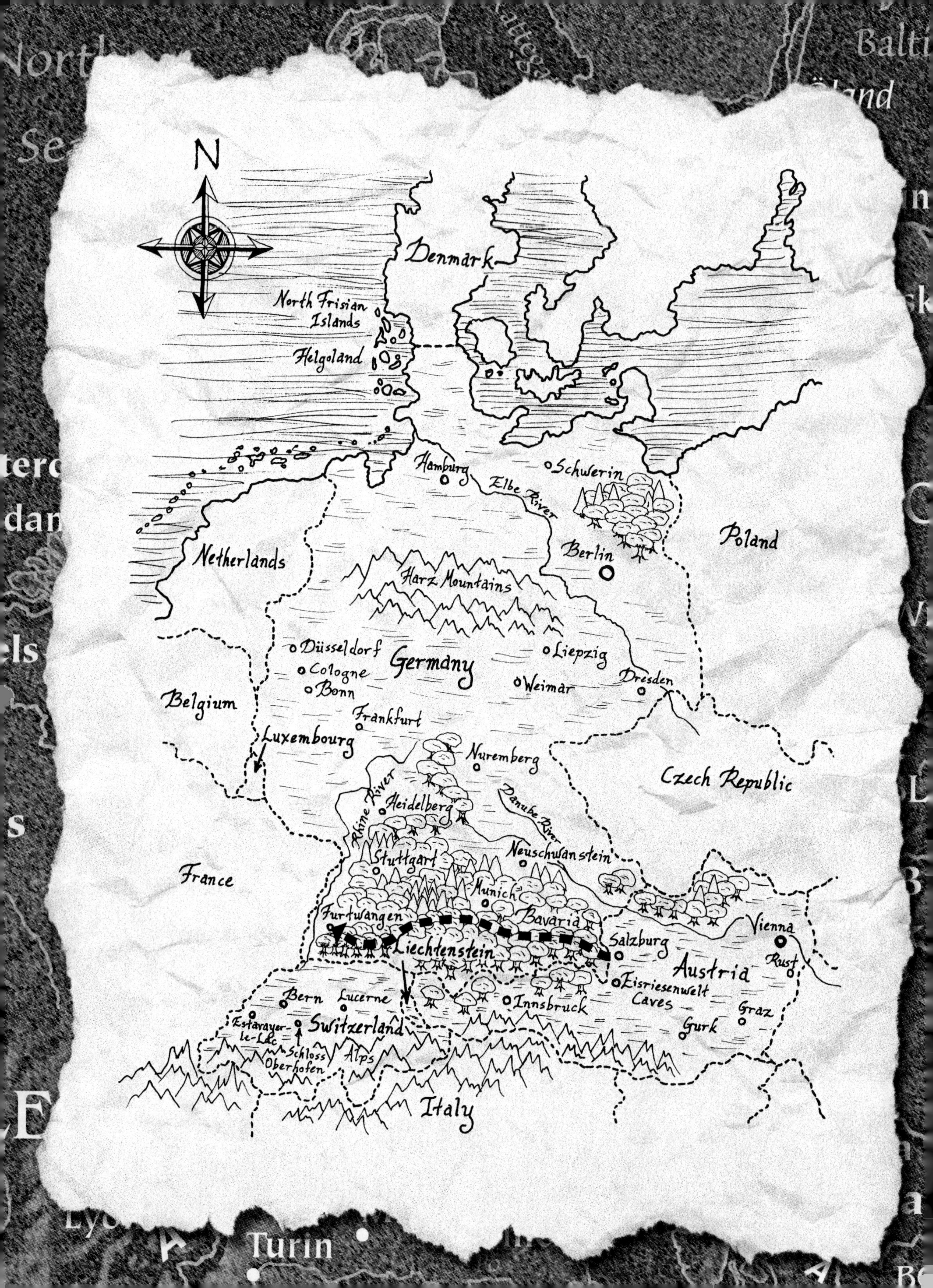

The Factory at Furtwangen

As you pull into the town of *Furtwangen*, you and Spinne quickly gather your things and exit the train. An old man sitting on a bench by the train station plays a haunting song on a harmonica.

"Entschuldigen Sie bitte, mein Herr," you say approaching the elderly musician.

"Ja?" he answers gruffly. It's clear he doesn't appreciate your interruption.

"Wo finden wir die cuckoo clock factory?" Spinne asks.

"If you don't know, I'm not going to tell you," he barks. "Too many strangers come through here these days. I don't like strangers."

"We're sorry for the interruption," you say.

You and Spinne move away from the station to find the factory. As you turn onto a nearby street, you look back and notice that the old man is gone from his perch on the bench.

"Keep your eyes peeled, Spinne," you say. "It looks like the old man may be on his way to tip someone off."

Turning the corner, you see smoke coming from a large building a few blocks away. You and Spider assume this is the factory, and as you come up on the driveway, you are happy to see the sign "Black Forest Cuckoo Clocks."

Entering the building, you ask for the factory manager, and a man named Herr Alder comes out to greet you.

"Hallo," Herr Alder says and offers his hand. "What can I do for you?"

You and Spinne explain your quest, and Herr Alder rubs his forehead with concern.

"Is anyone else looking for these keys?" he asks.

"Why do you ask?" you say.

"Let me show you why," Herr Alder answers. He leads you into the factory.

In this section you will:
→ Use repetition to gain full comprehension.
→ Learn the rules of the genitive case.
→ Test your knowledge of the genitive case.
→ Comprehend the meaning of a story.

 Disc **2**   Track **7**

SECTION 1.2.2

As he opens the doors, both you and Spinne gasp. The factory is a shambles. Workers are cleaning up what looks like the wreckage after a hurricane.

"What happened here?" you ask.

Herr Alder, looking tired, scratches his head and replies, "Someone was looking for something and obviously couldn't find it. This mess was here when I opened the factory this morning. We have been cleaning all day, and it still looks like this."

"Was anything missing?" you ask.

"Not that I can tell, but we still haven't gotten through the entire mess," says Herr Alder.

He leads you and Spinne back to the office. It is a tiny workshop, and pieces of clocks are strewn across a workbench and his office desk.

"Please forgive the mess," says Herr Alder. "I enjoy restoring old clocks along with running the factory." Intricate antique gears, carved wood birds and figures, and pieces of clock houses are stacked in bins along the work bench. One particularly beautiful clock sits on his desk. It is over-sized and intricately carved. The carved wood around the house gable is so delicate it looks like wooden lace. Stories from the Black Forest are painted along the sides and back of the clock.

"This clock is incredible," you comment.

"Each of the doors and the contents behind each door represent a day of the week," says Herr Alder. "This is a very special clock," he adds. "This is one of the oldest clocks I have ever worked on. It once belonged to one of the Bavarian kings. Here, let me show you how it works."

Herr Alder moves the hands to the hour, and a happy tune plays. As the tune sings on, each door opens in turn. Figures of a baker, a butcher, a silver smith, and a teacher reveal themselves under the days Sunday, Monday, Tuesday, and Wednesday. Thursday reveals a cobbler, and Friday and Saturday are both fishermen.

"I can't quite get the fishermen to tuck in neatly when they are done," says Herr Alder, and he starts fiddling with the figures.

"What days to do the fishermen talk?" says Spinne. "May I see that clock?"

"Certainly, but be careful. It is very old and not very sturdy," says Herr Alder, handing over the clock.

Spinne fiddles with the figures until one comes loose.

"Oh dear, be very careful please," Herr Alder warns.

"Don't worry, I think we may have found what we are looking for," says Spinne, pulling a wooden key out from behind the Friday door.

"The key!" you exclaim.

"No wonder I couldn't get it to work," says Herr Alder.

"And here is the next clue," says Spider, lifting the Saturday fisherman figure from its resting place to reveal a folded sheet of music.

"Sheet music?" asks Herr Alder.

"We're following clues left by an employee of the scientist who released the plague. He hid clues to the cure within a certain piece of sheet music," you explain.

"Interesting," says Herr Alder, popping the fishermen back into place. "I'm glad my office was locked last night and that whoever ransacked the factory did not find this clock."

"*Wir sind genauso froh*," you reply. *"Vielen Dank für Ihre Hilfe."*

"My pleasure," Herr Alder says. "I am happy to be of help."

As you leave the factory, the sun is setting. Pink and orange streams of light color the tops of the evergreen trees that surround the factory. Herr Alder is kind enough to loan you a truck from the factory.

You and Spinne drive to the nearest town, where you find a quaint bed and breakfast. As you sit in the restaurant eating dinner, you review the clues and what you have left to accomplish. You pull out the sheet music, holding it up to the candle on your table. Again, the heat from the candle reveals the next clue. Letter by letter, the words *"Schau in die Mitte der Einheit,"* are revealed.

"Hmm, I wonder what that could mean?" asks Spinne.

"I don't know," you yawn. "I am too tired to think about it now."

"Yes," says Spinne. "Me too. Let's try and figure this out in the morning."

"Good idea," you say.

You and Spinne pay for dinner and climb the carved stairs to your respective rooms. You may be imagining it, and you are too tired to check and make sure, but you think you saw the old man from the train station step out of a hidden corner and look up the stairs after you.

The next morning, you and Spinne meet again in the restaurant for breakfast. Hot *bratwurst* and eggs are served with a selection of fresh-baked breads and pastries. A glass of drinkable yogurt goes down smoothly with the delicious food.

"I did some research last night," says Spinne. "I think that the clue "Stone, mixed with bitter salt, lies deep underground,' has something to do with a salt mine. After looking at the map, it looks like one of the most famous is near Innsbruck, Austria."

After making a phone call, Herr Alder agrees to sell you the truck from the factory. You meet him outside the inn and give him the money.

"Don't look now, *meine Freunde*, but I fear you are begin watched," Herr Alder says quietly. Across the street you see the drapes from an upstairs window quickly close.

"*Danke, Herr Alder,*" you say, shaking his hand.

"My pleasure. Now, go quickly and safely," says Herr Alder. "All our lives depend on your success."

You and Spinne drive carefully out of the quaint town. While driving to Innsbruck, both you and Spinne watch all the cars behind you, looking for possible followers.

For many miles, you see nothing, and you both start to relax as you roll through the green hills and thatched-roof villages of the countryside. You take turns driving, each studying while the other drives.

The Key of the Kingdom 3

INSTRUCTIONS Read through this story and try to recite it in German on your own!

English	German
Here is the key of the kingdom.	*Hier ist der Schlüssel zum Königreich.*
In the large kingdom there is a small town.	*In dem großen Königreich ist eine kleine Stadt.*
In the small town there is a wide street.	*In der kleinen Stadt ist eine breite Straße.*
By the wide street there is a narrow lane.	*Neben der breiten Straße ist eine enge Gasse.*
In the narrow lane there is a green garden.	*In der engen Gasse ist ein grüner Garten.*
In the green garden there is a tall house.	*In dem grünen Garten ist ein hohes Haus.*
In the tall house there is an empty room.	*In dem hohen Haus ist ein leeres Zimmer.*
In the empty room there is a Chinese vase.	*In dem leeren Zimmer ist eine chinesische Vase.*

In this activity you will:

→ Use repetition to gain full comprehension.

Rooster Clocks?

Wood from the Black Forest has been used to craft and carve intricate clocks since 1630. The first clocks crowed like a rooster every hour and half hour. It wasn't until 1738 that Franz Ketterer thought of carving a cuckoo bird for a clock. He designed two bellows to produce two distinct sounds like a cuckoo's call. On the hour, the carved cuckoo bird would come out from behind a small door as the clock made the two sounds of a cuckoo bird.

English (cont.)	German
In the Chinese vase there are pretty flowers.	*In der chinesischen Vase sind schöne Blumen.*
The pretty flowers in the Chinese vase,	*Die schönen Blumen in der chinesischen Vase,*
the Chinese vase in the empty room,	*die chinesische Vase in dem leeren Zimmer,*
the empty room in the tall house,	*das leere Zimmer in dem hohen Haus,*
the tall house in the green garden,	*das hohe Haus in dem grünen Garten,*
the green garden in the narrow lane,	*der grüne Garten in der engen Gasse,*
the narrow lane by the wide street,	*die enge Gasse neben der breiten Straße,*
the wide street in the small town,	*die breite Straße in der kleinen Stadt,*
the small town in the large kingdom.	*die kleine Stadt in dem großen Königreich.*
And here's the key of the kingdom.	*Und hier ist der Schlüssel zum Königreich.*

Performance Challenge

Individual   Research the Matterhorn in Switzerland. Write a story about a King, a flower, a garden, a street, and a Chinese vase, using the Matterhorn as part of your setting. Share your story with a family member or friend. Rough out some ideas below.

....

....

....

....

....

....

....

....

....

....

....

....

....

....

....

....

....

....

....

....

....

....

....

....

Performance Challenge

Group   Set up a pen pal program for your students (go through local school administration or a pen pal agency). Ask students to include a description of their town in the first letter, and to ask at least five questions about the recipient's town.

Discovery of Grammar 13

ACTIVITY 31

 In this activity you will:

➡ Learn the rules of the genitive case.

Genitive: The "of" Relationship Between Two Things

Model Strings

INSTRUCTIONS Study these examples and get a feel for how the preposition "of" is used in German.

	English	German
1.	The name of the man is Karl.	*Der Name <u>des</u> Mannes ist Karl.*
2.	The name of the lady is Marie.	*Der Name <u>der</u> Dame ist Marie.*
3.	The name of the child is Johann.	*Der Name <u>des</u> Kindes ist Johann.*
4.	The price of this vase is ten marks.	*Der Preis <u>dieser</u> Vase ist zehn Mark.*
5.	The price of this coat is ten marks.	*Der Preis <u>dieses</u> <u>Mantels</u> ist zehn Mark.*
6.	The price of this book is only two marks.	*Der Preis <u>dieses</u> <u>Buches</u> ist nur zwei Mark.*
7.	That was the end of my letter.	*Das war das Ende <u>meines</u> <u>Briefes</u>.*
8.	That is the end of my street.	*Das ist das Ende <u>meiner</u> Straße.*
9.	Here is the house of our friends.	*Hier ist das Haus <u>unserer</u> Freunde.*
10.	I'm reading the diary of my grand-mother.	*Ich lese das Tagebuch <u>meiner</u> Groß-mutter.*
11.	Today is Mozart's birthday, and also the birthday of my brother.	*Heute ist <u>Mozarts</u> Geburtstag und auch der Geburtstag <u>meines</u> <u>Bruders</u>.*

Commentary

The preposition "of" describes a relationship of ownership between two nouns in a sentence. For example, "He must think he's the king <u>of</u> the road" means "He must own or control the road."

However, ownership or possession is not the only relationship indicated by "of." Look over the following phrases for the various "genitive" relationships indicated in English by "of."

Phrase	"of" Relationship
the road of a king	(the road that a king uses)
the color of lead	(the color that lead displays)
the price of victory	(the price that victory requires)
the heat of summer	(heat that summer produces)
the source of evil	(the source from which evil comes)
a feeling of pride	(a feeling engendered by pride)
the diary of my father	(the diary written by my father)

In English you can make reference to a house owned by your father by saying "the house of my father," or the shorter form "my father's house." In German there are parallel ways of expressing the same relationship: *das Haus meines Vaters* or the shorter form, with *-s* (minus the apostrophe we use in English): *mein Vaters Haus*.

In phrases where a proper name joins in a genitive relationship with another noun, as in Mozart's birthday, where there's no modifying word—no my, the, this, etc. to mark the genitive relationship—only the short form can be used: *Mozarts Geburtstag*. One cannot say *Geburtstag des Mozart*.

Chart of Genitive Forms

INSTRUCTIONS   Study these genitive forms.

	Genitive Singular		
n	*des Mannes*	*eines Mannes*	*dieses Mannes*
	'of the man'	'of a man'	'of this man'
l	*der Katze*	*einer Katze*	*dieser Katze*
	'of the cat'	'of a cat'	'of this cat'
s	*des Kindes*	*eines Kindes*	*dieses Kindes*
	'of the child'	'of a child'	'of this child'

	Genitive Plural		
u	*der Männer*	*meiner Männer*	*dieser Männer*
	'of the men'	'of my men'	'of these men'
u	*der Katzen*	*meiner Katzen*	*dieser Katzen*

	Genitive Plural *(cont.)*		
	'of the cats'	'of my cats'	'of these cats'
u	*der Kinder*	*meiner Kinder*	*dieser Kinder*
	'of the children'	'of my children'	'of these children'

Observations

INSTRUCTIONS   Read through the following observations carefully. Make sure you understand each one before moving on to the next.

○ Singular masculine and neuter nouns represented in the chart by *nMann* and *sKind*, have the suffix *-s* or *-es*: *des Mannes, des Kindes* 'of the man, of the child.'

○ Plural masculine and neuter nouns do not have the suffix *-s* or *-es*: *der Männer, der Kinder* 'of the men, of the children.'

○ Singular feminine nouns, represented in the chart by *lKatze* do not have the suffix *-s* or *-es*: *der Katze* 'of the cat.'

○ Plural feminine nouns likewise do not have the suffix *-s* or *-es*: *der Katzen* 'of the cats.'

Right vs. Wrong Strings

INSTRUCTIONS   Read through the English sentences and translate them without looking at the "Right" column. Then check your answers. Notice some common mistakes in the "Wrong" column (denoted with an asterisk). Did you make some of these mistakes?

		Right	Wrong
1.	the address of my brother	*die Adresse <u>meines</u> Bruders*	**die Adresse meines Bruder*
2.	the address of my sister	*die Adresse <u>meiner</u> Schwester*	**die Adresse meiner Schwesters*
3.	the book of this child	*das Buch <u>dieses</u> Kindes*	**das Buch dieses Kind*
4.	the diary of this man	*das Tagebuch <u>dieses</u> Mannes*	**das Tagebuch dieses Mann*
5.	the diary of this lady	*das Tagebuch <u>dieser</u> Dame*	**das Tagebuch dieser Dames*
6.	the things of our parents	*die Dinge <u>unserer</u> Eltern*	**die Dinge unserer Elterns*

But: *Mutters Buch* 'Mother's book'

The Cuckoo Clock Industry

The cuckoo clock industry developed rapidly in the Black Forest region. It began around 1630 and by 1808, there were already 688 clock makers in just two of the Black Forest districts, or areas. Since farms were snowed in during the long winter months, Black Forest clock makers had time to spend carving and crafting exquisite cuckoo clocks out of various woods.

Self Quiz 1

INSTRUCTIONS   Review the German model strings, the chart of genitive forms, and the right vs. wrong strings before taking this quiz. Fill in the missing parts. Check your answers in Appendix A, on page 391.

English	German
1. the name of the dog	der Name ____ Hund__
2. the price of the cat	der Preis ____ Katze
3. the birthday of my son	das Geburtstag ____ Sohn__
4. the diary of my daughter	das Tagebuch ____ Tochter
5. the telephone number of our friends	die Telefonnummer ____ Freunde
6. the address of our grandmother	die Adresse ____ Großmutter
7. This is the address of Your friends.	Das ist die Adresse ____ Freunde.
8. The house of my friends is here.	Das Haus ____ Freunde ist hier.
9. The color of his car is yellow.	Die Farbe ____ Auto__ ist gelb.
10. "We must flee," said one of the soldiers.	"Wir mussen fliehen," sagte einer ____ Soldaten.
11. "No," whispered one of the children.	"Nein," flüsterte eines ____ Kinder.
12. Such was the genius of Mozart.	So war Mozart__ Genie.
13. Oh, the worth of this diary!	Ach, der Wert ____ Tagebuch.

Self Quiz 2

INSTRUCTIONS   Form phrases using masculine, feminine, and neuter nouns in the genitive form with the noun *Tagebuch* (diary). Check your answers in Appendix A, on page 391. Before taking this quiz, review the model strings. Be sure you can correctly translate each of them from German to English and from English to German. Also make sure to review the chart of genitive forms.

Example	Other Words to Practice
1. Das Tagebuch of ■ mein Bruder	(Vater, Sohn, Onkel, Freund)
2. Das Tagebuch of ● deine Schwester	(Mutter, Tochter, Tante, Freundin)
3. Das Tagebuch of ▲ dieses Kind	(Mädchen, Fräulein)

Example *(cont.)*	Other Words to Practice
4. Das Tagebuch of ■ der König	*(Präsident, Doktor, Senator)*
5. Das Tagebuch of ● die Königin	*(Prinzessin, Studentin)*

Performance Challenge

Individual   Using the Power-Glide Flash Cards, see how many correct sentences you can create using genitive forms in five minutes. Keep trying until you get up to twenty.

Performance Challenge

Group   Separate students into pairs. Give each pair six to ten Power-Glide Flash Cards and ask them to write a song or poem using the nouns on the cards. Make sure they use genitive forms at least five times in their work.

Discovery of Grammar 13: Understanding

 In this activity you will:

→ Test your knowledge of the genitive case.

Self Quiz

INSTRUCTIONS   Translate the following sentences. Check your answers in Appendix A, on page 391.

1. The name of the child is Marie.

   ....

2. The name of my cat is Smokey.

   ....

3. The price of this book is five marks.

   ....

4. The price of these two books is only ten marks.

   ....

   ....

5. The price of this vase is ten marks.

   ....

6. Today is the birthday of my sister.

   ....

7. Yesterday was the birthday of my brother.

   ....

8. We're reading (*lesen*) the diary of our grandfather.

   ....

   ....

9. Have You read (*gelesen*) the diary of Your grandfather?

....

....

10. What is the address of Your uncle (*Onkel*) in Berlin?

....

....

11. "We must sleep," said one of the men.

....

12. "No," whispered (*flüsterte*) one of the children.

....

13. Here are Marie's book and Richard's diary.

....

14. Here are my father's house and my mother's car.

....

....

Unity is Strength

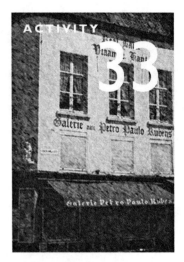

INSTRUCTIONS Listen to and read this story. Focus on understanding every word.

English	German
A man had several sons who often quarreled with each other.	Ein Mann hatte mehrere Söhne, die oft miteinander stritten.
The father tried to teach them to live in peace, but they would not listen.	Der Vater versuchte sie zu lehren, friedlich miteinander zu leben, aber sie wollten nicht hören.
Finally he hit on an idea.	Schließlich hatte er eine Idee.
He gathered several sticks and tied them in a bundle.	Er sammelte mehrere Stöcke und schnürte sie zu einem Bündel zusammen.
Then he called his sons to him and said:	Dann rief er seine Söhne zu sich und sagte:
"Let's see if you can break this bundle of sticks!"	"Lasst uns sehen, ob ihr dieses Bündel von Stöcken zerbrechen könnt!"
Each of the sons took the bundle of sticks and tried with all his might to break it, but they could not.	Jeder von den Söhnen nahm das Bündel von Stöcken und versuchte es mit aller Macht zu zerbrechen, aber sie konnten es nicht.
After they had tried and given up, the father said:	Nachdem sie es versucht hatten und aufgaben, sagte der Vater:
"Now I'll untie the bundle, and each of you take one stick and see if you can break it."	"Nun werde ich das Bündel auseinander schnüren und jedem von euch einen Stock geben und sehen, ob ihr den zerbrechen könnt."
This they did without difficulty.	Das machten sie ohne Schwierigkeiten.
Then the father said:	Dann sagte der Vater:
"When the sticks were bound together you saw how strong they were.	"Ihr habt gesehen, wie stark die Stöcke waren als sie zusammen gebunden waren.
You couldn't break them.	Ihr konntet sie nicht zerbrechen.

In this activity you will:

→ Comprehend the meaning of a story.

  Disc **2** Track **8**

Clock Peddlers

Clocks that were made in the winter were sold all over Europe during the summer. Hundreds of clock peddlers traveled throughout Europe carrying the finely carved clocks on their backs. Each clock was secured onto a wooden frame, which kept the clocks from knocking into each other and being damaged.

English (cont.)	German
But one stick at a time you could break easily.	*Aber einen einzelnen Stock konntet ihr leicht zerbrechen.*
If you stop quarreling and live in peace with each other you'll be like the bundle of sticks.	*Wenn ihr aufhört euch zu streiten und friedlich zusammen lebt, werdet ihr wie das Bündel von Stöcken sein.*
But if you quarrel with each other and live in disunity, you will be as weak as one of the sticks all by itself."	*Aber wenn ihr euch streitet und in Uneinigkeit lebt, werdet ihr schwach sein, wie ein einzelner Stock allein."*
Unity is strength.	*Einigkeit ist Stärke.*

Performance Challenge

Individual   Choose a German sport that is in season. Research and choose a team to follow. Keep track of the team's performance throughout the season. At the end, write an article on the season, using as much German as possible. Rough out some ideas below.

....

....

....

....

....

....

....

Performance Challenge

Group   Split your students into teams. Have them research sports teams from different German-speaking countries and have each group follow its chosen teams' performances. Have students write brief articles on their teams' performances and the high points of the season.

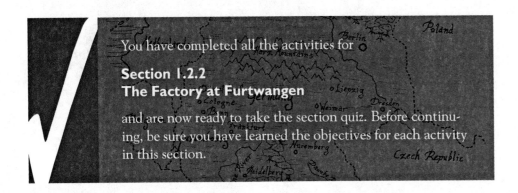

You have completed all the activities for

Section 1.2.2
The Factory at Furtwangen

and are now ready to take the section quiz. Before continuing, be sure you have learned the objectives for each activity in this section.

Section 1.2.2 Quiz

INSTRUCTIONS   Choose the correct response. Check your answers in Appendix D, on page 402.

1. In "The Key of the Kingdom," which of the following cannot be found in the kingdom?

   A. *die Prinzessin*

   B. *das leere Zimmer*

   C. *der engen Gasse*

   D. *die chinesische Vase*

2. How do you translate "of a child?"

   A. *einer Kindes*

   B. *eines Kindes*

   C. *eine Kindes*

   D. *einen Kindes*

3. Which does NOT describe the location of the house in The Key of the Kingdom?

   A. *auf der breiten Straße*

   B. *in dem grünen Garten*

   C. *in der chinesischen Vase*

   D. *in die Stadt*

4. How do you translate "of the cats?"

   A. *der Katzen*

   B. *meiner Katzen*

   C. *dieser Katzen*

   D. *eines Katzen*

SECTION 1.2.2

5. **What is the capital city of Liechtenstein?**

   A. Rapal

   B. Prague

   C. Vaduz

   D. Terrort

6. **What object does the father compare his sons to in "Unity is Strength?"**

   A. *ein starkes Haus*

   B. *eine Idee*

   C. *ein Bündel von Stöcken*

   D. *ein Mann*

7. **How would you translate "the address of my brother?"**

   A. *die Adresse dieses meiner Bruders*

   B. *das Adresse meiner Bruders*

   C. *die Adresse meines Bruder.*

   D. *die Adresse meines Bruders*

8. **Which of the following is not an official language of Liechtenstein?**

   A. Italian

   B. French

   C. German

   D. English

9. **In the story "Unity is Strength," what will happen to the man's sons if they quarrel with each other?**

   A. *Sie es versucht hatten.*

   B. *Werder ihr schwach sein, wie ein einzelner Stock allein.*

   C. *Versuchte sie zu lehren.*

   D. *Dan machten sie ohne Schwierigkeiten.*

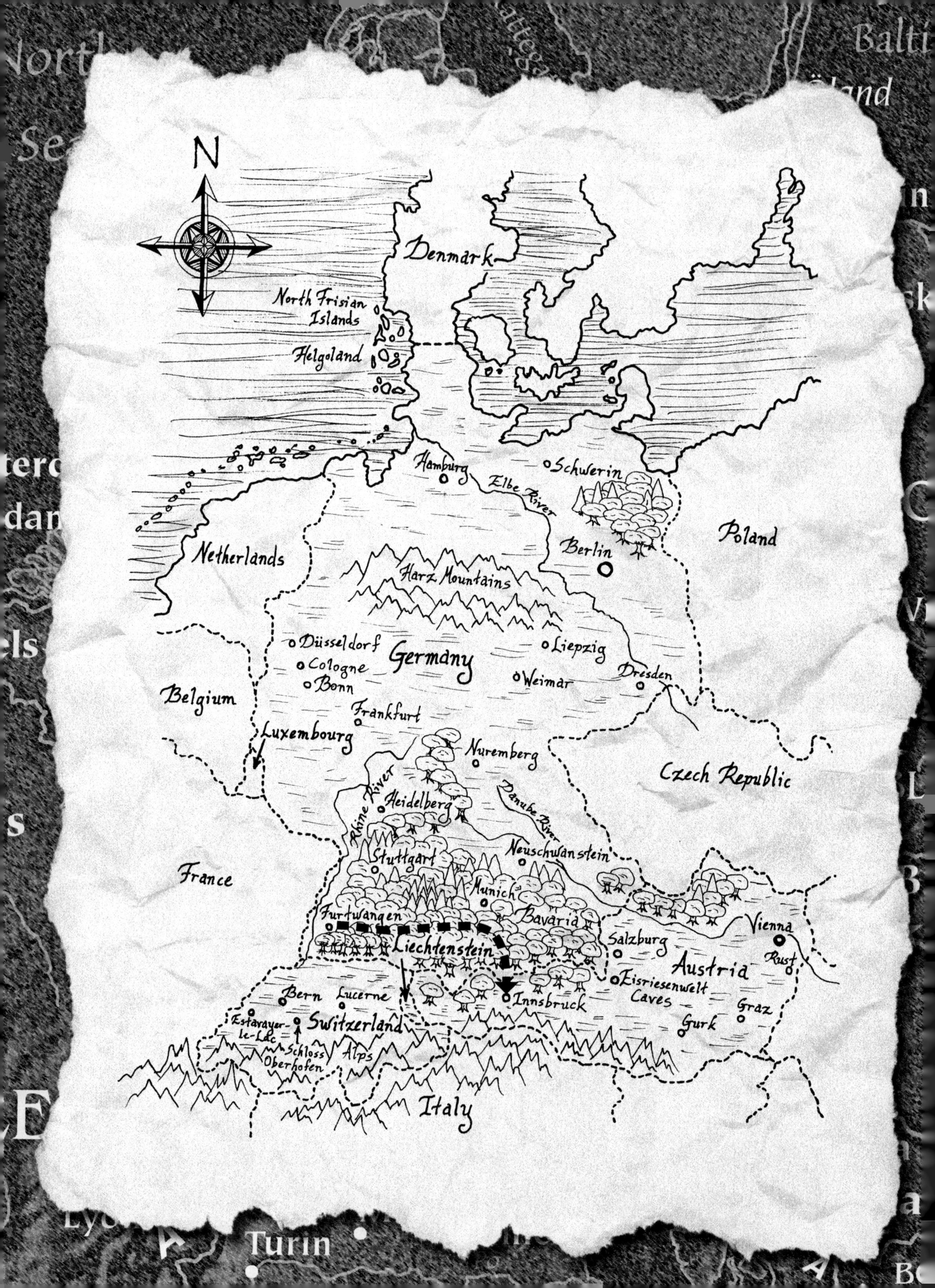

Two Narrow Escapes

After a few hours, you see the skyline of Innsbruck in the distance. You exit the freeway and follow the signs to a hotel. As you stop at a downtown traffic light, though, cars from every direction pull into the intersection. A man wearing sunglasses gets out of one of the cars and walks over to your truck.

"Follow my lead," you say, nodding to Spinne.

The man gestures for you to roll your window down. You comply.

"*Hallo, mein Freund,*" the man says to you. *"Du hast ein paar Sachen, die dir nicht gehören."*

"I'm sorry, I don't speak German," you reply. "We are here for an exchange at the local university."

"The university?" the man repeats.

"Yes, we are here studying weather patterns." You turn to Spinne who shrugs like he doesn't understand the man either.

"Du sprichst kein Deutsch?" he says. *"Ich glaube dir nicht. Gib uns jetzt die Schlüssel."*

"I'm sorry, what?" you ask. "Do you speak English?"

Frustrated, the man reaches into the truck cabin, just as you hit the gas with your truck in reverse. The man is knocked off balance and falls to the street. By the time he rises and runs to his car, you and Spider have backed up at least two blocks. Turning off into a side street, you hear the tires of several cars screeching away from the intersection to follow you.

You drive as fast as you can on such a small street, careful not to hit the vendors selling fruits and vegetables along the side of the road.

"They're closing in on us! Step on it!" Spinne yells. The sounds of screaming can be heard as the five cars knock over fruit and vegetable stands.

"Move it! Move it!" Spinne's voice sounds panicked.

One of the cars is right on your tail. The passenger of the car leans out of the window and points what looks like a harpoon at the truck.

In this section you will:

→ Use more small talk on a formal level.

→ Expand your comprehension toward complete understanding.

→ Comprehend the meaning of a story.

→ Learn how to use possessives.

→ Test your knowledge of possessional case.

→ Follow a *Geschichte* with full comprehension.

 Disc **2**   Track **9**

"Whoa! If you can turn, now is the time!" yells Spinne.

Just then, the road widens into a plaza filled with vendor stands. You turn right just as the passenger shoots the harpoon with a long cable attached to it. Instead of latching onto the back of your truck, the anchor hits a power pole. The car slams on it brakes, but it still smashes into the pole, spouting steam from the engine while sparks rain down from the damaged pole.

The other cars are delayed for a few seconds, finding safe passage around the crashed car. That doesn't stop them, though. You see an opening between two vendors of brightly woven area rugs. You steer the truck through the opening and conceal the truck behind one booth. The cars following your truck pull into the plaza, then drive out through one of the streets meeting the plaza without noticing your hiding place.

You swiftly explain the situation to the rug vendor, who's looking puzzled and worried. He nods after listening to your story and gives you directions to the salt mine. After a few minutes of cautious waiting, you pull out from behind the rug vendor's booth. You follow his directions and arrive safely at the salt mine just outside of Innsbruck.

The mine no longer produces salt but has been converted into a museum of sorts. You find the quickest way inside is to join a tour. Upon purchasing your tickets, you are given a white jumpsuit and booties.

"What are these for?" you ask.

"For the slides," says the guide. "We don't have staircases here. We use huge wooden slides to get from level to level within the mine. The suits protect the slides and your clothes."

You and Spinne zip up the white suits and place the booties over your shoes. As you move into the mine, the tour guide drones on about the formation of natural salt and the process of mining it.

"Please stay close to the crowd. There are certain areas of the mine that are not safe for the tourists," says the tour guide. "Now, this mine has over 35 shafts which move out like a wheel around a central area."

"Hey Spinne, look," you say, pointing to a ten-foot wide wooden semicircle leading downward behind you. "It's a slide, come on."

You and Spinne break away from the group and sit on the edge of the slide. Letting go, you slide down a 30-foot wooden half-tube. The breeze gets cooler as you descend. You and Spinne spill out onto the next level. It's pitch black. This area obviously is not on the tour route. You switch on a flashlight and take in your surroundings. You're standing in a long tunnel, much narrower than the one a level above you. Not 20 feet from where you are standing, the tunnel has collapsed, completely blocking the tunnel that way.

"I guess that means we go this way," Spinne says, walking away from the collapsed area. "I sure hope this was a good idea, Fliege."

As you're turning to follow him, though, you hear something other than Spinne's voice. Other voices, harsh and unfriendly, drift down the slide from above.

"*Wo sind sie?*" asks one voice. "*Ich weiß genau, dass sie hier entlang gekommen sind. Ihr LKW steht draußen vor der Tür.*"

"*Ich weiß nicht,*" answers a second voice. "*Sie müssen mit der Reisegruppe gegangen sein. Los. Wir können sie noch einholen.*"

The voices fade, moving away from the slide, and you hurry after Spinne. After you've walked for half an hour, the tunnel opens into a salty, man-made cavern. In one corner of the cavern, you see a dark shape that stands out against the pale white of the cavern walls. You rush up to it. It's a bundle of twigs, tightly bound together. A bundle of twigs. Unity. You suddenly remember the story you studied.

"This is it!" you tell Spinne.

You untie the bundle. In a padded cloth pouch at the center of the bundle is a heavy key carved of obsidian. Next to it is an envelope in which you find another sheet of music. Spinne places the stone key with the silver and wood keys, while you tuck the new sheet of music into a secret compartment of your bag with the other sheets.

"Come on, let's get out of here," you say.

Just then, somewhere nearby, an explosion shakes the ground. Salt showers down, irritating your eyes so badly that you can barely see, and boulders tumble down the cavern walls, narrowly missing you.

"This way!" you hear Spinne shouting. Blindly, you follow his voice. After several minutes, the air clears, and you're able to see where you are. You're in another narrow tunnel. There's light up ahead that's not coming from Spinne's flashlight, and fresh, cool air flows down the tunnel toward you. Moments later, you emerge into the soft, late afternoon sunshine. Carefully, you make your way back around the mountain to the salt mine's parking lot. After checking to make sure no one's following you, you steer the truck out of the parking lot and back toward Innsbruck.

Back at your hotel in Innsbruck, you and Spinne study for a while, then head to your rooms for some much-needed rest. Hopefully, what you're learning will help you get the next key.

Conversation Snatches 10

ACTIVITY

34

✓ **In this activity you will:**

→ Use more small talk on a formal level.

 Disc **2** Track **10**

INSTRUCTIONS Listen to and read these dialogues. Then make up new dialogues of your own!

English	German
How late is it, please?	*Wie spät ist es, bitte?*
I'm sorry, but I don't know.	*Es tut mir leid, aber ich weiß es nicht.*
It's six o'clock.	*Es ist sechs Uhr.*
Why are we still working? It's late.	*Warum arbeiten wir noch? Es ist schon spät.*
Let's quit then.	*Los, hören wir auf.*
Yeah, let's go home.	*Ja, gehen wir nach Hause.*
You're smarter than I am.	*Sie sind klüger als ich.*
Yes, and don't forget that!	*Ja, und vergessen Sie das nicht!*
Do you guys know the latest?	*Wisst ihr schon das Neueste?*
Tell us.	*Erzähl es uns.*
My wife is going to have a baby.	*Meine Frau wird ein Baby bekommen.*
What do you want to see in Germany?	*Was willst du in Deutschland sehen?*
As much as possible.	*So viel wie möglich.*
How do you like Germany?	*Wie gefällt dir Deutschland?*
I feel very much at home here.	*Ich fühle mich hier sehr zu Hause.*
Germany is very beautiful, a beautiful land.	*Deutschland ist sehr schön, ein schönes Land.*
I'm of the same opinion.	*Der Meinung bin ich auch.*
Give him one dollar and me one dollar, please.	*Geben Sie ihm bitte einen Dollar und mir einen.*

Clock Making Today

Cuckoo clocks are still manufactured in the Black Forest, although the dimly lit workshops of the past have given way to the well-lit, well-equipped workshops of today. Modern methods are used to manufacture the moving clock parts inside each cuckoo clock are manufactured, but the art of clock making really hasn't changed that much since its beginnings 200 years ago. Some of the same designs and patterns used then are still in use today. The intricate carving done on the outside of each clock is still done by hand by skilled masters.

English *(cont.)*	German
I'll give you one and her one and them one, OK?	*Ich werde dir einen und ihr einen und ihnen einen geben, OK?*
Thanks for Your help.	*Danke für Ihre Hilfe.*
We thank You.	*Wir danken Ihnen.*
We're there.	*Wir sind da.*
Finally!	*Endlich!*
Do You understand Russian?	*Verstehen Sie Russisch?*
I have studied Russian four years, but I speak German better than Russian.	*Ich habe vier Jahre Russisch gelernt, aber ich spreche Deutsch besser als Russisch.*
Don't You know who I am?	*Wissen Sie nicht, wer ich bin?*
No, I don't know.	*Nein, das weiß ich nicht.*
I am Professor Dr. Heinrich Jäger.	*Ich bin Professor Dr. Heinrich Jäger.*
Well that is very nice.	*Das ist aber sehr schön.*

Performance Challenge

Individual   Choose one of the conversation snatches and fill in the rest of the conversation. What might people have been saying before that snatch to lead up to it? How might the conversation have gone afterward? Have fun, and be creative!

Performance Challenge

Group   Divide students into pairs or small groups, and have each group choose one of the conversation snatches. Have them develop it into a full conversation, using as much German as possible. Then, have them perform the conversation for their classmates.

The Wind and the Sun

In this activity you will:

→ Expand your comprehension toward complete understanding.

Disc **2**   Track **11**

INSTRUCTIONS   Listen to and read the following story. Read along with the German voice on the audio.

Der Wind und die Sonne

Eines Tages stritten die Sonne und der Wind miteinander. Der Wind rühmte sich seiner Macht.

"Mit meinem Atem kann ich große Stürme hervorrufen. Ich kann große Schiffe versenken, große Bäume umstürzen, und sogar Städte zerstören. Du kannst nichts von diesem tun. Du musst sicher zugeben, dass deine Macht nicht so groß ist, wie meine." Die Sonne sprach bescheiden:

"Ich gebe zu, dass deine Macht wahrhaftig groß ist, aber du bist zu prahlerisch. Was hältst du von einem Wettkampf? Siehst du den Mann, der da unten entlang läuft? Er trägt eine Jacke. Lass uns sehen, wer es von uns beiden schafft, dass er die Jacke auszieht."

"Fein," sagte der Wind.

"Ich werde es zuerst versuchen." Der Wind ging hinab und begann zu blasen, aber der Mann hielt seine Jacke noch stärker fest. Um so stärker der Wind blies, desto stärker hielt der Mann seine Jacke fest. Schließlich gab der Wind auf. Und die Sonne sagte:

"Nun lass mich es versuchen." Die Sonne bewegte sich von hinter den Wolken hervor und fing auf den Mann zu scheinen an. Bald fing der Mann zu schwitzen an und es dauerte nicht lange bevor er seine Jacke auszog. Die Sonne sagte:

"Überzeugung ist besser als Zwang. Und wenn du prahlen musst, dann nicht mit dem Schaden den du verursachen kannst, sondern mit den guten Dingen, die du vollbringen kannst."

Innsbruck, Part I

Innsbruck is the only major city located in Austria's Eastern Alps. Because of its location high in the mountains, Innsbruck has become a winter sports capital. Many tourists are drawn to Innsbruck's first-rate ski resorts and sports facilities every year. Tourists even like to come to Innsbruck during the summer to go hiking in the Alps and to enjoy the natural beauties of this mountain city.

★ Performance Challenge

Individual   Go on the Internet and find the weather forecast for your city for the next week. Translate it into German and share it with a family member or friend. Write your translation below.

....

....

....

....

....

....

....

....

....

....

....

....

....

....

★ Performance Challenge

Group   Take the nouns out of this story and write them on flashcards. Divide the group into two teams. Each team takes a stack of flashcards and creates as many sentences in German as they can in three minutes.

Two Stubborn Goats

In this activity you will:

→ Comprehend the meaning of a story.

Disc **2**   Track **12**

INSTRUCTIONS   Listen to and read the following story. Do your best to comprehend some of the new vocabulary.

English	German
In ancient Greece there was once a man called Aesop who could tell stories.	Im alten Griechenland war einmal ein Mann namens Aesop, der Geschichten erzählen konnte.
The stories he told took place more than 2000 years ago.	Die Geschichten, die er erzählte, handelten vor mehr als 2000 Jahren.
One of the stories he told is about two stubborn goats.	Eine Geschichte, die er erzählte, handelte von zwei dickköpfigen Ziegen.
One day a large tree fell across a river, making a narrow bridge.	Eines Tages fiel ein großer Baum quer über einen Fluss, und bildete eine Brücke.
It happened that two goats wanted to cross the bridge at the same time from opposite sides, but the bridge was so narrow that only one after another could cross it at a time.	Es begab sich, dass zwei Ziegen die Brücke zur gleichen Zeit von entgegengesetzter Seite überqueren wollten, aber die Brücke war so schmal, dass nur eine nach der anderen sie überqueren konnte.
What do you think happened?	Was denkst du, was geschah?
Of course, they knocked heads at the middle of the bridge, but each obstinately refused to give way to the other.	Natürlich stießen sie mit ihren Köpfen mitten auf der Brücke zusammen, aber beide waren hartnäckig und gaben der anderen nicht nach.
Both struggled to push the other back.	Beide kämpften, um die andere zurück zuschieben.

English *(cont.)*	German
They pushed until both fell into the river and drowned.	*Sie schoben so lange, bis beide in den Fluss fielen und ertranken.*

Innsbruck, Part II

The Winter Olympics were held in Innsbruck in both 1964 and 1976. As a result, many buildings were constructed for the purpose of accommodating the thousands of athletes and visitors who came to Innsbruck to participate in and watch the Olympic games. An entire residential development, Olympic Village, was created. This still thriving village is centered around the Olympia Eishalle, which was originally used solely for sporting events. Now concerts and other non-sporting events can be attended at the Olympia Eishalle.

Performance Challenge

Individual Find a copy of Aesop's Fables. Choose your favorite fable, and write a one page paper on it, in German. Share your what you have written with your family or friends. Rough out some ideas below.

Performance Challenge

Group Play "Tug of War" with the group in two teams. The team that wins the tug has to answer a question about the story, in German. If they answer correctly, they get a point. If they answer incorrectly, the other team gets a point.

Discovery of Grammar 14

 In this activity you will:

➡ Learn how to use possessives.

Possession and Belonging

Model Strings

INSTRUCTIONS   Study the following sentences to get a feel for how each word is used.

	English	German
1.	Who does this book belong to? It's mine.	*Wem gehört dieses Buch? Es ist meines.*
2.	Who do these keys belong to?	*Wem gehören diese Schlüssel?*
3.	They belong to us. They are ours.	*Sie gehören uns. Sie sind unsere.*
4.	This key is not ours; it is Yours.	*Dieser Schlüssel ist nicht unserer; er ist Ihrer.*
5.	Ours is the big one; Yours is the small one.	*Unser ist der große; Ihrer ist der kleine.*
6.	Hers is the red one; his is the green one.	*Ihrer ist der rote; seiner ist der grüne.*
7.	Mine is the white one; Karl's is the blue one.	*Meiner ist der weiße; Karls ist der blaue.*
8.	This blouse is not mine; it is mother's.	*Diese Bluse ist nicht meine; sie ist Mutters.*
9.	This book is not mine; it is yours.	*Dieses Buch ist nicht meines; es ist deines.*
10.	These books are not ours; they are theirs.	*Diese Bücher sind nicht unsere; sie sind ihre.*
11.	Whose ring is this? Mine. It belongs to me.	*Wessen Ring ist das? Meiner. Er gehört mir.*

English (cont.)	German
12. Whose vase is this? Does it belong to You?	*Wessen Vase ist das? Gehört sie Ihnen?*
13. No, it belongs to my sister.	*Nein, sie gehört meiner Schwester.*

Right vs. Wrong Strings

INSTRUCTIONS   Read through the English sentences and translate them without looking at the "Right" column. Then check your answers. Notice some common mistakes in the "Wrong" column. Did you make some of these mistakes?

		Right	Wrong
1.	This key is yours.	*Dieser Schlüssel ist deiner.*	*Dieser Schlüssel ist dein.*
2.	This book is his...Karl's.	*Dieses Buch ist seines...Karls.*	*Dieses Buch ist sein...Karls.*
3.	This blouse is hers...Ruth's.	*Diese Bluse ist ihre...Ruths.*	*Diese Bluse ist ihrer...Ruths.*
4.	This vase is Yours.	*Diese Vase ist Ihre.*	*Diese Vase ist Ihrer.*
5.	This vase is ours.	*Diese Vase ist unsere.*	*Diese Vase ist unser.*
6.	Are these things yours?	*Sind diese Dinge eure?*	*Sind diese Dinge eurer?*
7.	Whose ring is this?	*Wessen Ring ist das?*	*Wesser Ring ist das?*

Observations

INSTRUCTIONS   Read through the following observations. Make sure you understand each one before moving on to the next.

○ Names and persons indicate possession by the suffix -s (without an apostrophe). *Karls* (Karl's), *Maries* (Marie's), *Vaters* (father's), *Mutters* (mother's), *Omas* (grandma's), *Opas* (grandpa's)

○ The verb *gehören* (to belong) governs the dative case. *Das gehört mir.* (That belongs to me.) *Diese Dinge gehören dir.* (These things belong to you.)

○ 'Whose' is *wessen*, as in 'Whose watch is this?' *Wessen Armbanduhr ist das?*

○ *Das ist unserer* is a grammatically correct and possible response to the question: *Wessen Schlüssel ist das?*

Chart of Possessive Pronouns

The possessive pronouns (my / mine, your / yours, our / ours, etc.) need special attention and review. Below is a chart of the possessive pronouns (*meiner, deiner, seiner, Ihrer / ihrer, unserer, eurer*) as observed in sentences like the following:

1. This ring is mine, and this book is mine, and this vase is also mine.
   Dieser Ring ist meiner und dieses Buch ist meines und diese Vase ist auch meine.

2. Take my ring, my book, and my vase.
   Nehmen Sie meinen Ring, mein Buch und meine Vase.

3. Give the ring to my father, the book to my mother, and the vase to my child.
   Geben Sie den Ring meinem Vater, das Buch meiner Mutter und die Vase meinem Kind.

4. Give the things of my parents to my grandparents.
   Geben Sie die Dinge meiner Eltern meinen Großeltern.

5. Here are the book of my father, the car of my mother, and the house of my parents.
   Hier sind das Buch meines Vaters, das Auto meiner Mutter und das Haus meiner Eltern.

Singular

	Nominative	Accusative	Dative	Genitive
■	mein / meiner	meinen	meinem	meines
●	meine	meine	meiner	meiner
▲	mein	mein	meinem	meines

Plural

	Nominative	Accusative	Dative	Genitive
	meine	meine	meinen	meiner

Dealing With Real Communication

As before, place three books in front of you: one you identify as your brother's, the second you identify as your sister's, the third as your parents' (*Eltern*). Your task is to see how many meaningful statements you can make about the books and their "owners" in two minutes. You may take two minutes for planning things to say before you begin. You know how to make a variety of statements such as "This book is not mine, and that book is not yours." Gradually move from simple to more complex statements. Say each sentence out loud. Aim for fluency and confidence in speaking.

Prepositions

Some prepositions that govern the genitive case: *während, außer, anstatt* (or *statt*), *diesseits, jenseits, wegen.*

Model Strings

INSTRUCTIONS Read through these sentences so that you can get a feel for how these words are used.

English	German
1. They came during the war.	*Sie kamen während des Krieges.*
2. Everyone is here except for your mother.	*Alle sind hier außer deiner Mutter.*
3. My father and mother went instead of my brother and sister.	*Mein Vater und meine Mutter gingen anstatt meines Bruders und meiner Schwester.*
4. My house is [on] this side of the river.	*Mein Haus ist diesseits des Flusses.*
5. My brother's house is on the far side of the park.	*Das Haus meines Bruders ist jenseits des Parks.*
6. Because of this situation, I must work tomorrow.	*Wegen dieser ⬤? Situation muss ich morgen arbeiten.*

Right vs. Wrong Strings

INSTRUCTIONS Read through the English sentences and translate them without looking at the "Right" column. Then check your answers. Notice some common mistakes in the "Wrong" column. Did you make some of these mistakes?

	Right	Wrong
1. instead of my father	*anstatt <u>meines</u> <u>Vaters</u>*	*anstatt mein Vater*
2. instead of my mother	*anstatt <u>meiner</u> Mutter*	*anstatt meine Mutter*
3. except for Your sister	*außer <u>Ihrer</u> Schwester*	*außer Ihr Schwester*
4. except for Your brother	*außer <u>Ihres</u> <u>Bruders</u>*	*außer Ihr Bruder*
5. during the picnic	*während <u>des</u> ▲ <u>Picknicks</u>*	*während das Picknick*
6. during the class	*während <u>der</u> ⬤ Klasse*	*während die Klasse*
7. this side of the lake	*diesseits <u>des</u> ■ Sees*	*diesseits des See*

Hall, Innsbruck's Neighbor

When Innsbruck was just a small village, Hall was a rich, salt-mining center. Today, visitors escaping the busy, big city of Innsbruck come to the modest town of Hall where they can tour an old salt mine, drink fresh milk from one of the three dairy farms nearby, and make a coin the traditional way at Hall's 500-year-old mint.

What happens when you add adjectives after {DER} or {EIN} words?

Model Strings (With Adjectives)

INSTRUCTIONS   See the words you've learned being used in sentences. Study these examples and get a feel for how each word is used.

	English	German
1.	the phone number of my good (f) friend	*die Telefonnummer meiner guten Freundin*
2.	the diary of a poor old man	*das Tagebuch eines armen, alten Mannes*
3.	the diary of the old lady	*das Tagebuch der alten Dame*
4.	the price of the new book	*der Preis des neuen Buches*
5.	the price of a new book	*der Preis eines neuen Buches*
6.	the worth of a good man	*der Wert eines guten Mannes*
7.	the worth of a good woman	*der Wert einer guten Frau*
8.	the blue vase instead of a red vase	*die blaue Vase anstatt einer roten Vase*
9.	because of Your younger brother	*wegen Ihres jüngeren Bruders*
10.	because of Your younger sister	*wegen Ihrer jüngeren Schwester*

Observations

Adjectives are known to be either "weak" or "strong."

Weak Form   An adjective is considered in its "weak form" when one of the following conditions apply:

- When adjectives come after a {DER}, {EIN} or {DIES} word
- When adjectives modify a masculine, feminine or neuter noun

For both of these conditions, the adjective takes the suffix *-en*.

Strong Form   When there is no {DER}, {EIN} or {DIES} word before an adjective, and / or when it does not modify a masculine, feminine or neuter noun, the adjective is in its "strong form." This means that it stands by itself in front of a noun.

Which of these sentences have strong form adjectives? See Activity 43 if you need any help.

English	German
1. Good tea is expensive here.	_Guter_ ▪ _Tee ist hier teuer._
2. Good milk is also expensive.	_Gute_ ● _Milch ist auch teuer._
3. But good water is free.	_Aber gutes_ ▲ _Wasser ist kostenlos._
4. without good tea and without good milk	_ohne guten Tee und ohne gute Milch_
5. with good tea and good milk	_mit gutem Tee und mit guter Milch_
6. with the good tea and the good milk	_mit dem guten Tee und mit der guten Milch_
7. without my good tea and my good milk	_ohne meinen guten Tee und ohne meine gute Milch_
8. the price of good milk and good tea	_der Preis guter Milch und guten Tees_
9. the price of the good milk and the good tea	_der Preis der guten Milch und des guten Tees_
10. the worth of good men and good women	_der Wert guter Männer und guter Frauen_

★

Performance Challenge

Individual   Research the famous German scientist Werhner von Braun. Teach a friend or family member about his life and his accomplishments. Also teach at least five German phrases and how they are pronounced.

★

Performance Challenge

Group   Assign groups of students to teach a short science lesson on rockets and space travel. Then watch the footage of the US landing on the moon in 1969. Have a group discussion about what you have learned using as much German as possible.

Discovery of Grammar 14: Understanding

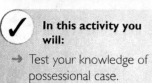

In this activity you will:

→ Test your knowledge of possessional case.

Self Quiz

INSTRUCTIONS Translate the following sentences. Check your answers in Appendix A, on page 391.

1. My key is red.

   ....

2. This red key is mine.

   ....

3. Karl's key is blue.

   ....

4. Mother's key is green.

   ....

5. This book is not ours; it is Yours.

   ....

6. Our book is green; Your book is blue.

   ....

7. Yes, Yours is the blue one; ours is the green one.

   ....

8. Her glass is the red one; his is the green one.

   ....

9. This vase is not mine; it is father's.

   ....

10. This vase is not ours; it is theirs.

....

11. Whose watch (● *Armbanduhr*) is this? Mine. It belongs to me.

....

....

12. Does this ring belong to You?

....

13. Yes, it is mine.

....

14. And this one belongs to my sister.

....

15. Who does this thing belong to? To us.

....

39

Questions of a Small Child 7

✓ **In this activity you will:**

→ Follow a *Geschichte* with full comprehension.

 Disc **2**   Track **13**

INSTRUCTIONS   Listen to and read the following conversation.

English	German
Who is my cousin?	*Wer ist mein Cousin?*
Dieter is your cousin.	*Dieter ist dein Cousin.*
I know, but what is a cousin?	*Ich weiß, aber was ist denn ein Cousin?*
Dieter is your uncle's son.	*Dieter ist der Sohn deines Onkels.*
But what is an uncle?	*Aber was ist ein Onkel?*
Your uncle is the brother of your father or of your mother.	*Dein Onkel ist der Bruder deines Vaters oder deiner Mutter.*
So a cousin is the son of my father's brother?	*So, ein Cousin ist der Sohn meines Vaters Bruders?*
Exactly.	*Genau!*

Performance Challenge

Individual   Choose a family member in this activity and write about your favorite memory of him or her. Use as much German as possible. Then share what you have written with that family member. Rough out some ideas below.

....

....

....

....

The Salt Mines of Hall

In the days when salt was money, Hall was a wealthy town. Salt was mined in deep, underground pits and shafts, which can still be seen today. Salt is literally what gave this small town its name. Hall, is an ancient word for salt.

....

....

....

....

....

....

....

....

....

....

....

....

....

....

....

....

....

....

Performance Challenge

Group   Have students write three-generation family pedigree charts.
Once completed, have them tell choose a family member they are most
like and describe in German their similar characteristics.

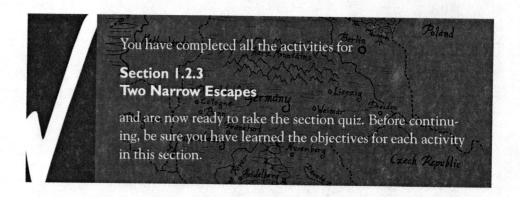

You have completed all the activities for

Section 1.2.3
Two Narrow Escapes

and are now ready to take the section quiz. Before continuing, be sure you have learned the objectives for each activity in this section.

Section 1.2.3 Quiz

INSTRUCTIONS   Choose the correct response. Check your answers in Appendix D, on page 402.

1. **In Conversation Snatches, what is the latest?**

    A. *Das ist aber sehr schön.*

    B. *Meine Frau wird ein Baby bekommen.*

    C. *Wir danken Ihnen.*

    D. *Ich spreche Deutsch besser als Russisch.*

2. **Also in Conversation Snatches, why do they quit working?**

    A. *Es ist sechs Uhr.*

    B. *Ich weiß es nicht.*

    C. *Erzähl es uns.*

    D. *Ja, und vergessen Sie das nicht.*

3. **Who is stronger, the wind or the sun?**

    A. the sun

    B. the wind

    C. they are the same

4. **What ultimately happened to the two stubborn goats?**

    A. *Beide kämpften, um die andere zurück zuschieben.*

    B. *Stießen sie mit ihren Köpfen mittenauf der Brücke zusammen.*

    C. *Sie schoben so lange, bis beide in den Fluss fielen und ertranken.*

    D. *Aber die Brücke was so schmal.*

5. **Which of the following is the correct translation of "The vase is ours?"**

    A. *Diese Vase ist Ihre.*

    B. *Diese Vase ist Ihrer.*

    C. *Diese Vase ist unser.*

    D. *Diese Vase ist unsere.*

6. **Which of the following it the correct translation of "instead of my father?"**

    A. *anstatt meines Vaters*

    B. *anstatt mein Vater*

    C. *anstatt meines Vater*

    D. *anstatt mein Vaters*

7. **Which of the following is not a characteristic of a "strong adjective?"**

    A. It does not modify a masculine or feminine noun.

    B. There is no *der, ein,* or *dies* word before the adjective.

    C. It does not modify a neuter noun.

    D. It does not modify a singular noun.

8. **Which of the following is in the singular accusative form?**

    A. *mein*

    B. *meinem*

    C. *meiner*

    D. *meines*

9. **Which of the following is in the plural genitive form?**

    A. *meine*

    B. *meiner*

    C. *meinen*

    D. *meines*

10. **As a small child would ask, what is an uncle?**

    A. *Ist dein Cousin*

    B. *Ist der Sohn meines Vaters Bruders*

    C. *Ist der Bruder deines Vaters oder deiner Mutter.*

    D. *Ist der Sohn deines Onkels.*

You have completed all the sections for

Module 1.2

and are now ready to take the module test. Before continuing, be sure you have learned the objectives for each activity in this module.

Module 1.2 Test

INSTRUCTIONS   Choose the correct German translation of the English word or phrase. Check your answers in Appendix D, on page 401.

1. **dog**
    A. *das Schwein*
    B. *der Wolf*
    C. *der Vogel*
    D. *der Hund*

2. **cat**
    A. *die Katze*
    B. *der Adler*
    C. *Das Nilpferd*
    D. *Das Krokodil*

3. **why**
    A. *was*
    B. *wie*
    C. *warum*
    D. *weil*

4. **oh my**
    A. *na nu*
    B. *wieso*
    C. *ach, meine Gute*
    D. *nein*

5. **because**

   A. *was*

   B. *warum*

   C. *wenn*

   D. *weil*

6. **imagine that**

   A. *glauben Sie*

   B. *stellen Sie sich das vor*

   C. *wissen Sie*

   D. *denken Sie*

7. **together**

   A. *getrennt*

   B. *zusammen*

   C. *zwischen*

   D. *verschleppen*

8. **worse than**

   A. *besser als*

   B. *dicker als*

   C. *schlechter als*

   D. *mehr besser*

9. **How late is it?**

   A. *Wieviel Uhr ist es?*

   B. *Wie spat ist es?*

   C. *Was ist die Zeit?*

   D. *Wie kommt es?*

10. **I'm sorry, but I don't know.**

    A. *Ich weiß nicht.*

    B. *Es ist halb zwei.*

    C. *Es tut mir leid.*

    D. *Es tut mir leid, aber ich weiß nicht.*

11. **It's 6 o'clock.**

    A. *Es ist halb sechs.*

    B. *Es ist sieben Uhr.*

    C. *Es ist sechs Uhr.*

    D. *Es ist elf Uhr.*

12. **Why are we still working?**

    A. *Warum laufen wir?*

    B. *Warum schlafen wir spät?*

    C. *Warum arbeiten wir spat?*

    D. *Warum arbeiten wir noch?*

13. **Let's quit then.**

    A. *Fahren wir auf.*

    B. *Hören wir auf.*

    C. *Fangen wir an.*

    D. *Kommen wir an.*

14. **You're smarter than I am.**

    A. *Sie sind schneller als er.*

    B. *Du bist größer als ich.*

    C. *Sie sind klüger als ich.*

    D. *Du bist langsamer als ich.*

15. **Yes, and don't forget it.**

    A. *Ja, und vergeben Sie es nicht.*

    B. *Ja, und vergessen Sie es nicht.*

    C. *Nein, das gibt's doch nicht.*

    D. *Ja, und was soll das?*

16. **How do you like Germany?**

    A. *Fahren wir nach Deutschland?*

    B. *Wie gefällt es dir Deutschland?*

    C. *Gefällt es dir Eisland?*

    D. *Wird Deutschland vereinigen?*

MODULE 1.2

INSTRUCTIONS   Choose the correct English translation of the German word or phrase.

17. *rühmte sich*
   A. prided itself
   B. boasted
   C. lied
   D. lost

18. *Macht*
   A. weakness
   B. breath
   C. strength
   D. destructiveness

19. *Atem*
   A. breath
   B. sound
   C. strength
   D. power

20. *Stürme*
   A. hurricanes
   B. tornadoes
   C. storms
   D. earthquakes

21. *Schiffe*
   A. trains
   B. airplanes
   C. trees
   D. ships

22. *umstürzen*
   A. throw
   B. destroy
   C. overturn
   D. burn

23. **zerstören**
    A. destroy
    B. overturn
    C. overthrow
    D. bury

24. **Dingen**
    A. items
    B. disasters
    C. earthquakes
    D. things

25. **groß**
    A. weak
    B. small
    C. big
    D. strong

Module 1.3

Throughout this module we'll be learning about Bavarian coats of arms and Lucerne, Switzerland.

Keep these tips in mind as you progress through this module:

1. Read instructions carefully.

2. Repeat aloud all the German words you hear on the audio CDs.

3. Learn at your own pace.

4. Have fun with the activities and practice your new language skills with others.

5. Record yourself speaking German on tape so you can evaluate your own speaking progress.

N

North Sea

Baltic

Denmark

North Frisian Islands

Helgoland

Netherlands

Hamburg

Schwerin

Elbe River

Berlin

Poland

Harz Mountains

Düsseldorf

Germany

Liepzig

Cologne

Bonn

Weimar

Dresden

Belgium

Frankfurt

Luxembourg

Nuremberg

Czech Republic

Rhine River

Heidelberg

Danube River

France

Stuttgart

Neuschwanstein

Munich

Furtwangen

Bavaria

Liechtenstein

Salzburg

Vienna

Bern

Lucerne

Innsbruck

Austria

Rust

Estavayer-le-Lac

Switzerland

Eisriesenwelt Caves

Graz

Schloss Oberhofen

Alps

Gurk

Italy

Turin

Racing South

Morning comes too soon, and you wake up still sleepy. You check out, then meet Spinne downstairs for breakfast, where you review the riddle for the next leg of your quest.

"Fire in the lion's heart," you read from the riddle. "This can't be literal."

"No," says Spinne, "unless it's a lion with a bad case of heartburn."

You laugh and then start looking for lion-shaped geographic formations, businesses with "Lion" in the name, and famous people with the last name of Lion, but to no avail.

As you are poring over a guide book and the daily newspaper, you notice a black van with dark windows and no license plates pull into the parking lot opposite the window where you are enjoying your breakfast.

"Spinne," you say. "Look." You nod at the van, trying to be inconspicuous.

The van circles the parking lot, stopping at your truck. A man and a woman emerge from it wearing sunglasses and wigs. They peer into the truck windows. Then, after looking around, they pull out what looks like a regular refrigerator magnet and place it next to the door lock. A red light beeps for a few seconds, then the man opens the driver-side door. You immediately jump to your feet.

"Don't," warns Spinne. "Everything is right here in our packs. They won't find anything."

"We need to make sure they don't plant any bugs," you answer.

"Or worse," says Spinne.

You both watch as the man and woman examine your truck and look carefully around the parking lot. You can tell they're not finding what they wanted. After a few minutes, obviously frustrated, they get back in their van and start its engine. Relieved, you and Spider begin sipping your yogurt and reading the newspaper again.

As you read, something out of the corner of your eye catches your attention. It is the black van, parked facing the restaurant. Rather than leaving, the car is simply sitting in its place.

"Great," you start. "It looks like we are going to have to go through the ba…"

In this section you will:

- Comprehend the meaning of a story.
- Read a dialogue for comprehension and then repeat it.
- Understand vocabulary in the areas of geometry.
- Learn proper adjective use.
- Test your knowledge of adjective use.
- Use more small talk on a formal level.
- Master new vocabulary.

Disc **3**   Track **1**

SECTION 1.3.1

Just then the van revs its engine, and the wheels start to screech, smoke pouring off the back tires. Spinne's eyes get wide as you both realize what is about to happen. You grab your packs and leap out of the way as the van barrels into the side of the restaurant, breaking a huge hole in the wall where you were previously sitting. Smoke and dust move through the restaurant as the other patrons scream in confusion.

"Fliege, we can get out this way," Spinne whispers, and you both move through the swinging kitchen doors. In the kitchen, servers, chefs, and the host are all yelling and moving into the dining room. Yelling can be heard from the dining room as you and Spinne run out of the side door and jump into your truck. The man and the woman watch through a 15-foot wide hole in the restaurant wall as you and Spinne peel out of the parking lot.

You head for the freeway, not sure which way to turn. The nearest entrance is facing south, and with no firm plan, you move onto the freeway littered with signs pointing the way to Italy and Switzerland.

"I hope the lion is south of here," you say. Spinne is thumbing through the tour guide given to you by your boss.

"Lions, lion, lyon," Spinne reads aloud.

"Many of the Bavarian family crests used lions," you suggest.

"True, but, I wouldn't know where to start. There are so many," says Spinne.

"What about art?" you ask, remembering the large black statues of lions in Trafalgar Square in London.

"That is one I haven't checked," says Spinne. "Maybe our boss gave us some hints in the activities she left with us."

You and Spinne continue south as you both work through the activities, hoping to make some sense of the clues from the riddle.

The Arab and His Camel

INSTRUCTIONS   Listen to and read the following story. Try to come up with different possible endings to the story in German.

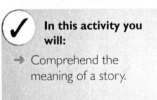

In this activity you will:

→ Comprehend the meaning of a story.

Der Araber und sein Kamel

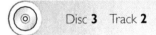

Disc **3**   Track **2**

Einmal schlief ein Araber in einer kalten Winternacht in seinem Zelt. Plötzlich streckte sein Kamel die Nase ins Zelt und sagte:

"Meister, darf ich hereinkommen um mich aufzuwärmen?" Nach etwas Zögern, sagte der Araber:

"Du darfst." Nach einer Weile streckte das Kamel seinen Hals in das Zelt und sagte:

"Mir ist kalt. Darf ich meinen Hals hier hereinstrecken?"

"Ja, du darfst," sagte der Araber. Nach einer Weile sagte das Kamel:

"Mir ist immer noch sehr kalt. Darf ich meine Vorderbeine hereinstellen?"

"Ja, du darfst," sagte der Araber. Nun musste der Araber zurückrücken, um mehr Platz zu machen. Das Kamel sprach wieder:

"Wenn ich hier so stehen bleibe, bleibt das Zelt offen und es ist uns beide kalt. Lass mich herein und den Eingang schließen. Dann wird es uns beiden warm sein."

"Gut," sagte der Araber. Und das Kamel trat herein und schloss den Eingang. Aber nun war nicht genügend Platz für beide. Das Zelt war zu klein. Nach einer Weile sagte das Kamel:

"Hier gibt es nicht genügend Platz für uns beide. Du bist kleiner als ich. Es wäre für dich besser, das Zelt zu verlassen. Dann gibt es hier Platz für mich. Wenigstens einer von uns wird es bequem haben." Dann schob das Kamel seinen Meister aus das Zelt. Der Araber sagte sich selbst:

"Es war falsch von mir. Ich hätte es nicht einmal den Kopf hereinstrecken lassen dürfen."

Performance Challenge

Individual   Camping is a fun way to vacation. Write about a time that you went camping with your family or friends in German. Share what you have written with them and teach them at least 10 new words in German. Rough out some ideas below.

....

....

....

....

....

....

....

....

....

....

....

....

Performance Challenge

Group 1   Perform the story for a group of younger children. Do it first in English and then in German. See how many of the German words they are able to recognize.

Performance Challenge

Group 2   Plan a field trip to a local zoo. Before you go, write down in German a list of animals that can be found there. Split the students into teams and give them each a list. Have them go on a scavenger hunt in teams to find each animal.

Questions of a Small Child 8

ACTIVITY

41

ACTIVITY 41

INSTRUCTIONS Listen to and read the following dialogue.

English	German
Ruth is my cousin, isn't she?	*Ruth ist meine Cousine, nicht wahr?*
Yes, Ruth is your cousin.	*Ja, Ruth ist deine Cousine.*
How so?	*Wieso?*
She is the daughter of your aunt.	*Sie ist die Tochter deiner Tante.*
What is an aunt?	*Was ist eine Tante?*
Your aunt is your father's sister.	*Deine Tante ist die Schwester deines Vaters.*
Or your mother's sister.	*Oder die Schwester deiner Mutter.*
The sister of one of your parents.	*Die Schwester einer deiner Eltern.*
So Ruth is my cousin because she's my mother's sister's daughter?	*Also Ruth ist meine Cousine, weil sie die Tochter der Schwester meiner Mutter ist?*
Right, and if your father's brother Karl had a daughter, she would be your cousin also.	*Richtig, und wenn deines Vaters Bruder Karl eine Tochter hätte, würde sie auch deine Cousine sein.*

In this activity you will:

→ Read a dialogue for comprehension and then repeat it.

  Disc **3** Track **3**

Challenge

INSTRUCTIONS Try to answer the following question. Check your response to the sample answer in Appendix A, on page 391.

• *Was ist eine Schwägerin?*

ACTIVITY **41**

INSTRUCTIONS Now write a parallel conversation that explains in German what a *Schwager* is.

....

....

....

★

Performance Challenge

Individual   Write an essay on five people you love and why you love them, in German. Write them each a letter telling them how you feel. Teach them at least five German words in each letter. Rough out some ideas below.

....

....

....

....

....

....

....

....

....

....

★

Performance Challenge

Group   Have each student tell about a favorite aunt or cousin. Have them use as much German as possible.

A Geometry Lesson

INSTRUCTIONS   Listen to and read this following lesson. Learn new geometry-related vocabulary in German.

English	German
A rectangle, like a square, has four straight lines and four right angles, right?	*Ein Rechteck hat, genau wie ein Quadrat, vier gerade Linien und vier rechte Winkel, nicht wahr?*
Then what is the difference between a rectangle and a square?	*Was ist dann der Unterschied zwischen einem Rechteck und einem Quadrat?*
Listen.	*Hören Sie zu.*
I will explain it to You.	*Ich werde es Ihnen erklären.*
A square is one kind of rectangle.	*Ein Quadrat ist eine Art Rechteck.*
Like any rectangle, a square has four sides.	*Wie jedes Rechteck hat ein Quadrat vier Seiten.*
But different from other rectangles, the four sides of a square are equal in length.	*Aber, anders als andere Rechtecke, sind die vier Seiten des Quadrats gleich lang.*
Each side and its opposite side are parallel.	*Jede Seite und ihre gegenüberliegende Seite sind parallel.*
This is a rectangle.	*Das ist ein Rechteck.*
This is one side.	*Das ist eine Seite.*
This is the opposite side.	*Das ist die gegenüberliegende Seite.*
This side and the opposite side are parallel.	*Diese Seite und die gegenüberliegende Seite sind parallel.*
Also the top side and the bottom side are parallel.	*Auch die obere Seite und die untere Seite sind parallel.*

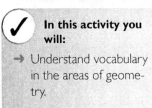

In this activity you will:

→ Understand vocabulary in the areas of geometry.

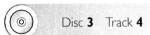

Disc **3**   Track **4**

The Guards of Switzerland

Over the years, the Swiss have, in general, remained politically neutral. Because of this neutrality, Swiss guards have gained a reputation of being effective and loyal mercenaries for foreign governments.

English (cont.)	German
What's the difference between a circle and an oval?	*Was ist der Unterschied zwischen einem Kreis und einer Ellipse?*

Performance Challenge

Individual   Choose three homework problems from an algebra, geometry, trigonometry, or calculus book. Rewrite each problem in German and then try to solve the problems.

....

....

....

....

....

....

....

....

....

....

....

....

Performance Challenge

Group   Create cards with geometric shapes on them. Have someone direct students, using only German, to create patterns of shapes within a specific time frame. The team that completes the most patterns within the time limit wins.

Discovery of Grammar 15

INSTRUCTIONS Study these charts and learn about adjectives in their strong form.

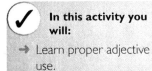

In this activity you will:

→ Learn proper adjective use.

Adjectives in Their Strong Form

Singular

	Nominative	Accusative	Dative	Genitive
■	frisch_er_ Tee	frisch_en_ Tee	frisch_em_ Tee	frisch_en_ Tees
●	frisch_e_ Milch	frisch_e_ Milch	frisch_er_ Milch	frisch_er_ Milch
▲	frisch_es_ Wasser	frisch_es_ Wasser	frisch_em_ Wasser	frisch_en_ Wassers

Plural

	Nominative	Accusative	Dative	Genitive
	gut_e_ Leute	gut_e_ Leute	gut_en_ Leuten	gut_er_ Leute

If you compare the strong form of adjectives—the form they have when they stand in front of nouns but with no supporting article—you'll see that they take endings you have previously encountered. Compare the forms of {DER}, {EIN}, {DIES} words in the chart below with those of strong-form adjectives in the chart above.

Singular

	Nominative	Accusative	Dative	Genitive
■	d_er_ Mann	d_en_ Mann	d_em_ Mann	d_es_ Mannes
●	d_ie_ Dame	d_ie_ Dame	d_er_ Dame	d_er_ Dame

Singular *(cont.)*

	Nominative	Accusative	Dative	Genitive
▲	das Kind	das Kind	dem Kind	des Kindes
■	ein Mann	einen Mann	einem Mann	eines Mannes
●	eine Dame	eine Dame	einer Dame	einer Dame
▲	ein Kind	ein Kind	einem Kind	eines Kindes
■	dieser Mann	diesen Mann	diesem Mann	dieses Mannes
●	diese Dame	diese Dame	dieser Dame	dieser Dame
▲	dieses Kind	dieses Kind	diesem Kind	dieses Kindes

Plural

Nominative	Accusative	Dative	Genitive
die	die	den	der
(Männer, Damen, etc.)	(Männer, Damen, etc.)	(Männern, etc.)	(Männer, etc.)
meine	meine	meinen	meiner
(Männer, Damen, etc.)	(Männer, etc.)	(Männern, etc.)	(Männer, etc.)
diese	diese	diesen	dieser
(Männer, Damen, etc.)	Männer, etc.)	(Männern, etc.)	(Männer, etc.)

Self Quiz

INSTRUCTIONS   Write-in the correct response. Check your answers in Appendix A, on page 391.

English	German
1. Warm milk is good.	Warm__ ● Milch ist gut.
2. Cold tea is not good.	Kalt__ ■ Tee ist nicht gut.
3. Cold water is free.	Kalt__ ▲ Wasser ist kostenlos.
4. the price of good milk and good tea	der Preis gut__ Milch und gut__ Tees
5. the worth of good people	der Wert gut__ Leute
6. without good water and without good milk	ohne gut__ Wasser und ohne gut__ Milch
7. with the good water and the good milk	mit <u>dem</u> gut__ Wasser und mit <u>der</u> gut__ Milch
8. with good water and with good milk	mit gut__ Wasser und mit gut__ Milch
9. the price of the good milk and the good tea	der Preis der gut__ Milch und des gut__ Tees
10. the price of good milk and good tea	der Preis gut__ Milch und gut__ Tees

Performance Challenge

Individual   Research the Rhine River and the castles along the river, which were built to protect the land from marauders. Write a one page paper in German on the castle you would most like to visit and why you would like to go there. Rough out some ideas below.

....

....

....

....

....

....

....

....

....

....

....

....

....

....

....

....

....

....

....

....

....

....

....

....

Performance Challenge

Group   Find a German newspaper and circle all the adjectives on one page. Use these words to write your own news story. Be as creative as you can!

Discovery of Grammar 15: Understanding

 In this activity you will:

→ Test your knowledge of adjective use.

Self Quiz

INSTRUCTIONS   Translate the following sentences. Check your answers in Appendix A, on page 392.

1. Warm milk is good.

   ....

2. The warm milk is good.

   ....

3. Cold water is good.

   ....

4. The cold water is good.

   ....

5. Cold tea is not good.

   ....

6. The cold tea is not good.

   ....

7. They live without good water.

   ....

8. He doesn't drink (*trinkt*) the good milk.

   ....

9. They make it with cold milk.

   ....

10. They make it with the cold milk.

....

11. The price of the little red book.

....

12. Here is a little red book.

....

13. We're reading the little red book.

....

14. We live (*leben*) without the little red book.

....

Conversation Snatches 11

INSTRUCTIONS Listen to and read these dialogue fragments. Try to come up with a dialogue of your own using these sentences!

In this activity you will:

→ Use more small talk on a formal level.

  Disc **3** Track **5**

English	German
Everyone is sleeping but us.	*Alle schlafen außer uns.*
I'm not tired.	*Ich bin nicht müde.*
Everyone has eaten but us.	*Alle haben gegessen außer uns.*
I wasn't hungry.	*Ich war nicht hungrig.*
Let's not argue anymore.	*Lass uns nicht länger streiten.*
OK. As you wish.	*OK. Wie du willst.*
Now the big show begins.	*Jetzt beginnt die große Show.*
Yes, now the curtain goes up.	*Ja, jetzt geht der Vorhang auf.*
We are happy You came to visit us.	*Wir freuen uns über Ihren Besuch bei uns.*
It was our pleasure.	*Es war uns eine Freude.*
When do You go back to America?	*Wann gehen Sie nach Amerika zurück?*
The sooner the better. I'm homesick.	*Je eher, desto besser. Ich habe Heimweh.*
Ow, that hurts!	*Au, das tut Weh!*
Don't be a baby!	*Sei kein Baby!*
Why is he so poor?	*Warum ist er so arm?*
He earns no money.	*Er verdient kein Geld.*
But why?	*Aber warum?*
He doesn't like to work.	*Er arbeitet nicht gern.*
Do you like to go to the theater?	*Gehst du gern ins Theater?*

Swiss Guards in France

Once such example of this loyalty was demonstrated in 1792 when more than 700 Swiss officers died defending the French Royal family in the Tuileries Palace in Paris.

English *(cont.)*	German
Now and then, but I'd rather go to a concert.	*Hin und wieder, aber ich gehe lieber zu einem Konzert.*

Review

INSTRUCTIONS   Take some time now for review, if you feel you need it. Go back over any words or sentences that you had difficulty with until you are comfortable with them. When you are ready, move on.

Performance Challenge

Individual   Rent a DVD that has German language and German subtitles. Watch the movie (or set of scenes) once in English, then in English with German subtitles, then only in German. See how much you can understand and learn.

Performance Challenge

Group   Rent a DVD that can play with both German language and German subtitles. Have students watch the movie (or part of the movie), first in English, then in German with English subtitles, then in German alone.

Meeting at the University 2

INSTRUCTIONS Listen carefully to this conversation and follow along. How much can you understand without using the English?

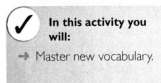

In this activity you will:
→ Master new vocabulary.

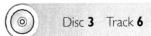 Disc **3** Track **6**

English	German
●●: Vincent?	Vincent?
●: Rosa, hello.	Rosa, hallo.
●●: Hi, Vincent. You forgot my name. It's Annelise.	Hallo, Vincent. Sie haben meinen Namen vergessen. Ich heiße Annelise.
●: Annelise, forgive me. Somehow I have Rosa in my head.	Annelise, entschuldigen Sie mich. Irgendwie habe ich den Namen Rosa im Kopf.
●●: Who is this Rosa?	Wer ist Rosa?
●: She's just a friend…many years ago. So be it. How are things, actually?	Nur eine Freundin von mir…von vor vielen Jahren. Wie auch immer. Wie geht es Ihnen eigentlich?
●●: Quite well, thanks.	Ganz gut, danke.
●: And how is Your husband?	Und wie geht es Ihrem Mann?
●●: Fine. Everything's fine with us. How are you doing? Is everything OK? I haven't seen You for a long time.	Gut. Bei uns ist alles in Ordnung. Wie geht es Ihnen? Alles in Ordnung? Ich habe Sie schon seit langem nicht mehr gesehen.
●: I haven't seen You since fall. And it's already January. By the way, Happy New Year!	Ich habe Sie seit dem Herbst nicht gesehen. Ja, und es ist schon Januar. Apropos, ein frohes neues Jahr!
●●: Same to You. Are You coming from work?	Gleichfalls. Kommen Sie von der Arbeit?
●: No, from a singing lesson. I'm going to the library.	Nein, von meinem Gesangsunterricht. Ich gehe zur Bibliothek.

English *(cont.)*	German
●●: Are You still working at the post office?	*Arbeiten Sie immer noch beim Postamt?*
●: No. I quit in February. To tell the truth, they fired me.	*Nein. Ich habe im Februar gekündigt. Ehrlich gesagt, ich wurde entlassen.*
●●: That's too bad! What happened? Why did they fire You?	*Das ist schade! Was ist passiert? Warum haben sie Sie entlassen?*
●: Because I couldn't come on time.	*Weil ich nicht pünktlich sein konnte.*
●●: How so?	*Wie kommt das?*
●: I always study until midnight in the library. And then I can't get up at 5 in the morning.	*Ich lerne in der Bibliothek immer bis Mitternacht. Und dann kann ich nicht um 5 Uhr morgens aufstehen.*
●●: I understand that.	*Das kann ich verstehen.*
●: But now my father is angry with me.	*Aber mein Vater ist jetzt böse auf mich.*
●●: Why is that?	*Warum denn?*
●: He says I'm a fool. I should have bought an alarm clock.	*Er sagt, dass ich dumm bin. Ich hätte mir einen Wecker kaufen sollen.*
●●: In my opinion, it would have been better to go to bed <u>earlier</u>.	*Meiner Meinung nach wäre es besser gewesen, wenn Sie <u>früher</u> ins Bett gegangen wären.*
●: And get bad grades in my courses?	*Dann hätte ich schlechte Noten in meinen Kursen bekommen.*
●●: Such is life! Are You looking for a job?	*So ist das Leben! Suchen Sie eine Arbeitsstelle?*
●: Of course. Otherwise I'll run out of money.	*Natürlich. Andernfalls wird mir das Geld ausgehen.*
●●: Where do You work now?	*Wo arbeiten Sie jetzt?*
●: At the bookstore.	*In der Buchhandlung.*
●●: That's where my sister works.	*Meine Schwester arbeitet dort.*
●: Really. I didn't know. What is her name?	*Wirklich. Ich habe das nicht gewusst. Wie heißt sie?*
●●: Rosa. Her name is Rosa, believe it or not!	*Rosa. Sie heißt Rosa, ob Sie es glauben wollen oder nicht!*
●: You're kidding!	*Sie machen Witze!*

English *(cont.)*	German
••: No, I'm not kidding. I'm telling the truth. She works in the computer section.	*Nein, ich mache keine Witze. Ich sage die Wahrheit. Sie arbeitet in der Computerabteilung.*
•: Introduce me to her, will You?	*Könnten Sie mich ihr vorstellen?*
••: I will do that some day.	*Das werde ich eines Tages tun.*
•: Got to go now. I'm going to a piano lesson. Nice to see You again.	*Jetzt muss ich gehen. Ich gehe zu meiner Klavierstunde. Es hat mich gefreut, Sie wiederzusehen.*
••: So long.	*Auf Wiedersehen.*

Performance Challenge

Individual Make a clock with movable hands. Practice telling time in German. Then write about what time of the day you do certain things (wake up, study German, eat lunch, practice the piano) in German. Rough out some ideas below.

....

....

....

....

....

....

....

....

Performance Challenge

Group Have each student research and write about German New Year, or *der Silvesterabend*. Then have them describe in German their own family's traditions for the holiday and their goals for the current year.

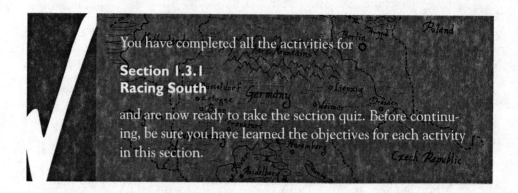

You have completed all the activities for

**Section 1.3.1
Racing South**

and are now ready to take the section quiz. Before continuing, be sure you have learned the objectives for each activity in this section.

Section 1.3.1 Quiz

INSTRUCTIONS   Choose the correct response. Check your answers in Appendix D, on page 402.

1. **Was hat der Araber nicht?**

   A. *ein Zelt*

   B. *ein Kamel*

   C. *ein Pferd*

   D. *ein Problem*

2. **Was ist die Schwester deines Vaters?**

   A. *die Oma*

   B. *die Mutter*

   C. *die Cousine*

   D. *die Tante*

3. **Was ist eine Cousine?**

   A. *der Sohn der Tante*

   B. *die Schwester des Onkels*

   C. *die Tochter des Onkels*

   D. *der Sohn des Onkels*

4. **Wieviele Seiten hat ein Quadrat?**

   A. 3

   B. 4

   C. 6

   D. 8

5. **Was ist ein Rechteck?**

   A. a rhombus

   B. a trapezoid

   C. a triangle

   D. a rectangle

6. **____ Milch ist gut.**

   A. *Warmer*

   B. *Warme*

   C. *Warmes*

   D. *Warm*

....

INSTRUCTIONS   Choose the correct translation of the following phrases.

7. **That hurts!**

   A. *Das tut Weh!*

   B. *Aber warum!*

   C. *Das herzt!*

   D. *Wie du willst!*

8. **aber warum**

   A. that hurts

   B. around the room

   C. but why

   D. anyway

9. **gleichfalls**

   A. why is that

   B. how so

   C. too bad

   D. same to you

10. **What happened?**

   A. *Was ist passiert?*

   B. *Was verstehe ich?*

   C. *Warum denn?*

   D. *Wie heisst?*

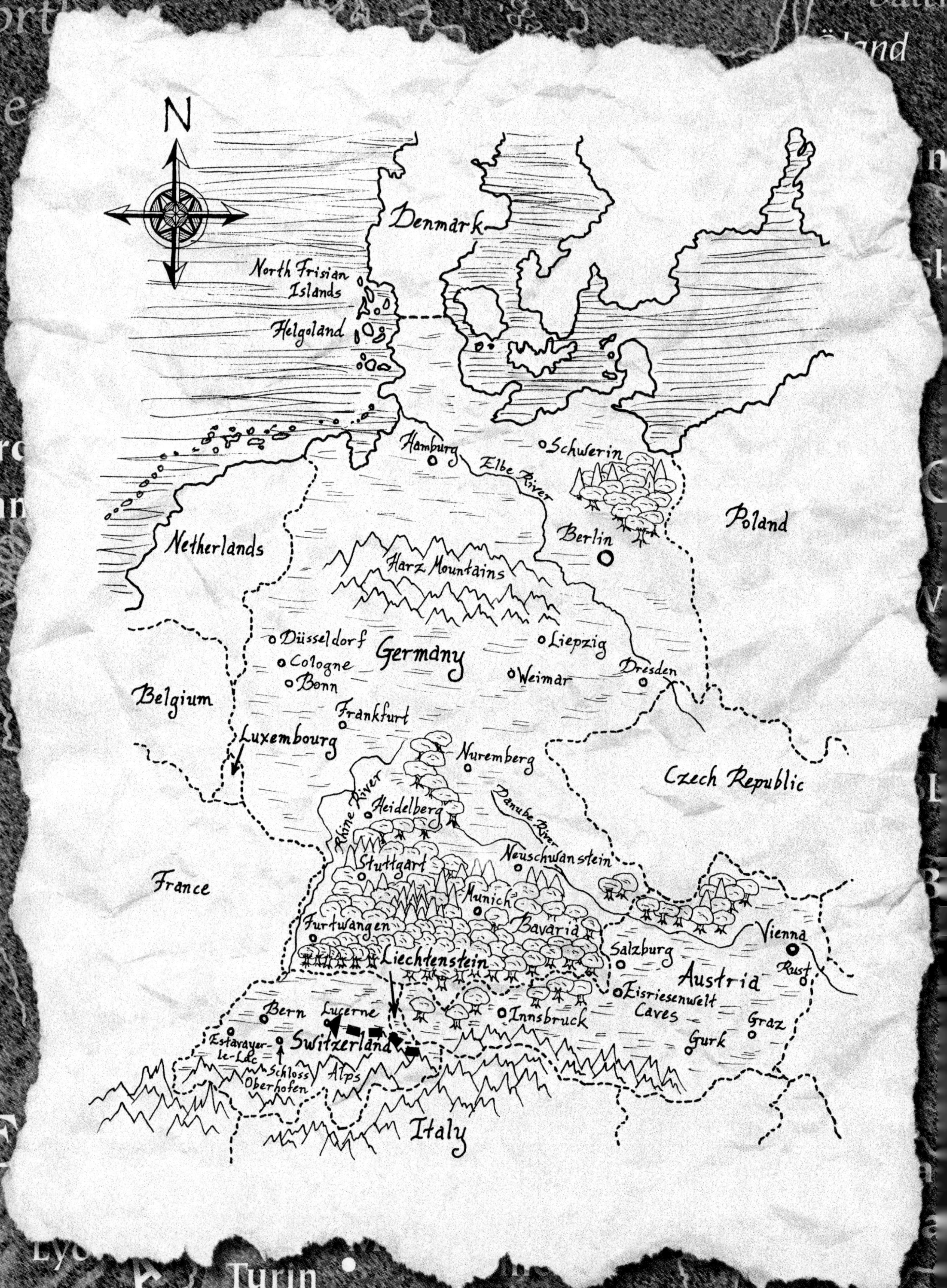

Fire in the Lion's Heart

You begin to get a little drowsy from the drive and from working through the activities. Suddenly, you turn a corner, and there at the side of the road is a terrible car crash. You swerve to miss it, then slam on your brakes to avoid hitting the emergency vehicles parked in the street. Your heart beats quickly from the adrenaline, and you are no longer drowsy.

"Whoa!" you exclaim. "That was close. I wonder what happened. Maybe we can help."

You and Spinne, being certified in CPR, tumble from the truck and move quickly to the accident scene.

"Hallo, können wir Ihnen helfen?" you say in your best German accent.

"Ja, bitte," a pretty red-haired emergency technician answers. "Please give these soldiers juice and warm blankets while we tend to those that have been more severely hurt."

You pour out juice to help stop the soldiers from going into shock, then dole out the blankets from the back of the emergency vehicle. As you move down the line, you learn that the soldiers are French. They were traveling to a monument in Lucerne, Switzerland, dedicated to Swiss soldiers who died in the French revolution.

"Das klingt interessant," you say to one of the soldiers. "I didn't know such a monument existed. You move on to the next soldier. *"Was ist passiert… bei dem accident?'*

"Schafe," he says, in his best German accent.

"Sheep?" you ask. "What do you mean?"

"Sheep… crossing the road," he answers, then gestures to show a car swerving to miss something and crashing into a tree trunk.

"Oh, I see," you say, wrapping a bandage around the arm of a nearby soldier. The French soldiers continue to discuss the trek in their native tongue, but you hear a few German words sprinkled into their conversation. You sit up straight. You

In this section you will:

→ Follow a conversation and understand its meaning.
→ Master new vocabulary.
→ Read a dialogue for comprehension and then repeat it.
→ Recognize your ability to understand German.
→ Increase reading comprehension, and vocabulary usage.

 Disc **3**   Track **7**

SECTION **1.3.2**

don't understand the soldiers' French conversation, but those German words sound very familiar. The soldier says them again, and you lean in to ask him a question.

"Did you say '*das Löwendenkmal?*'" you ask.

The soldier nods and pulls the blanket around him tighter.

You turn to the emergency technician and ask her, "Where was this truck headed?"

The technician answers, "The Lion Monument, in Lucerne, Switzerland."

You and Spinne look knowingly at each other.

"Where is this monument, exactly?" you ask.

The technician pulls out a map of Lucerne from her map book and circles a square near the middle of town. "Here," she says.

"May we keep this?" you ask.

"Sure," she answers. "And thank you for your help. I think we have everything under control now."

Moving quickly to the truck, you are glad you chose to go south, as Lucerne is now only about an hour away.

In a little less than an hour, you arrive at a plaza where a majestic carved lion sits next to the flags of both France and Switzerland.

"So, where do you think the key is?" asks Spinne. "What was the clue about a man's coat?"

You pull out the sheet music again, as you move from the car to the monument. Using your flashlight, you heat the paper and see the words, *"Wende dich demjenigen zu, der den Mann nicht dazu bewegen konnte, seinen Mantel abzunehmen,"* appear clearly through the notes.

"Make what man take off his coat?" asks Spinne. Just then, a gust of wind blows the paper from your hand, and you run down the street, chasing the buffeted sheet music.

Laughing, Spinne helps you retrieve it. "I think we'll need a little more studying to solve this one," he tells you. Using the large statue as shelter from the wind, you settle down and work through a few more activities.

Questions of a Small Child 9

INSTRUCTIONS Listen to this conversation. Try to learn the words it uses. Can you make your own sentences using these words?

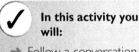

In this activity you will:

→ Follow a conversation and understand its meaning.

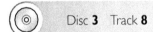

Disc **3** Track **8**

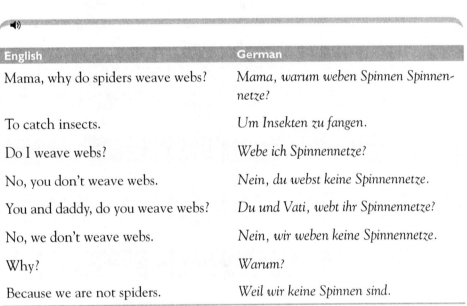

English	German
Mama, why do spiders weave webs?	*Mama, warum weben Spinnen Spinnennetze?*
To catch insects.	*Um Insekten zu fangen.*
Do I weave webs?	*Webe ich Spinnennetze?*
No, you don't weave webs.	*Nein, du webst keine Spinnennetze.*
You and daddy, do you weave webs?	*Du und Vati, webt ihr Spinnennetze?*
No, we don't weave webs.	*Nein, wir weben keine Spinnennetze.*
Why?	*Warum?*
Because we are not spiders.	*Weil wir keine Spinnen sind.*

Performance Challenge

Individual I   Write 10 "Why" questions in German. Research the answers and share them with a friend or family member.

1. ....

2. ....

3. ....

4. ....

ACTIVITY 47

5. ....

6. ....

7. ....

8. ....

9. ....

10. ....

Performance Challenge

Individual 2   Find a German-speaker in your town or city. Interview them using at least 10 "Why" questions. Write an article or essay based on the information you collect from the interview.

Performance Challenge

Group 1   Choose a variety of Power-Glide Flashcards and place them in a hat. Create teams and have them play "Twenty Questions" using the words from the hat.

Performance Challenge

Group 2   Have students choose a song that contains at least three questions. Have them each translate as many of the lyrics into German as they can. Next, have each student (or student group) perform their songs.

A Treatment for Depression

ACTIVITY

48

ACTIVITY 48

INSTRUCTIONS Listen to this story and use it to learn German vocabulary. Listen a second time in German only.

✔ **In this activity you will:**
→ Master new vocabulary.

◎ Disc **3** Track **9, 10**

English	German
A man went to see a doctor.	*Ein Mann ging zum Doktor.*
The doctor asked him:	*Der Doktor fragte ihn:*
"What are Your complaints?"	*"Wo liegen Ihre Beschwerden?"*
"I am depressed," said the man.	*"Ich bin deprimiert," sagte der Mann.*
"I am not happy.	*"Ich bin nicht glücklich.*
I am always sad.	*Ich bin immer traurig.*
I often cry.	*Ich weine oft.*
I never laugh.	*Ich lache nie.*
It is years since I have laughed.	*Es ist Jahre her, seitdem ich gelacht habe.*
Is there anything that can cure me of my depression?	*Gibt es etwas, was meine Depressionen heilen kann?*
Can You prescribe medication?	*Können Sie mir eine Medizin verschreiben?*
Can You treat me or counsel me?	*Können Sie mich behandeln oder mir Ratschläge geben?*
Is there something that can make me laugh again?"	*Gibt es etwas, was mich wieder zum Lachen bringen kann?"*
"I believe Your depression can be cured.	*"Ich glaube Ihre Depressionen können geheilt werden.*
Go to the circus.	*Gehen Sie zum Zirkus.*
The circus has a clown who is extremely funny.	*Der Zirkus hat einen Clown, der äußerst lustig ist.*

The Lion Monument

To commemorate the bravery and sacrifice of this group of Swiss officers, the Danish artist Bertel Thorvaldsen was commissioned to create a monument. The beautiful reclining Lion Monument, *Löwendenkmal*, is sculpted of sandstone rock taken from a cliff above the city of Lucerne, near the Glacier Garden and the Panorama.

English (cont.)	German
For sure he'll make You laugh."	*Er wird Sie sicher zum Lachen bringen.*"
"No he won't."	*"Nein, das wird er nicht."*
"Why don't You believe it?	*"Warum glauben Sie das nicht?*
I guarantee You the clown will make You laugh until You're sick to Your stomach."	*Ich garantiere Ihnen, dass der Clown Sie zum Lachen bringen wird bis Ihnen der Bauch weh tun wird."*
"No, You are wrong," said the poor man.	*"Nein, bestimmt nicht," sagte der arme Mann.*
"Why not?" said the doctor.	*"Warum nicht?" sagte der Doktor.*
The man said:	*Der Mann sagte:*
"Because I am the clown."	*"Weil ich der Clown bin."*

Performance Challenge

Individual   Ask a doctor to allow you to spend time in his or her office. Make a list of familiar and unfamiliar words in English. When you get home, translate those words into German and then share them with the doctor.

Performance Challenge

Group   Study *Deutsches* Theater and a German film director, screenwriter, or actor. Choose one of their movies to watch and then critique it as a group.

Questions of a Small Child 10

INSTRUCTIONS Listen to and read this dialogue.

English	German
Mama, who is that in this picture?	*Mama, wer ist das auf diesem Bild?*
My grandfather.	*Mein Großvater.*
Where did he live?	*Wo hat er gelebt?*
He lived in England.	*Er lebte in England.*
What did he do?	*Was hat er gemacht?*
He was a blacksmith.	*Er war ein Hufschmied.*
Why was he a blacksmith?	*Warum war er ein Hufschmied?*
Because his father was a blacksmith.	*Weil sein Vater ein Hufschmied war.*
When did he die?	*Wann ist er gestorben?*
He died a long time ago.	*Er ist vor einer langen Zeit gestorben.*
How did he die?	*Wie ist er gestorben?*
An anvil fell on his foot.	*Ein Amboss fiel auf seinen Fuß.*
Which foot?	*Welchen Fuß?*
The left one, I think.	*Ich denke auf den linken.*
Oh!	*Oh!*

In this activity you will:

→ Read a dialogue for comprehension and then repeat it.

Disc **3** Track **11**

215

Performance Challenge

Individual   Study the history of blacksmithing in Germany, which included building wagons, shoeing horses, making cooking pans, and fixing farm equipment. Write a one page report on your findings. Rough out some ideas below.

....

....

....

....

....

....

....

....

....

....

....

....

....

....

....

Performance Challenge

Group   Have each student find a picture of their grandfather and learn as much as they can about his profession. Then have them write a short, biographical sketch of their grandfather in German and share it with the rest of the class.

The Lazy Carpenter

INSTRUCTIONS Listen to and read this story. Learn new German vocabulary.

In this activity you will:

→ Increase reading, listening comprehension, and vocabulary usage.

 Disc **3**   Track **12**

English	German
Once there was a man who had a three year-old son.	Es war einmal ein Mann, der einen drei Jahre alten Sohn hatte.
The father wanted to have a bed built for his son.	Der Vater wollte ein Bett für seinen Sohn bauen lassen.
So he went to a carpenter and asked him to build a bed for the little one.	So ging er zu einem Zimmermann und bat ihn, ein Bett für den Kleinen zu bauen.
The carpenter agreed and said the bed would be ready in a week.	Der Zimmermann war einverstanden und sagte, dass das Bett in einer Woche fertig sein würde.
One, two, three weeks passed by, and still the carpenter hadn't finished the bed.	Eine, zwei, drei Wochen vergingen und der Zimmermann hatte das Bett immer noch nicht fertig.
Every time the father went to him the carpenter had an excuse.	Jedesmal, wenn der Vater zum Zimmermann ging, hatte er eine Ausrede.
He would say:	Er sagte:
"Come back in another week and I'll have it ready."	"Komm in einer Woche zurück, dann wird es fertig sein."
More weeks went by, until finally the man got tired of hearing the carpenter's excuses and gave up.	Mehrere Wochen vergingen, bis der Mann schließlich genug davon hatte sich die Entschuldigungen des Zimmermanns anzuhören und aufgab.
The boy grew up, married, and had a son.	Der Junge wuchs heran, heiratete und hatte einen Sohn.
He asked his father to give him a bed for his son.	Er fragte seinen Vater nach einem Bett für seinen Sohn.

ACTIVITY 50

English (cont.)	German
The father said:	*Der Vater sagte:*
"Go to the carpenter and ask him for the bed."	*"Geh zum Zimmermann und frag ihn nach dem Bett."*
So the son went to the carpenter and asked him for the bed, which had been ordered years before.	*So ging der Sohn zu dem Zimmermann und fragte ihn nach dem Bett, welches Jahre vorher bestellt worden war.*
The carpenter said to him:	*Der Zimmermann sagte:*
"Here, take your money back.	*"Hier, nimm dein Geld zurück.*
I don't like being rushed in my work!"	*Ich mag es nicht, wenn man mich bei meiner Arbeit antreibt!"*

Performance Challenge

Individual   Take a walk around your block. On a piece of paper write the German names of 15 actions that you saw on your walk that could be described as "lazy."

....

....

....

....

....

....

....

Performance Challenge

Group   Many of the German immigrants to the U.S. in the 1850s worked in bakery and carpentry. Divide the students into two groups. Have them prepare and give a presentation to the class in German using visual aids.

Meeting at the University 3

INSTRUCTIONS Listen to and read this dialogue—work toward full comprehension.

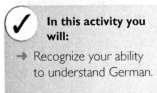

In this activity you will:
→ Recognize your ability to understand German.

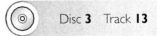

Disc **3**   Track **13**

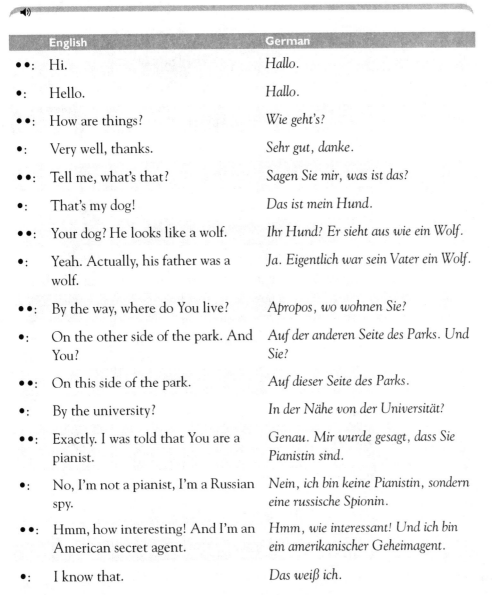

English	German
••: Hi.	*Hallo.*
•: Hello.	*Hallo.*
••: How are things?	*Wie geht's?*
•: Very well, thanks.	*Sehr gut, danke.*
••: Tell me, what's that?	*Sagen Sie mir, was ist das?*
•: That's my dog!	*Das ist mein Hund.*
••: Your dog? He looks like a wolf.	*Ihr Hund? Er sieht aus wie ein Wolf.*
•: Yeah. Actually, his father was a wolf.	*Ja. Eigentlich war sein Vater ein Wolf.*
••: By the way, where do You live?	*Apropos, wo wohnen Sie?*
•: On the other side of the park. And You?	*Auf der anderen Seite des Parks. Und Sie?*
••: On this side of the park.	*Auf dieser Seite des Parks.*
•: By the university?	*In der Nähe von der Universität?*
••: Exactly. I was told that You are a pianist.	*Genau. Mir wurde gesagt, dass Sie Pianistin sind.*
•: No, I'm not a pianist, I'm a Russian spy.	*Nein, ich bin keine Pianistin, sondern eine russische Spionin.*
••: Hmm, how interesting! And I'm an American secret agent.	*Hmm, wie interessant! Und ich bin ein amerikanischer Geheimagent.*
•: I know that.	*Das weiß ich.*

Bavarian Coats of Arms, Part I

Like the English, Bavarian aristocracy also used family crests as a means of differentiation during tournaments and battle. Also in the same tradition as their neighbors to the North, the Bavarian ruling class created the crests or "Coats of Arms" using different symbols, each with their own meaning. For example, lions represent courage; peacocks, beauty or knowledge; and even a simple color like blue painted on a crest represents an individual who displays truth and loyalty.

English *(cont.)*	German
••: How did You find out?	*Wie haben Sie das herausgefunden?*
•: My husband is also a secret agent. He told me that.	*Mein Mann ist auch Geheimagent. Er hat es mir gesagt.*
••: How about that!	*Was soll man dazu sagen?*
•: Well, I got to go now.	*Ich muss jetzt gehen.*
••: Wait a second, I've got one last question.	*Warten Sie eine Sekunde, ich habe eine letzte Frage.*
•: Yes?	*Ja?*
••: Tell me, what's Your dog's name?	*Sagen Sie mir, wie heißt Ihr Hund?*
•: Rover. His name is Rover.	*Rover. Er heißt Rover.*
••: Why do you call him Rover?	*Warum heißt er Rover?*
•: Hard to say…	*Schwer zu sagen…*
••: Well, I got to go now. Goodbye, Rover. Goodbye, Isabelle.	*Nun, ich muss jetzt gehen. Auf Wiedersehen, Rover. Auf Wiedersehen, Isabel.*
•: Good luck!	*Viel Glück!*

Performance Challenge

Individual   The Berlin Wall fell in November of 1989. Research East and West Germany prior to its fall and compare it to the Federal Republic of Germany today. Use as much German as possible in your paper. Rough out some ideas below.

....

....

....

....

....

....

....

....

....

....

....

....

....

....

....

....

....

....

....

Performance Challenge

Group   Divide the group into two teams. Write words from the story and attach one word to each student. Then play "Red Rover," calling out a word used in the story. The team must give the English translation before they can add that player.

ACTIVITY

52

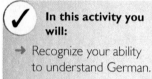

✓ **In this activity you will:**

→ Recognize your ability to understand German.

Chicken Little

INSTRUCTIONS   Read the following story. You will learn German words for various animals.

Das kleine Hühnchen

Dies ist die Geschichte eines kleinen Hühnchens, ein Küken das sich ängstigte, weil es sich einbildete, dass der Himmel herunterfällt. Eines Tages war das Küken im Garten, als plötzlich ein Blatt, ein sehr großes Blatt, auf seinen Kopf fiel. Das arme Küken erschreckte sich und bildete sich ein, dass der Himmel herunterfällt und es begann herumzulaufen und schrie:

"Piep, piep, Mammi, wo bist du Mammi?"

"Gluck, gluck, hier bin ich, Küken, was ist passiert?"

"Der Himmel fällt herunter! Der Himmel fällt herunter!"

"Woher weißt du das, Küken?"

"Ich sah es mit meinen eigenen Augen und ein Stück fiel BOING! auf meinen Kopf. Ich sage dir die Wahrheit."

"Lass uns fliehen!" sagte die Henne.

"Lass uns fliehen, lauf!"

"Ente, Ente, wo bist du?"

"Quack, Quack, ich bin hier. Was ist passiert? Was ist passiert?"

"Der Himmel fällt herunter! Der Himmel fällt herunter!"

"Woher weißt du das, Henne?"

"Das Küken hat es mir erzählt."

"Woher weißt du das, Küken?"

"Ich sah es mit meinen eigenen Augen und ein Stück fiel BOING! auf meinen Kopf. Ich sage dir die Wahrheit."

"Lasst uns fliehen!" schrie die Ente.

"Lasst uns fliehen! Lasst uns fliehen! Lauft!"

"Gans, Gans, wo bist du, Gans?"

"Honk, honk, ich bin hier, Ente. Was ist passiert?"

"Der Himmel fällt herunter! Der Himmel fällt herunter!"

"Woher weißt du das, Ente?"

"Die Henne hat es mir gesagt."

"Woher weißt du das, Henne?"

"Das Küken hat es mir gesagt."

"Woher weißt du das, Küken."

"Ich sah es mit meinen eigenen Augen und ein Stück fiel BOING! auf meinen Kopf. Ich sage dir die Wahrheit."

"Lasst uns fliehen!" schrie die Gans.

"Lasst uns fliehen! Lauft!"

"Truthahn, Truthahn, wo bist du, Truthahn?"

"Gobble, gobble. Ich bin hier, Gans. Was ist passiert? Was ist passiert?"

"Der Himmel fällt herunter! Der Himmel fällt herunter!"

"Woher weißt du das, Gans?"

"Die Ente hat es mir gesagt."

"Woher weißt du das, Ente?"

"Die Henne hat es mir gesagt."

"Woher weißt du das, Henne?"

"Das Küken hat es mir gesagt."

"Woher weißt du das, Küken?"

"Ich habe es mit meinen eigenen Augen gesehen und ein Stück fiel BOING! auf meinen Kopf. Ich sage dir die Wahrheit."

"Lasst uns fliehen!" schrie der Truthahn.

"Lasst uns fliehen! Lauft!"

"Fuchs, Fuchs, wo bist du, Fuchs?"

"Yif, Yif. Ich bin hier. Was ist passiert?"

"Der Himmel fällt herunter! Der Himmel fällt herunter!"

"Woher weißt du das, Truthahn?"

"Die Gans hat es mir gesagt."

"Woher weißt du das, Gans?"

"Die Ente hat es mir gesagt."

Bavarian Coats of Arms, Part II

Although commonly called "Family Crests," coats of arms do not actually belong to a family. These representations are often associated with families due to surname association, but are actually awarded to individuals. Subsequently, the same German surname may have several coats of arms that are associated with their family. Tracking specific family ancestry will help any modern-day family understand the coats of arms that belong to their individual ancestors.

"Woher weißt du das, Ente?"

"Die Henne hat es mir gesagt."

"Woher weißt du das, Henne?"

"Das Küken hat es mir gesagt."

"Woher weißt du das, Küken?"

"Ich habe es mit meinen eigenen Augen gesehen und ein Stück fiel BOING! auf meinen Kopf. Ich sage dir die Wahrheit." Der Fuchs dachte ein bisschen nach und sagte:

"Habt keine Angst. Ich werde euch retten. Kommt mit mir zu meiner Höhle." Und alle Tiere gingen mit dem Fuchs in seine Höhle. Dann tötete der Fuchs sie und fraß sie alle. Die armen Tiere.

Performance Challenge

Individual   Using stuffed animals and any other props you can find, retell the story to a small child in German as a Diglot Weave™.

Performance Challenge

Group   Ask several different people to come in and talk about their jobs. Then have the students write about what profession interests them and why, in German.

A Language Lesson 2

INSTRUCTIONS This activity will help you increase your German comprehension skills.

English	German
That black line is long, and this white line is long.	*Jene schwarze Linie ist lang, und diese weiße Linie ist lang.*
That short chalk is colored and this one is white.	*Jene kurze Kreide ist farbig und diese ist weiß.*
This black line is not long.	*Diese schwarze Linie ist nicht lang.*
And this white line is not long either.	*Und diese weiße Linie ist auch nicht lang.*
Aren't these black lines short?	*Sind diese schwarzen Linien nicht kurz?*
No, these black lines are not short.	*Nein, diese schwarzen Linien sind nicht kurz.*
These black lines are not long either.	*Diese schwarzen Linien sind auch nicht lang.*
This line is long, but it is not black.	*Diese Linie ist lang, aber sie ist nicht schwarz.*
Give me one black line.	*Geben Sie mir eine schwarze Linie.*
Give her the white line.	*Geben Sie ihr die weiße Linie.*
Take the white line, and put (lay) it here.	*Nehmen Sie die weiße Linie und legen Sie sie hierher.*
Take the black line, and put (lay) it there.	*Nehmen Sie die schwarze Linie und legen Sie sie dorthin.*
Take all the lines, and put (lay) them here.	*Nehmen Sie alle Linien und legen Sie sie hierher.*
Take that line, and give it to me.	*Nehmen Sie jene Linie und geben Sie sie mir.*

✓ **In this activity you will:**

→ Increase reading comprehension, and vocabulary usage.

English *(cont.)*	German
That long line is not upright. It is lying down.	*Diese lange Linie steht nicht. Sie liegt.*
These white lines are not lying down; they are upright.	*Diese weißen Linien liegen nicht; sie stehen.*
Don't give me the black chalk; give me the white one.	*Geben Sie mir nicht die schwarze Kreide; geben Sie mir die weiße.*
Don't put the black one on the white one.	*Legen Sie nicht die schwarze auf die weiße.*
Don't take this white chalk.	*Nehmen Sie nicht diese weiße Kreide.*
Don't take that black chalk either.	*Nehmen Sie auch nicht jene schwarze Kreide.*
Here is the short white chalk.	*Hier ist die kurze, weiße Kreide.*
Take it, but don't put it on the black chalks.	*Nehmen Sie sie, aber legen Sie sie nicht auf die schwarzen Kreiden.*
Take the other two white chalks.	*Nehmen Sie die anderen zwei weißen Kreiden.*

Translation Exercise

INSTRUCTIONS   Give the German equivalent for the following. Note: These commands are all addressed to the formal You - *Sie*. Check your answers in Appendix A, on page 392.

1. Give him the long white line.

   ....

2. Take all the lines, and put them here.

   ....

3. Aren't these black lines short?

   ....

4. These black lines are not long either.

   ....

5. These white lines are not lying down; they are standing.

   ....

   ....

6. Don't give me the black line; give me the white one.

....

....

7. Don't take that black line either.

....

8. Here is the short white line. Take it, but don't put it on the black lines.

....

....

9. Take the other two short white lines.

....

10. Don't give him these lines.

....

★ **Performance Challenge**

Individual   Did you know that Albert Einstein was trained as a Physics and Mathematics teacher? Research his life and teach a family member or friend about what you have learned.

★ **Performance Challenge**

Group   Play "Simon Says" in German. Choose one student to be "Simon" and have them use the words and phrases from the activity. Rotate turns until everyone has had a chance to be "Simon."

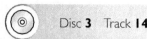

Disc **3**   Track **14**

Fire in the Lion's Heart *(cont.)*

"The wind!" you say enthusiastically.

"Yes, it's pretty windy," answers Spinne.

"No, you don't understand! That's the answer to the riddle," you explain. "In the story, wind couldn't make the man take off his coat."

"Hey, you're right!" says Spinne, smiling at the discovery.

You both stand and turn to face the monument. You lick a finger and stick it up into the wind.

"It's coming from this direction," you say, turning to face your pointing hand.

Spinne turns to face the same direction and surveys the monument.

"I don't see anything. Do you?" Spinne asks.

"No," you say. "Perhaps I was wrong about the clue."

Just then, a taxi drives up to the monument and lets out an elderly woman. The windows of the car are open, and the news is blaring over the cab's radio.

"Another 4,000 people have been admitted to Swiss hospitals with the mysterious plague," says the radio announcer. "Scientists working on a cure say that if an antidote is not found soon, the majority of citizens in Switzerland will be infected within a month."

Spinne moves quickly to the monument and starts feeling around the base. "We have to move faster. We need that antidote," he says urgently.

Suddenly the wind picks up, blowing cold and brisk from the nearby mountains. As the wind blows, one of the bricks on the base of the statue seems to creak slightly. You run over to the brick and roll it open.

"That's it!" says Spinne.

The brick opens to reveal a fiery red interior with a box inside it. On the box are red lacquered flames and a gold clasp. Opening the clasp, you find the next sheet of music and a black stone key.

"What is this key made out of?" you ask.

Spinne turns it over and over, then smiles widely. "Fire in the Lion's Heart," Spinne says. Spinne then takes the key and strikes it briskly against the base of the statue.

"What are you doing?" you bark. "Don't break it!"

As Spinne smacks the key hard against the statue's base, sparks fly out and sizzle the hair on your arm.

"Hey!" you protest.

"Fire in the Lion's Heart!" says Spinne. "It's flint, like flint and steel. It's the stone you use to make fire."

"Oh!" you say rolling the sheet music up and placing it in your pack. "That makes sense. Now, we better get going. We have no time to lose."

You jump in the truck and head into the mountains.

About two miles out of town, you notice another dark black van following you at a fast pace.

"Spinne, they found us," you say, watching closely through the rear-view mirror. "Hang on, this could get bumpy."

You step on the accelerator, trying to lose the van on the twisting mountain roads. You swerve through curve after curve, with Spinne hanging on to the handle above the seat. The van gains on you. Through a straight place in the road, you see the woman lean out of the passenger side of the car and throw a spike at your rear tire. Unfortunately, she hits it, blowing the tire out and sending you swerving along the road.

Without your back tire, the truck is almost impossible to control, and as you take the next curve, your truck can't quite make it. You plow headlong off the steep road and into a patch of trees and rocks.

When you wake up, aching and bruised, you lean over to check that Spinne is okay. To your horror, Spinne is gone, as is his pack where the keys were kept. You quickly open your pack and unzip the false bottom to reveal the sheet music still in place.

"Whew! At least they didn't find that," you say to yourself. "Now, where is Spinne?"

You let yourself out of the truck and search around the crash site, yelling for Spinne. As you round the front of the truck, you see a piece of paper tucked in the passenger-side door. You open the paper to find a scrawled message that makes your stomach turn:

"We have your companion and your keys. We want the music. If you want to see your partner alive, come to Estavayer-le-Lac, and we will trade his life for the music."

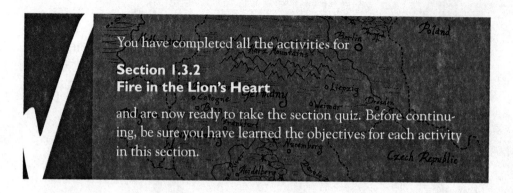

You have completed all the activities for

Section 1.3.2
Fire in the Lion's Heart

and are now ready to take the section quiz. Before continuing, be sure you have learned the objectives for each activity in this section.

Section 1.3.2 Quiz

INSTRUCTIONS   Choose the correct response. Check your answers in Appendix D, on page 402.

1. **Wir ... keine Spinnennetz, weil wir keine Spinnen ...**

    A. *webt; sind*

    B. *weben; bist*

    C. *webt; bin*

    D. *weben; sind*

2. **Why don't you believe it?**

    A. *Wo liegen Ihre Beschwerden?*

    B. *Weil ich der Clown bin?*

    C. *Warum glauben Sie das nicht?*

    D. *Wirst du das nicht?*

3. **Was ist richtig?**

    A. *immer, nie, oft*

    B. *nie, oft, immer*

    C. *oft, immer, nie*

    D. *nie, immer, oft*

INSTRUCTIONS   Choose the correct German translation of the English sentence.

4. **He died a long time ago.**

    A. *Er ist einer langen Zeit vor gestorben.*

    B. *Er ist gestorben einer langen Zeit vor.*

    C. *Er ist gestorben vor einer langen Zeit.*

    D. *Er ist vor einer langen Zeit gestorben.*

5. **Go to the carpenter and ask him for the bed.**

   A. *Geh zu dem Zimmermann und frag ihn nach dem Bett.*

   B. *Gehst du zu dem Zimmermann und fragen ihn nach dem Bett.*

   C. *Gehen du zu dem Zimmermann und fragen du ihn nach dem Bett.*

   D. *Geht sie zu dem Zimmermann und fragt ihn nach dem Bett.*

....

INSTRUCTIONS   Choose the correct response.

6. **Wie geht's? You answer**

   A. *Immer zu Fuß.*

   B. *Mein Name ist …*

   C. *Sehr gut, danke.*

   D. *Nein, danke.*

7. **Was passt nicht? (does not match)**

   A. *die Henne*

   B. *die Ente*

   C. *die Gans*

   D. *die Maus*

8. **Was ist richtig?**

   A. *Die Henne gesagt es hat mir.*

   B. *Gesagt es mir hat die Henna.*

   C. *Die Henne hat gesagt es mir.*

   D. *Die Henne hat es mir gesagt.*

9. **Diese Stange ist lang, aber sie ist nicht schwarz. We know**

   A. This chalk is not short and it is white.

   B. This rod is not short and it could be green.

   C. This chalk is long, and it is black.

   D. This rod is long, and it is black.

10. **Wie sagt man "Don't take the white chalk" auf Deutsch?**

    A. *Nehmen Sie nicht die weiße Kreide.*

    B. *Geben Sie mir nicht die weiße Kreide.*

    C. *Nehmen Sie nicht die weiße Stange.*

    D. *Geben Sie mir nicht die weiße Kreide.*

You have completed all the sections for

Module 1.3

and are now ready to take the module test. Before continuing, be sure you have learned the objectives for each activity in this module.

Module 1.3 Test

INSTRUCTIONS   True or False. The following sentences are translated correctly. Check your answers in Appendix D, on page 401.

1. **As you wish. = *Wie du willst.***
   A. True
   B. False

2. **It was our pleasure. = *Es war eine Freude.***
   A. True
   B. False

3. **Do you like to go to the theater? = *Gehst du gern in dem Theater?***
   A. True
   B. False

4. **Do you still love me? = *Liebst du mich noch?***
   A. True
   B. False

5. **Now and then. = *Ab und zu.***
   A. True
   B. False

....

INSTRUCTIONS   Choose the correct translation of the phrase or sentence.

6. **How are things?**

   A. *Wie sind Dinge?*

   B. *Wie geht's?*

   C. *Was gibt's?*

   D. *Was ist los?*

7. ***Sehr gut, danke.***

   A. Very well, thanks.

   B. Not well, thanks.

   C. No, thanks.

   D. Much thanks.

8. **Yes. Tell me, what's that?**

   A. *Ja. Was ist das?*

   B. *Ja. Sagt mir was?*

   C. *Ja. Sagen Sie mir, was soll das?*

   D. *Ja. Sagen Sie mir, was ist das?*

9. ***Das ist mein Hund.***

   A. That is my hand.

   B. That is her friend.

   C. My dog is brown.

   D. That is my dog.

10. **Your dog? He looks like a wolf!**

   A. *Dein Hund? Er sieht aus wie einen Wolf!*

   B. *Dein Hund? Er sieht aus wie ein Wolf!*

   C. *Ihr Hund? Ist er ein Wolf?*

   D. *Ihr Hund? Er sieht aus wie den Wolf!*

11. ***Ja. Eigentlich war sein Vater ein Wolf.***

   A. Yes. Actually his father was a wolf.

   B. Yes. His father was a wolf.

   C. Yes. His father was part wolf.

   D. Yes. Actually his father was not a wolf.

12. **By the way, where is your home?**

    A. *Apropos, wohin gehst du?*

    B. *Apropos, wo wohntest Sie?*

    C. *Apropos, wo wohnen Sie?*

    D. *Apropos, wo wohnt ihr?*

13. ***Auf der anderen Seite des Parkes. Und Sie?***

    A. On the other side of town. And you?

    B. Near the park. And you?

    C. On the other side of the tracks. And you?

    D. On the other side of the park. And you?

14. **on this side of the park**

    A. *auf dieser Seite des Parkes*

    B. *auf jener Seite des Parkes*

    C. *auf diesem Seite der Stadt*

    D. *an dieser Seite dieses Parkes*

15. ***in der Nähe von der Universität***

    A. by the university

    B. next to the university

    C. where's the university

    D. do you go to the university

16. **the rectangle**

    A. *der Kreis*

    B. *das Quadrant*

    C. *das Rechteck*

    D. *die Linie*

17. **the square**

    A. *der Kreis*

    B. *das Quadrant*

    C. *das Rechteck*

    D. *das Oval*

18. **the angle**

   A. *der Kreis*

   B. *das Quadrat*

   C. *der Hufschmied*

   D. *der Winkel*

19. **the line**

   A. *der Kreis*

   B. *die Linie*

   C. *der Winkel*

   D. *der Hufschmied*

20. **the circle**

   A. *der Kreis*

   B. *die Linie*

   C. *das Quadrant*

   D. *das Rechteck*

21. **the oval**

   A. *der Kreis*

   B. *die Linie*

   C. *das Recheck*

   D. *das Oval*

22. **bad**

   A. *gut*

   B. *besser*

   C. *schlecht*

   D. *schlimmer*

23. **the truth**

   A. *das Wert*

   B. *das Wort*

   C. *die Sache*

   D. *die Wahrheit*

24. **the medicine**
    A. *der Hufschmied*
    B. *die Medizin*
    C. *die Zahncreme*
    D. *die Aspirin*

25. **the blacksmith**
    A. *der Hufschmied*
    B. *der Zimmermann*
    C. *der Zahnarzt*
    D. *der Bäckerei*

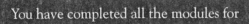

You have completed all the modules for

Semester 1

Review any material in this semester that you feel needs extra attention. When you're ready, move on to Semester 2.

Semester 2

Module 2.1

Throughout this module we'll be learning about Estavayer-le-Lac, Switzerland.

Keep these tips in mind as you progress through this module:

1. Read instructions carefully.
2. Repeat aloud all the German words you hear on the audio CDs.
3. Learn at your own pace.
4. Have fun with the activities and practice your new language skills with others.
5. Record yourself speaking German on tape so you can evaluate your own speaking progress.

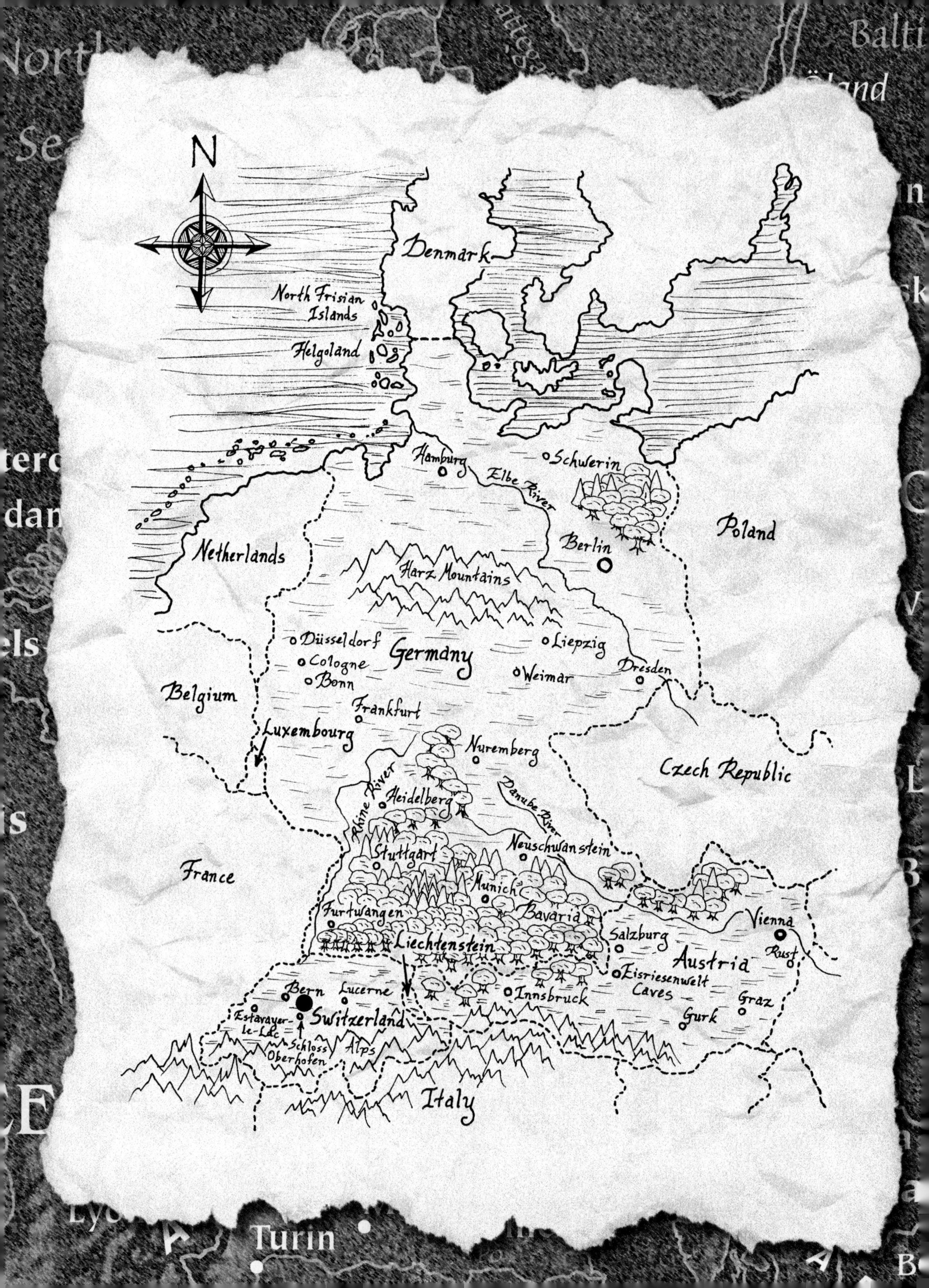

Unfortunate Delays

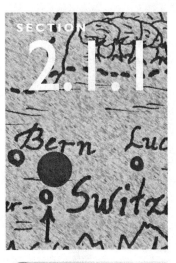

It takes the rest of the night to stagger to the nearest town. Once there, you're required to file a report on the car accident, and the well-intentioned police officers won't let you out of their sight until a doctor has made sure you're all right. You chafe at the delays. Who knows what could be happening to Spinne while you're stuck here?

It's after noon by the time the doctor pronounces you fit to travel. Not wasting a moment, you rush out of his office—only to discover that this small town has no car rental shops. You don't have time to walk to Estavayer-le-Lac. After inquiring at the town hall, you learn that a bus bound for Estavayer-le-Lac will stop here this afternoon. It won't arrive for a couple of hours, though. Frustrated, you make your way to a local café for a late lunch.

While waiting for your meal, you examine the sheet of music that you retrieved from the Lion Monument. *"Suche nach den Fröschen, die eine Nadelsuppe kochen,"* its hidden clue reads. What on earth does that mean? You try to figure it out over lunch but still don't have an answer when you go to catch the bus. On the bus, you study some more German activities, hoping that one of them will tell you what the new clue means. You also ask the driver to tell you about Estavayer-le-Lac. You have no intention of surrendering the music sheets you've collected so far, so you need to know all you can about the town. After all, it will do no good to rescue Spinne if you get caught yourself.

✓ In this section you will:

→ Master new vocabulary.

→ Recognize your ability to understand German.

→ Read and understand a *Geschichte auf deutsch*.

→ Read and listen to a *Geschichte* and understand new vocabulary from context.

→ Read to increase all skill levels of language learning.

◎ Disc **4** Track **I**

SECTION **2.1.1**

243

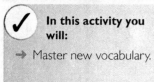

In this activity you will:

→ Master new vocabulary.

Disc **4** Track **2**

Toward Fluency 4

Words and Patterns

INSTRUCTIONS Learn these vocabulary words. See them used in sample sentences.

English	German
a spy	ein(e) Spion(in)
a double agent	ein(e) Doppelagent(in)
an imposter	ein(e) Schwindler(in)
a soccer player	ein(e) Fußballspieler(in)
so / then	dann
perhaps	vielleicht
That means nothing.	Das bedeutet überhaupt nichts.
there is / there are	es gibt
everything	all / alles
That is all.	Das ist alles.
in reality	in Wirklichkeit
probably	wahrscheinlich
precisely	genau
with	mit

Sample Sentences

English	German
There's a princess here.	Es gibt hier eine Prinzessin.
Now there are two princesses here.	Jetzt gibt es hier zwei Prinzessinnen.
There is a double agent here.	Es gibt hier einen Doppelagenten.
Mary is with him.	Maria ist bei ihm.
She is a double agent, too, perhaps.	Sie ist vielleicht auch eine Doppelagentin.
Indeed. Precisely.	Tatsächlich. Genau.

Sample Sentences (cont.)

English	German
Terrible!	*Schrecklich!*
That means nothing.	*Das bedeutet überhaupt nichts.*

Rapid Oral Translation Exercise 1

INSTRUCTIONS Translate the following sentences into German. Check your answers in Appendix A, on page 392.

1. Who is the spy? Who knows? I don't know.
2. It's certain that there is an imposter here, a double agent.
3. The soccer player, is he an imposter?
4. I believe he is the soccer player.
5. No, he is not the soccer player, but he is probably a double agent.
6. The princess from Monaco, is she a friend of the spy?
7. Probably, but that's nothing. She is also a friend of the prince.

Review

1. Go through the three oral translation exercises again, aiming for rapid, smooth delivery. Speak with expression and confidence. Imagine you are telling a story to children.

2. See how many meaningful statements you can generate from this material in 2 minutes. Keep a tally. Your goal is to create 16 statements in 2 minutes. Can you reach this goal?

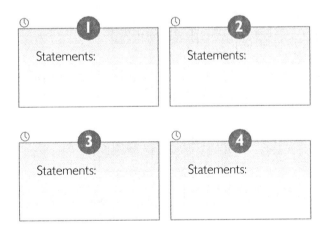

Words and Patterns

INSTRUCTIONS Learn these vocabulary words. See them used in sample sentences.

English	German
He / she / it must be.	Er / sie / es muss sein.
He / she / it can be.	Er / sie / es kann sein.
They are here.	Sie sind hier.
They are friends.	Sie sind Freunde.
strange	merkwürdig
Rather strange, isn't it?	Ziemlich merkwürdig, nicht wahr?
without doubt	zweifellos
a man and a woman	ein Mann und eine Frau
a dangerous woman	eine gefährliche Frau
I'm in accord / I agree.	Ich stimme zu.
Is it true? It is true.	Wirklich? Wirklich.
Why?	Warum?
because	weil
the palace	das Schloss
The situation is very grave.	Die Situation ist sehr schwerwiegend.

Sample Sentences

English	German
But the princess isn't in the garden; she is in the palace.	Aber die Prinzessin ist nicht in dem Garten; sie ist in dem Schloss.
Is it true? Yes, I believe it is so.	Wirklich? Ich glaube, ja.
Rather strange, isn't it?	Ziemlich merkwürdig, nicht wahr?
I agree with You.	Ich stimme Ihnen zu.
If she is in the palace with Robert...	Wenn sie mit Robert in dem Schloss ist...
Then she is a spy. She must be a spy.	Dann ist sie eine Spionin. Sie muss eine Spionin sein.
She must be. And Robert must be a spy too.	Sie muss eine sein. Und Robert muss auch ein Spion sein.
I agree with You.	Ich stimme Ihnen zu.
Now they are in the garden. But why?	Jetzt sind sie in dem Garten. Aber warum?

Sample Sentences *(cont.)*

English	German
Rather strange, but why not?	*Ziemlich merkwürdig, aber warum nicht?*
It's because they…perhaps…oh, who knows why?	*Es ist, weil sie…vielleicht…oh, wer weiß warum?*
Without doubt she is a dangerous woman.	*Zweifellos ist sie eine gefährliche Frau.*
And he is a dangerous man.	*Und er ist ein gefährlicher Mann.*
Oh, without doubt.	*Oh, zweifellos.*

Rapid Oral Translation Exercise 2

INSTRUCTIONS   Translate the following sentences into German. Check your answers in Appendix A, on page 392.

1. There is a spy in the garden.
2. Yes, and probably there is a woman with him.
3. Really? Do You know who she is?
4. I don't know, but she may be the double agent who is a friend of the prince.
5. Robert, the prince's friend, is no doubt an imposter and a dangerous man. He may be a spy.
6. Oh, that's rather strange.
7. Why? Why strange?
8. Because…because…Oh, I don't know, but it may be that…
9. The situation is grave, isn't it?
10. I agree with You, it's very grave.

Review

1. Go through the oral translation exercises again, aiming for smoothness. Speak with expression and confidence.
2. See how many meaningful statements you can generate from this material in two minutes. Your goal is to create 17 statements in 2 minutes. Can you reach this goal?

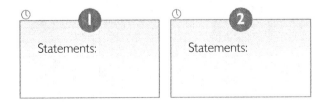

Statements:

Statements:

Estavayer-le-Lac

Estavayer-le-Lac is located on the shores of beautiful Lake Neuchâtel in the canton (state) of Neuchâtel, Switzerland. It is home to a regional museum which houses a 130-year old collection of frogs. In the 19th century, François Perrier spent most of his free time stuffing the frogs with sand and then arranging them in parodies of human situations such as attending school, dating, and playing games. He often used props to help him tell the story better. The museum is open to the public and free of charge.

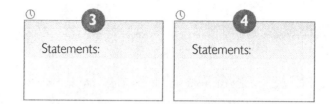

3. Quickly review the Toward Fluency lesson, then take the following test. Cover the opposite column except to check your interpretation.

Self Quiz

INSTRUCTIONS Review the material in this lesson. Then orally translate the following sentences.

1. Who is here? And who is there?
2. There is one princess here and one there.
3. Is there a princess in the garden?
4. Yes. And there is one in the palace.
5. One princess is there? Is it Anita?
6. No, she is not there. She is here.
7. The princess Johanna is there with Frank, right?
8. Probably. I believe that he is a spy.
9. Then she is a friend of a spy.
10. That's true.
11. Then she must be a spy too.
12. I agree. She may be a double agent.
13. But that's rather strange, isn't it?
14. Why? Because she is my friend?
15. Yes, because she is Your friend.
16. If Fritz is a spy…
17. Then Johanna is a spy too, right?
18. Frank may be a spy, but he is not a soccer player.
19. In reality, he is a formidable enemy.
20. Yes, without doubt, but…
21. That's all.

INSTRUCTIONS Now repeat the test three or four times, each time aiming for faster time and increased fluency.

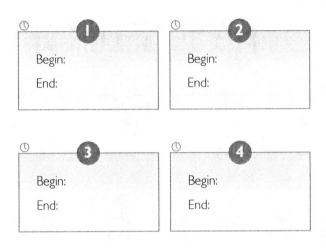

⭐

Performance Challenge

Individual   Choose a famous spy in history and write about him or her, using as much German as you can. Rough out some ideas below.

....

....

....

....

....

....

....

....

....

⭐

Performance Challenge

Group   Soccer is one of Germany's most popular sports. Read about the history of soccer in Germany and the current German National Soccer Team. Then divide the group into teams and have your own soccer match.

Conversation Snatches 12

ACTIVITY
55

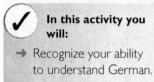

In this activity you will:

→ Recognize your ability to understand German.

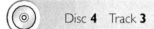

Disc **4**   Track **3**

INSTRUCTIONS   Listen to and read the following dialogues. Pay attention to all the new vocabulary. Circle all the vocabulary words you already know.

English	German
When I was small, nobody had anything.	*Als ich jung war, hatte niemand etwas gehabt.*
Not even a car?	*Nicht mal ein Auto?*
Not even a bicycle.	*Nicht mal ein Fahrrad.*
Now, all together, once more.	*Nun, alle zusammen, noch einmal.*
Heave ho!	*Heb' hoch!*
Where would You like to go?	*Wo wollen Sie denn hin?*
It doesn't matter.	*Es ist mir egal.*
Aren't Hans and Olga coming?	*Kommen Hans und Olga nicht?*
Olga yes, Hans no.	*Olga ja, Hans nicht.*
Hans isn't coming because he's sick.	*Hans kommt nicht, weil er krank ist.*
Hans feels better now.	*Hans fühlt sich jetzt besser.*
At last.	*Endlich.*
What do you want to tell me?	*Was willst du mir erzählen?*
Nothing. I have nothing to say.	*Nichts. Ich habe nichts zu sagen.*
They say where one door closes, another opens.	*Man sagt, dass wenn sich eine Tür schließt, sich eine andere öffnet.*
I'd like to believe that.	*Ich würde das gerne glauben.*
Will you dance with me?	*Wirst du mit mir tanzen?*
I have nothing against it.	*Ich habe nichts dagegen.*

The Frog Museum of München-stein

But frog collecting is not unique to Estavayer-le-Lac. In the city of Münchenstein, there is a more recent collection containing more than 10,000 frogs and frog-related items. This collection also has the stuffed frogs outfitted and arranged in scenes depicting everyday life.

English *(cont.)*	German
Can we help You now?	*Können wir Ihnen jetzt helfen?*
That is out of the question.	*Das kommt nicht in Frage.*

Performance Challenge

Individual   Research bicycle racing in Germany and the current Team Gerolsteiner. Write a short paper about this year's team members, their toughest competition for the current season, and the history of the team itself. Rough out some ideas below.

....

....

....

....

....

....

....

....

....

....

....

....

Performance Challenge

Group   Assign the students to research the *Deutsche Bahn* and travel in Germany. Have each of them choose a route and plan as if they were going to take the trip. Make sure they include hotels, car rentals, and tourist attractions along their route.

Chatter at a Royal Ball 5

In this activity you will:

→ Read and understand a *Geschichte auf deutsch*.

 Disc **4** Track **4**

Getting Ready for Conversation

INSTRUCTIONS Learn these words. Use them to master the conversation.

English	German
to dance	*tanzen*
to know / know how	*können*
He / she / it knows how to dance.	*Er / sie / es kann tanzen.*
he has	*er hat*
to joke	*Witze machen*
I'm not joking.	*Ich mache keine Witze.*
I know	*ich weiß*
Listen!	*Hören Sie mal!*
Listen to me!	*Hören Sie auf mich!*
Oh, my goodness!	*Ach, du meine Güte!*
in fact	*eigentlich*
Don't tell me!	*Sagen Sie nicht so etwas!*

Conversation

INSTRUCTIONS Concentrate on this conversation.

	English	German
••:	The king of France has a horse.	*Der König von Frankreich hat ein Pferd.*
•:	Of course he has a horse. What king doesn't have a horse?	*Natürlich hat er ein Pferd. Welcher König hat kein Pferd?*

Neuchâtel Chocolate

Switzerland is also famous for its chocolate. Because of the fresh ingredients that are used to make it, it is the finest, high-quality chocolate in the world. Neuchâtel is no exception. In fact, there is a company in Pennsylvania that was founded by a 5th generation Swiss Chocolatier that bears the name of Neuchâtel. He was given permission to use the name of the Swiss city, but under the strict guideline that the ingredients he uses are imported directly from Switzerland. The company is famous for their Swiss Truffles and other confections like the Swiss Chip which blends chocolate with potato chips; a surprisingly popular treat.

English (cont.)	German
●●: And You know, his horse is white.	*Und wissen Sie, sein Pferd ist weiß.*
●: Of course I know. What king doesn't have a white horse?	*Natürlich weiß ich das. Welcher König hat kein weißes Pferd?*
●●: Listen to me! His horse knows how to dance.	*Hören Sie auf mich! Sein Pferd kann tanzen.*
●: Whose horse knows how to dance?	*Wessen Pferd kann tanzen?*
●●: The horse of the king of France.	*Das Pferd des Königs von Frankreich.*
●: You are joking.	*Sie machen Witze.*
●●: I'm not joking. It's true. His horse knows how to do the cha-cha.	*Ich mache keine Witze. Es ist wahr. Sein Pferd kann Cha-Cha tanzen.*
●: Oh, my goodness!	*Ach, du meine Güte!*
●●: In fact, the horse and the dog and the cat dance together.	*Eigentlich tanzen das Pferd und der Hund und die Katze zusammen.*
●: Don't tell me! The white horse of the king of France dances with the dog and cat?	*Sagen Sie so etwas nicht! Das weiße Pferd des Königs von Frankreich tanzt mit dem Hund und der Katze?*
●●: Precisely.	*Genau.*

Task 1

INSTRUCTIONS Use your hands as puppets and dramatize the dialogue, looking only at the German. Visualize the situation and get into the spirit of the conversation. Aim for a flowing German quality, then go on.

Performance Challenge

Individual Research wildlife in three German-speaking countries of your choice. Write a one page report in German on each country and its wildlife. Rough out some ideas below.

....

....

....

ACTIVITY 56

....

....

....

....

....

....

....

....

....

....

....

....

....

....

....

....

....

....

....

....

....

Performance Challenge

Group Divide German-speaking countries among students. Have each student write an essay on wildlife in their assigned country in German.

Needle Soup

INSTRUCTIONS   Listen to and read this story. You will be learning vocabulary about different foods in German.

In this activity you will:

→ Read and listen to a *Geschichte* and understand new vocabulary from context.

   Disc **4**   Track **5**

English	German
There was once a boy named Sasha.	*Es war einmal ein Junge namens Sascha.*
His mother was a poor widow.	*Seine Mutter war eine arme Witwe.*
One day, her house caught on fire.	*Eines Tages brannte ihr Haus ab.*
She managed to save her son, but she died in the fire, leaving Sasha alone in the world.	*Sie schaffte es ihren Sohn zu retten, aber sie starb in dem Feuer und ließ Sascha allein in der Welt.*
The only thing he found in the ashes of the house was his mother's needle.	*Die Nadel seiner Mutter war das einzigste, was er in der Asche des Hauses fand.*
Poor Sasha was only ten years old.	*Der arme Sascha war erst zehn Jahre alt.*
He had no brother or sister, no grandmother or grandfather.	*Er hatte keinen Bruder und keine Schwester, keine Großmutter und keinen Großvater.*
Where could he go? What could he do?	*Wohin konnte er gehen? Was konnte er tun?*
He decided to leave the village and try his luck in the world.	*Er beschloss das Dorf zu verlassen um sein Glück in der Welt zu versuchen.*
Besides the clothes he was wearing and his mother's needle, he took nothing with him.	*Er nahm nichts weiter mit sich als die Nadel seiner Mutter und die Kleidung, die er anhatte.*
He wrapped the needle in paper and placed it in his pocket.	*Er wickelte die Nadel in Papier ein und packte sie in seine Tasche.*
He thought:	*Er dachte:*
"Because I have no money, I'll just have to live by my wits."	*"Weil ich kein Geld habe, werde ich nur von meinem Verstand leben müssen."*
For two days he wandered, cold and hungry.	*Er wanderte zwei Tage lang und es war ihm kalt und er war hungrig.*

English (cont.)	German
At last, he came to a village.	Schließlich kam er zu einem Dorf.
Weak and tired, he knocked on the door of a pretty house near the village gate.	Schwach und müde, klopfte er an eine Tür eines schönen Hauses nahe dem Dorfeingang.
A lady opened the door.	Eine Frau öffnete die Tür.
When she saw the ragged little boy, she thought:	Als sie den lumpigen kleinen Jungen sah, dachte sie:
"Such a ragged child must be a beggar.	"So ein lumpiges Kind muss ein Bettler sein.
I don't like beggars.	Ich mag keine Bettler.
I won't give him a thing."	Ich werde ihm nichts geben."
She was quite selfish and greedy, don't you think?	Denkst du nicht, dass sie sehr selbstsüchtig und gierig war?
"Ma'am, have You a small crust of bread for a hungry child?	"Haben Sie eine kleine Brotkruste für ein hungriges Kind?
Please!" Sasha asked.	Bitte!" fragte Sascha.
"No," the lady said.	"Nein," sagte die Frau.
"Beggars and thieves have taken all my food."	"Bettler und Diebe haben mein ganzes Essen gestohlen."
"Don't You have anything left to eat?"	"Haben Sie gar nichts zu essen übrig?"
"I already told you, I haven't even a crumb of bread."	"Ich habe dir bereits gesagt, dass ich nicht einmal einen Krümel Brot habe."
"Very well," said Sasha with a sigh.	"Na gut," sagte Sascha mit einem Seufzer.
"Then I shall have to have needle soup again."	"Dann muss ich wieder Nadelsuppe essen."
The selfish lady was about to close the door, but the little boy's words made her hesitate.	Die selbstsüchtige Frau war dabei die Tür zu schließen, aber wegen der Worte des kleinen Jungen zögerte sie.
"Needle soup?" she said, narrowing her eyes.	"Nadelsuppe?" sagte sie und verkleinerte ihre Augen.
"Yes, it's really quite tasty, only I've had it three nights in a row now.	"Ja, die ist wirklich sehr geschmackvoll, aber ich habe sie schon drei Abende hintereinander gegessen.

English (cont.)	German
I'd rather have a bit of bread tonight."	Heute Abend würde ich lieber ein Stück Brot essen."
The lady started to think:	Die Frau fing an nachzudenken:
"Wouldn't it be nice to know how to make soup from needles?	"Wäre es nicht schön zu wissen, wie man eine Suppe mit Nadeln kocht?
Then I would never want for food."	Dann wird es mir nie mehr an Speise mangeln."
She smiled at the boy and opened the door.	Sie lächelte den Jungen an und öffnete die Tür.
"I'm sorry I don't have any food for you, but if you like you may come inside and cook some needle soup in my pot."	"Es tut mir leid, dass ich keine Speise für dich habe, aber wenn du möchtest, kannst du hereinkommen und Nadelsuppe in meinem Kessel kochen."
Sasha smiled too and thought:	Sascha lächelte und dachte:
"I may not have food, but I have my wits."	"Ich habe zwar keine Speise, aber ich habe meinen Verstand."
Soon a large pot of water was boiling on the fire.	Bald kochte ein großer Kessel mit Wasser auf dem Feuer.
Sasha carefully took the package from his pocket.	Sascha holte vorsichtig das Päckchen aus seiner Tasche.
He unfolded the paper, took the needle out, and held it up for the lady to see.	Er entfaltete das Papier, nahm die Nadel und zeigte sie der Frau.
He said:	Er sagte:
"This needle has an especially good flavor."	"Diese Nadel hat einen besonders guten Geschmack."
Then he dropped the needle into the pot.	Dann ließ er die Nadel in den Topf sinken.
The lady watched, her eyes wide open, as Sasha busied himself stirring the pot.	Die Frau beobachtete Sascha mit weit geöffneten Augen, als er sich damit beschäftigte, den Topf umzurühren.
After a moment Sasha said:	Nach einer Weile sagte Sascha:
"With salt and pepper it's especially good.	"Mit Salz und Pfeffer ist es besonders gut.
Did the thieves and beggars take all your salt and pepper?"	Haben die Diebe und Bettler all dein Salz und Pfeffer gestohlen?"

Swiss Cheese, Part I

A variety of cheeses call Switzerland home: Emmental, Appenzeller, Vacherin Mont-d'Or, Vacherin Fribourgeois, Tilsiter, Tête de Moine, Bündnekäse and Gruyère.

English (cont.)	German
"No. I still have plenty of salt and pepper.	"Nein. Ich habe noch eine Menge Salz und Pfeffer.
Here!"	Hier!"
"Wonderful!" Sasha said, pouring some salt and pepper into the boiling water.	"Wunderbar!" sagte Sascha und schüttete Salz und Pfeffer in das kochende Wasser.
Then he stirred the pot some more, smacked his lips and said:	Dann rührte er den Topf wieder um, schmatzte mit seinen Lippen und sagte:
"Hmm, smell it!	"Hmm, riech es!
Doesn't it smell good already?	Riecht es nicht schon gut?
It's a pity the thieves and beggars took all your food.	Es ist schade, dass die Diebe und Bettler all deine Speise gestohlen haben.
An onion would give extra flavor to the soup."	Eine Zwiebel würde der Suppe einen Extrageschmack geben."
The lady said:	Die Frau sagte:
"Come to think of it, I did save one onion.	"Wenn ich so darüber nachdenke, habe ich eine Zwiebel gerettet.
I'll go get it."	Ich werde sie holen."
When she returned, she had not one but three onions.	Als sie zurück kam, hatte sie nicht nur eine Zwiebel, sondern drei.
"Wonderful!" Sasha said, and he peeled them and sliced them and dropped them into the boiling water.	"Wunderbar!" sagte Sascha, schälte und zerkleinerte sie und schüttete sie in den Kessel mit dem heißen Wasser.
Then he continued stirring the pot.	Dann rührte er den Kessel weiter um.
After a little while he said:	Nach einer Weile sagte er:
"A bit of cabbage would have really added a good taste.	"Ein bisschen Kohl hätte einen noch besseren Geschmack hinzugefügt.
What a pity the thieves and beggars took all your food."	Wie schade, dass die Diebe und die Bettler all deine Speise gestohlen haben."
The lady exclaimed:	Die Frau sagte:
"Come to think of it, they said they didn't like the cabbage, so they left two heads of it."	"Wenn ich so darüber nachdenke, sagten sie, dass sie kein Kohl mochten und so ließen sie zwei Köpfe Kohl zurück."
As soon as she had spoken, she was off to get the cabbage.	Als sie das gesagt hatte, holte sie den Kohl.

English (cont.)	German
"Wonderful!" Sasha said, and he sliced it with a knife and dropped it into the soup.	"Wunderbar!" sagte Sascha und zerkleinerte ihn mit einem Messer und schüttete ihn in die Suppe.
Soon, delicious smells filled the room where the soup was cooking.	Ein delikater Geruch füllte bald den ganzen Raum, wo die Suppe kochte.
"What a pity that all your food was stolen," said Sasha.	"Wie schade, dass all deine Speise gestohlen wurde," sagte Sascha.
"Oh, I nearly forgot about my garden.	"Oh, ich hätte fast meinen Garten vergessen.
Just this morning I noticed two carrots ready to pull."	Diesen Morgen habe ich festgestellt, dass zwei Karotten zum Ernten reif sind."
She went outside and in a moment came back with two big carrots and a nice big potato.	Sie ging hinaus und kam schnell wieder mit zwei großen Karotten und einer schönen, großen Kartoffel herein.
"Wonderful!" Sasha said as he peeled and washed them off.	"Wunderbar!" sagte Sascha als er sie schälte und wusch.
Then he cut them up and dropped them into the soup, and as he stirred, he said:	Dann schnitt er sie und schüttete sie in die Suppe, rührte sie um und sagte:
"If the beggars and thieves hadn't taken your food, we could have had some meat in our needle soup."	"Wenn die Bettler und Diebe nicht die ganze Speise gestohlen hätten, hätten wir etwas Fleisch in unsere Nadelsuppe tun können."
"Come to think of it," said the lady, "I hid a tiny scrap of meat from them."	"Wenn ich so darüber nachdenke," sagte die Frau, "habe ich ein kleines Stückchen Fleisch versteckt."
In a moment she was back with a nice big chunk of beef.	Nach einem Augenblick kam sie mit einem schönen, großen Stück Rindfleisch zurück.
"Marvelous!" Sasha said as he cut up the meat and dropped the pieces into the soup.	"Wunderbar!" sagte Sascha, schnitt das Fleisch und schüttete die Stücke in die Suppe.
Soon the kitchen was filled with a delicious smell.	Die Küche war bald mit einem delikaten Geruch gefüllt.
Sasha kept stirring the soup.	Sascha rührte die Suppe weiter um.
In a while he said:	Nach einer Weile sagte er:
"It will soon be ready!	"Es ist bald fertig!

English (cont.)	German
Perhaps you have a nice tablecloth and porcelain bowls and spoons for this special occasion."	*Vielleicht hast du ein schönes Tischtuch und Porzellanschüsseln und Löffel für diesen besonderen Anlass."*
"Indeed I do."	*"Das habe ich tatsächlich."*
The woman put a linen cloth on the table and placed her china bowls and glass spoons on top.	*Die Frau legte ein Leinentuch auf den Tisch und stellte ihre Porzellanschüsseln und Glaslöffel darauf.*
In a few minutes the soup was served in the fine china bowls.	*In wenigen Minuten war die Suppe in den schönen Porzellanschüsseln serviert.*
And the two sat down together and enjoyed the tasty soup.	*Und die beiden setzten sich zusammen hin und genossen die leckere Suppe.*
But the story does not end here.	*Aber die Geschichte endet hier noch nicht.*
The woman saw that Sasha was a very fine boy.	*Die Frau sah, dass Sascha ein sehr feiner Junge war.*
"What is your name, little boy?"	*"Wie heißt du kleiner Junge?"*
"Sasha."	*"Sascha."*
"And where do you live?"	*"Und wo wohnst du?"*
"I have no place to live. My mother and father are dead."	*"Ich habe keinen Platz zum Wohnen. Meine Mutter und mein Vater sind tot."*
"Where will you go now?"	*"Wohin wirst du nun gehen?"*
"Out into the cold, dark night."	*"In die kalte, dunkle Nacht hinaus."*
Now the woman realized how selfish she had been.	*Nun sah die Frau ein wie selbstsüchtig sie gewesen war.*
"I live alone here.	*"Ich lebe hier allein.*
I don't have any children.	*Ich habe keine Kinder.*
I apologize that I was so unkind to you.	*Es tut mir leid, dass ich so unfreundlich zu dir war.*
Here there is a warm fire.	*Hier ist ein warmes Feuer.*
Won't you stay with me and keep warm?"	*Willst du nicht hier bei mir im Warmen bleiben?"*
Sasha stayed.	*Sascha blieb.*
In the morning the woman gave him chores to do.	*Am Morgen gab die Frau ihm Hausarbeit zu erledigen.*

Swiss Cheese, Part II

The most famous cheese, of course, is Swiss Cheese, or Emmental. The story of Emmental cheese is an interesting one. Legend has it that there was once a young dairyman who fell in love with a farmer's daughter. The farmer did not approve of him and forbid his daughter to marry him. In those days, the father's will was law in the Emmental Valley.

English (cont.)	German
Sasha was very clever, and he was a willing worker.	Sascha war sehr klug und er war ein williger Arbeiter.
He liked the village and found the woman to be really very kind.	Er mochte das Dorf und fand heraus, dass die Frau wirklich sehr freundlich war.
When he was twenty, he was elected to be a member of the town council.	Mit zwanzig Jahren wurde er in den Ortsrat gewählt.
People came to him for advice.	Die Leute kamen zu ihm, um sich Rat zu holen.
And do you know what he told them?	Und weißt du, was er ihnen sagte?
"If you use your wits, you can find a solution to every problem."	"Wenn ihr euren Verstand benutzt, könnt ihr für jedes Problem eine Lösung finden."
Even today, Sasha keeps his mother's needle.	Sogar heute behält Sascha die Nadel seiner Mutter.
He wears it on his shirt.	Er trägt sie an seinem Hemd.
And when people ask him why he wears a needle on his shirt, he says:	Und wenn Leute ihn fragen, warum er die Nadel an seinem Hemd trägt, sagt er:
"One never knows what will happen tomorrow.	"Man weiß nie, was morgen geschehen wird.
But as long as I have my wits and this needle, I know I will never go hungry."	Aber solange ich meinen Verstand und diese Nadel habe, weiß ich, dass ich nie hungern werde."

Performance Challenge

Individual   Translate your favorite recipe for soup into German. Then teach someone how to make the soup, using the German directions. Tell the story of Needle Soup as you share it with your family or friends. Translate your recipe below.

....

....

....

....

....

....

....

....

....

....

....

....

....

....

....

....

....

....

....

....

....

....

....

Performance Challenge

Group Divide the students into groups. Have each group write a new ending for Needle Soup. Then have the groups perform or read their creative endings to the other students, in German.

The Shepherd Boy Who Cried "Wolf"

In this activity you will:

→ Read to increase all skill levels of language learning.

INSTRUCTIONS   Read the following story. Practice your pronunciation as you read, aiming for fluency and speed. Work toward full comprehension.

English	German
Once there was a shepherd boy who liked to play tricks on people.	*Es war einmal ein Hirtenjunge, der es liebte Leuten Streiche zu spielen.*
Every day he herded his sheep on the slope of a hill.	*Jeden Tag hütete er die Schafe am Berghang.*
One day, having nothing to do, he was bored, so he decided to play a trick on the villagers.	*Eines Tages, als er nichts zu tun hatte und sich langweilte, entschied er sich den Dorfbewohnern einen Streich zu spielen.*
He cried:	*Er schrie:*
"A wolf!	*"Ein Wolf!*
A wolf!	*Ein Wolf!*
Help!	*Hilfe!*
Help!"	*Hilfe!"*
The villagers heard the cries and rushed to the mountain with stones and sickles.	*Die Dorfbewohner hörten das Schreien und eilten zum Berg mit Steinen und Sicheln.*
But when they got there and looked around, there was simply no wolf to be seen.	*Aber als sie dort ankamen und sich umschauten, war einfach kein Wolf zu sehen.*
In anger the villagers scolded the boy:	*In Ärger schimpften die Dorfbewohner mit dem Jungen:*

English (cont.)	German
"Don't ever play such tricks again.	"Spiel uns nicht noch einmal solche Streiche.
That's very dangerous.	Das ist sehr gefährlich.
Do you understand?"	Verstehst du?"
The boy said:	Der Junge sagte:
"I'm sorry.	"Es tut mir leid.
I won't do it again."	Ich werde es nicht wieder tun."
A week went by.	Eine Woche ging vorbei.
With nothing to do, the boy was bored, so he decided to play the trick again.	Der Junge hatte nichts zu tun und war gelangweilt, und so entschied er sich wieder den Streich zu spielen.
He cried:	Er schrie:
"A wolf!	"Ein Wolf!
A wolf!	Ein Wolf!
Help!"	Hilfe!"
Hearing the desperate cries of the shepherd boy, the villagers rushed to the mountain to save the sheep.	Als die Dorfbewohner das verzweifelte Schreien des Hirtenjungen hörten, eilten sie zu dem Berg, um die Schafe zu retten.
When they saw again that there was no wolf but only a boy laughing and playing tricks, they were extremely angry.	Als sie wieder sahen dass dort kein Wolf war, sondern nur ein lachender Junge, der Streiche spielt, waren sie sehr wütend.
They severely scolded him again.	Sie schimpften wieder sehr mit ihm.
Finally he said:	Schließlich sagte er:
"I'm sorry.	"Entschuldigung.
I won't do it again."	Ich werde es nicht wieder tun."
The villagers went home, shaking their heads.	Die Dorfbewohner gingen kopfschüttelnd nach Hause.
A short time later, some wolves really came to attack the sheep.	Eine kurze Zeit später kamen wirklich einige Wölfe, um die Schafe anzugreifen.
The shepherd boy was desperate.	Der Hirtenjunge war verzweifelt.
He cried at the top of his voice:	Er schrie mit lauter Stimme:
"A wolf!	"Ein Wolf!

Swiss Cheese, Part III

The dairyman went home discouraged, but vowed to find a way to prove his worth to the farmer. That night, there was a horrible thunderstorm. While the dairyman was eating dinner, there was a knock at his door. When he answered, a stranger seeking shelter from the storm came right in and made himself at home. The dairyman fed and entertained his unexpected guest. As soon as the storm passed, the guest left, but on his way out, he handed the dairyman a note.

English (cont.)	German
A wolf!	Ein Wolf!
Help!	Hilfe!
Help!"	Hilfe!"
But the villagers shook their heads and said:	Aber die Dorfbewohner schüttelten ihre Köpfe und sagt
"The nasty little brat is playing another trick on us."	"Dieser widerliche kleine Knirps spielt uns noch einen Streich."
So no one went to help the poor boy.	Also ging niemand hin um dem armen Jungen zu helfen.
No one believed his words.	Niemand glaubte seinen Worten.
So the wolves killed many, many sheep.	Und so töteten die Wölfe viele, viele Schafe.

Performance Challenge

Individual   Write about a time when you felt like no one was listening to you, or write about a time when you played a trick on someone and it backfired. Use as much German as you can.

....

....

....

....

....

....

Performance Challenge

Group   Have a word scramble. Divide the group into two teams. Pin a sheet of paper with a word from the story on each child. Read a portion of the story in German. The first team to line up the words in the correct order wins.

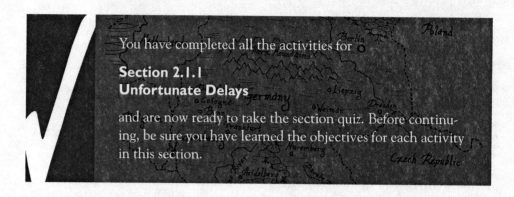

You have completed all the activities for

Section 2.1.1
Unfortunate Delays

and are now ready to take the section quiz. Before continuing, be sure you have learned the objectives for each activity in this section.

Section 2.1.1 Quiz

INSTRUCTIONS   Choose the correct response. Check your answers in Appendix D, on page 402.

1. **Wie sagt man "that means nothing?"**

    A. *Das ist alles.*

    B. *Das bedeutet überhaupt nichts.*

    C. *Das glaube ich.*

    D. *Das ist es vielleicht.*

2. **Wo ist der Mann?**

    A. *eine Doppelagentin*

    B. *eine Spionin*

    C. *eine Fußballspielerin*

    D. *ein Schwindler*

3. **Willst du mit mir tanzen?**

    A. *Heb' hoch.*

    B. *Nicht mal ein Fahrrad.*

    C. *Nichts.*

    D. *Ich habe nichts dagegen.*

4. **Hans fühlt sich jetzt besser.**

    A. *Das kommt nicht in Frage.*

    B. *Nichts.*

    C. *Endlich.*

    D. *Ich habe nichts zu sagen.*

5. **"in fact"** *ist*

   A. *wirklich*

   B. *endlich*

   C. *glauben*

   D. *eigentlich*

6. **Which sentence is grammatically correct?**

   A. *Sein Pferd kann Cha-Cha tanzen.*

   B. *Sein Pferd kann tanzen Cha-Cha.*

   C. *Sein Pferd Cha-Cha kann tanzen.*

   D. *Sein Pferd können Cha-Cha tanzen.*

7. **"whose"** *ist*

   A. *wes*

   B. *wem*

   C. *wessen*

   D. *wein*

8. **Woraus machte der Sascha Suppe?**

   A. *aus einer Nadel*

   B. *aus einer Tasche*

   C. *aus Kartoffeln*

   D. *aus Kohl*

9. **Was schrie der Hirtenjunge?**

   A. *ein Wunder*

   B. *nicht laug*

   C. *ein Wolf*

   D. *mein Schaf*

10. **Which sentence is grammatically correct?**

    A. *Glaubte niemand seinen Worten.*

    B. *Seinen Worten niemand glaubte.*

    C. *Worten seinen glaubte niemand.*

    D. *Niemand glaubte seinen Worten.*

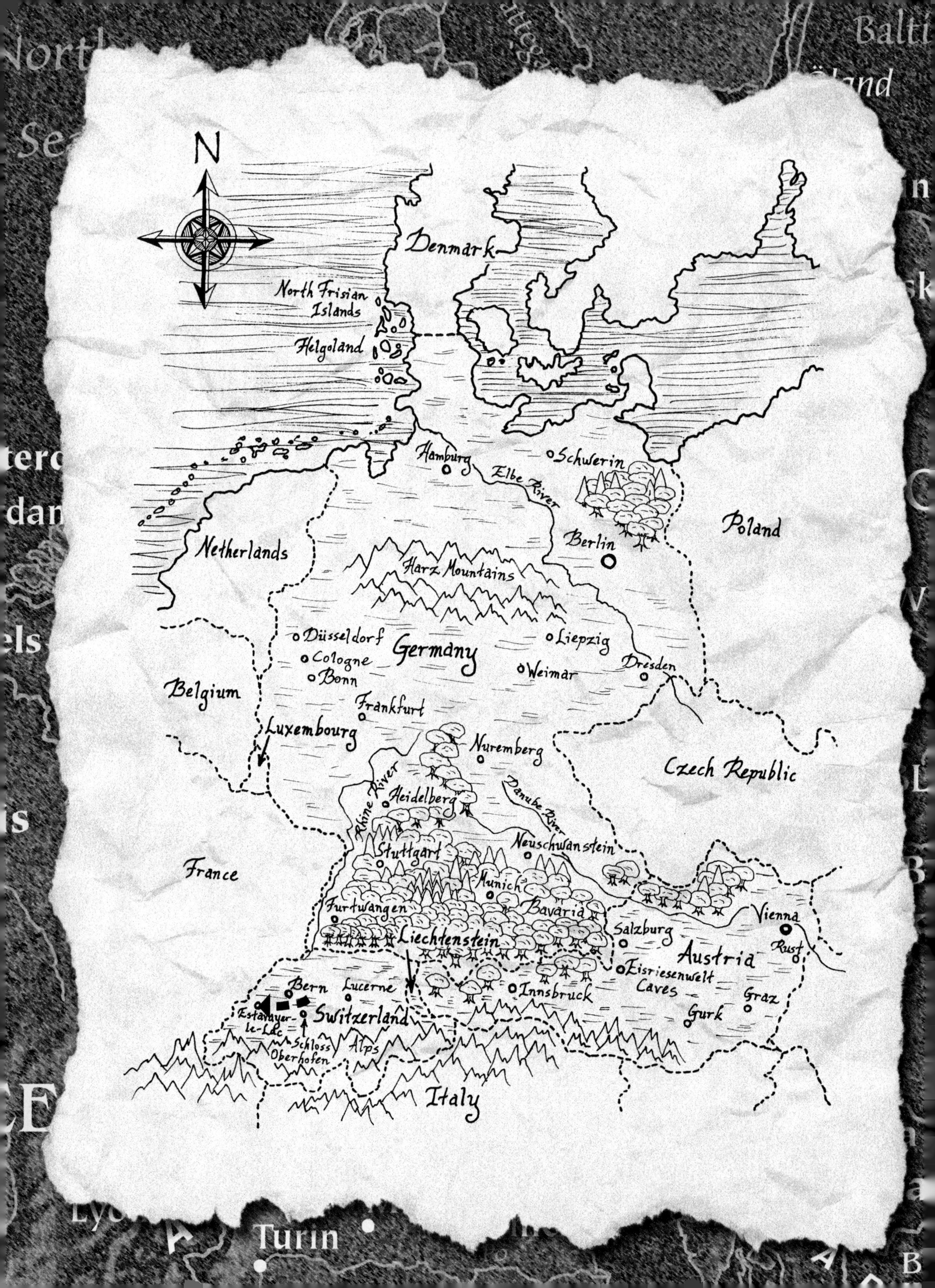

A Well Hidden Spider

By the time you arrive in Estavayer-le-Lac, it's well past dark. You thank the bus driver for his help. Between his stories and the town map he gave you, you believe that Spinne is being held captive in an abandoned 15th century storehouse in the town's medieval center. You also believe your next clue may be hidden in this town's Regional Museum, but that will have to wait until Spinne is safe.

Under cover of darkness, you approach the storehouse from behind and sneak through an open first-floor window. Crouched on the floor, you hear voices nearby. They seem to be coming from the next room. Your stomach turns as you realize this is Ungeschicklichkeit, the group that is trying to get the cure for themselves without sharing it with the rest of the world. From what you can understand, it sounds like they're plotting different ways of getting rid of both you and Spinne once they have the keys and clues you've collected so far. You shake your head and focus on the task at hand. You're good, but not good enough to take on the entire group by yourself. You look around. Obviously, this group isn't expecting you here. The silver, wood, and stone keys, still on Spinne's key ring, are lying on a small table in the hallway. You tuck them into your pocket and start looking for Spinne. He's not on the main floor, but in the last room, you find a trapdoor leading into a cellar. Carefully, you let yourself down into the cellar. It's pitch black down here. You pull a small flashlight from your pocket and switch it on. By its light, you can see that the cellar isn't very big, and about half of it is walled off in a crude cell. An old-fashioned iron-bound wooden door, with a heavy wrought-iron lock, marks the entrance to the cell.

Well, if Spinne is in the building, he must be in this cell. You take a chance and speak out loud. "Spinne? Are you in there?" you whisper through the narrow grating near the top of the door.

"Fliege? Bist du das?" comes a hoarse, familiar voice inside the cell.

"Hold on, we're going to get you out of there," you reply. You shine your flashlight on the lock. There's no visible keyhole. Molded onto the lock's surface are two figures—one of a roaring lion under a net, and one of a mouse.

"Hey, Spinne, you know anything about this lock on your door?" you ask.

In this section you will:

→ Read a *Geschichte auf deutsch* and recognize and understand new vocabulary from context.

→ Learn and use important phrases.

→ Increase reading, listening comprehension, and vocabulary usage.

→ Follow a story and understand its meaning.

Disc **4**   Track **6**

"Um…I heard one of them mumbling about some sort of story this morning. I think it was this morning, anyway…"

"Great," you mutter. You don't have time to sit down and study, not here in your enemies' lair. Also, Spinne's answer worries you. He's only been in here a little over a full day. He shouldn't be losing track of time already. You frown and shake your head.

"How often do people come down here?" you ask Spinne.

"Not that often…maybe twice a day," he answers.

You decide you're going to chance it. As far as you can see, the only way out of this cellar is the trap door through which you came. If you break open the lock, the noise will certainly attract the attention of the group upstairs. The only chance for both you and Spinne to escape is for you to open this strange lock the right way. You flip ahead in your set of German activities. There's a story called *Die Maus und der Löwe*. Perhaps it has the information you need. Concealing yourself behind some half-rotten wooden crates, you settle down for some studying.

Wrap-Up Activities

Summary: *Zusammenfassung*

INSTRUCTIONS   Read through this story and see how much you understand.

In dieser Geschichte gibt es einen König. Er ist der König, der trommelte. Er trommelte Trauerlieder. Aber jetzt trommelt er nicht. Jetzt singt er. Er singt mit der Königin, nicht wahr? Er singt Trauerlieder mit der Königin in dem Turm. Der König singt besser. Ja, er singt besser als sie…besser als die Königin. Sie singt mehr oder weniger gut…nicht sehr gut. Aber sie trommelt gut.

In der Geschichte gibt es auch einen Hund und eine Katze, die mit dem König und der Königin singen. Ja, und jetzt singen der Hund und die Katze. Sie singen mit dem König und der Königin in dem Turm. Stellen Sie sich das vor! Ein Hund und eine Katze, die singen…die Trauerlieder singen. Sie singen nicht gut, aber sie singen. Sehr seltsam! Unglaublich!

Es gibt einen Prinzen. Es gibt auch eine Prinzessin. Die Königin ist jetzt in dem Turm mit dem König. Beide singen, aber nur die Königin trommelt. Interessant, nicht wahr?

In this activity you will:
→ Read a *Geschichte auf deutsch* and recognize and understand new vocabulary from context.

Questions

INSTRUCTIONS   Answer the following questions as best as you can.

1. Wer ist sie ?

....

2. Ist er ?

....

3. Was macht der Prinz?

....

4. Mit wem spricht er?

....

5. *Wo sprechen der Prinz und die Prinzessin?*

....

6. *Warum trinkt sie nicht?*

....

7. *Was macht sie?*

....

8. *Singen der Hund und die Katze?*

....

9. *Mit wem singen sie?*

....

10. *Wo singen sie?*

....

11. *Singen der König und die Königin gut?*

....

12. *Singen der Hund und die Katze gut?*

....

13. *Wer singt besser, der Hund oder die Katze?*

....

14. *Was für Lieder singen sie?*

....

15. *Wer trommelt?*

....

16. *Trommelt sie gut?*

....

Some Explanations

These explanations will help you in understanding the German text. Read through them.

English	German
Why does the king sing?	*Warum singt der König?*
The king sings because he loves the queen.	*Der König singt, weil er die Königin liebt.*

English (cont.)	German
Why does the queen sing?	*Warum singt die Königin?*
The queen sings because she loves the king.	*Die Königin singt, weil sie den König liebt.*
Why do they love each other?	*Warum lieben sie einander?*
Who knows?	*Wer weiß?*
Why do kings and queens love each other?	*Warum lieben Könige und Königinnen einander?*
When does the king sing?	*Wann singt der König?*
The king sings when the queen is happy.	*Der König singt, wenn die Königin glücklich ist.*
When does the queen sing?	*Wann singt die Königin?*
The queen sings when the king is happy.	*Die Königin singt, wenn der König glücklich ist.*
They sing together when they both are happy.	*Sie singen zusammen, wenn sie beide glücklich sind.*
And when are they happy?	*Und wann sind sie glücklich?*
They are happy when they're singing.	*Sie sind glücklich, wenn sie singen.*

Generating Sentences

INSTRUCTIONS   Write a story using German vocabulary only. Here is a list of possible words to be used in a story of your own. Give it your best shot! Try to use as many words as you can! If you need any help, there are guidelines following this list which can help you approach the task.

Types of Words	German
Actor nouns	*Prinz, Königin, Prinzessin, Herzog, Herzogin, Hund, Katze*
Modifiers	*der, die, ein, eine, dieser, diese*
Pronouns	*er, sie, sie beide*
Location	*der Turm, das Badezimmer, die Kirche, hier, da*
Action-verb stems	*sing-, wein-*
Action-verb endings	*-t, -en*
Auxiliary verb	*ist (sind)*
Complements	*Spanisch, Chinesisch*
Manner	*besser/schlechter (als); (sehr) gut, schlecht*

Swiss Cheese, Part IV

The dairyman read the note and discovered it was a recipe that included a lot of milk and some other ingredients which didn't make any sense to him. But, the very next day, he went to work. When he was finished, he has a large loaf of cheese.

Types of Words (cont.)	German
Information-question words	Was? Wer? Welcher? Wo? Wie? Wann? Welcher? Warum?
Attestation preface	er weiß, dass; er denkt, dass; er beschwört; er sagt, dass; er liest, dass; er beobachtet, dass
Quantity information	viel, ein bisschen
Conjunctions and other words	aber, weder...noch, auch, auch nicht
Rejoinders/answers	ja, nein, stellen Sie sich das vor! endlich, alle, vermutlich, wirklich, das ist wahr, grausam, schrecklich, ich stimme damit überein, Ich glaube ja, wie seltsam!, genau, wahrscheinlich, Pech!, stellt euch vor!

Suggested Activities

INSTRUCTIONS   Using the above list, complete the following activities:

1. Take three actor-nouns and three action-words, e.g. {hund} {sing-}. By adding the proper grammatical details, make up three quick sentences on the model of *der Hund singt*.

2. Make your three sentences plural, on the model *die Hunde singen*. (Be sure to put the plural-marker *-en* on the action verb.)

3. Turn these sentences into yes-no questions by reversing the noun and the verb, on the model of *singt der Hund?* (the reverse of *der Hund singt*).

4. Turn the sentences into which-questions or where-questions as in: *Wer singt? wo singt die Prinzessin?*

5. Change the sentences to what-action questions as in: *Was macht der Hund?* or *was machen die Prinzessinnen?*

6. Make three new sentences by joining two actors as sentence subject, on the model *der Hund und die Prinzessin singen*. Be sure to put the plural-marker *-en* on the action verb.

7. Expand your last three sentences by adding modifiers such as *immer, nur*, or *auch* on the model "*der Hund singt immer viel.*"

8. Compose sentences with a "preface" construction: *er weiß, dass der Hund singt* ('he knows that the dog sings'), *er glaubt, dass die Katze spricht* ('he believes that the cat talks'), *er beobachtet, dass der König trommelt* ('he observes that the king plays the drum'), *er schwört, dass der Hund singt* ('he swears the dog sings').

9. Make up equally or even more complex sentences of your own choosing from this material.

Performance Challenge

Individual   Take three things that happened in this story and write a song about them in German. Put your song to music and then sing it for someone. Rough out some ideas below.

....

....

....

....

....

....

....

....

....

....

....

....

....

....

Performance Challenge

Group   Give the students a simple German quiz every day this week. The girl and boy who score the highest on the quizzes each day can be crowned "*Prinz*" and "*Prinzessin*" for the day. Make a crown for them to wear during their reign.

Creating Your Own Mini-Story Plots

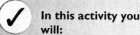

In this activity you will:

→ Learn and use important phrases.

INSTRUCTIONS Read through the following mini-story plots. Using them as a guide, create several mini-story plots of your own in German. Practice saying them out loud, working on your pronunciation.

English	German
The court poet...	*Der Hofdichter...*
composes a poem.	*verfasst ein Gedicht.*
reads his poem to the queen.	*liest der Königin sein Gedicht vor.*
The member of the cabinet...	*Das Mitglied des Kabinetts...*
considers the situation.	*betrachtet die Situation.*
observes the action.	*beobachtet die Handlung.*
The nice secretary...	*Die nette Sekretärin...*
listens with much interest.	*hört mit großem Interesse zu.*
works with enthusiasm.	*arbeitet mit Begeisterung.*
copies the document.	*kopiert das Dokument.*
has the key.	*hat den Schlüssel.*
The humble gardener...	*Der demütige Gärtner...*
has an idea.	*hat eine Idee.*
hides the flowers in the garden.	*versteckt die Blumen in dem Garten.*
hides <u>himself</u> among the flowers.	*versteckt <u>sich</u> zwischen den Blumen.*
The malicious thief...	*Der gemeine Dieb...*
hides <u>himself</u> in the garden.	*versteckt <u>sich</u> in dem Garten.*

English (cont.)	German
enters the treasury.	*betritt die Schatzkammer.*
steals the jewels.	*stiehlt die Juwelen.*
The inspector…	*Der Detektiv…*
investigates the crime.	*untersucht das Verbrechen.*
finds the jewels in the bathroom.	*findet den Schmuck in dem Badezimmer.*
encounters the thief.	*trifft den Dieb.*
The impartial judge…	*Der unparteiische Richter…*
denounces the crime.	*verurteilt das Verbrechen.*
pardons the gardener.	*entschuldigt den Gärtner.*
condemns the thief.	*verurteilt den Dieb.*
The vice-president…	*Der Vizepräsident…*
proposes a plan.	*schlägt einen Plan vor.*
contests the decision of the judge.	*bestreitet die Entscheidung des Richters.*
accuses the president.	*beschuldigt den Präsidenten.*
The innocent child…	*Das unschuldige Kind…*
answers the question.	*beantwortet die Frage.*
declares the truth.	*sagt die Wahrheit.*
The young engineer…	*Der junge Ingenieur…*
identifies the problem.	*identifiziert das Problem.*
explains the problem.	*erklärt das Problem.*
solves the problem.	*löst das Problem.*
The intrepid driver…	*Der unerschrockene Fahrer…*
divulges the secret.	*plaudert das Geheimnis aus.*
adopts the duchess's plan.	*akzeptiert den Plan der Herzogin.*
provokes an argument.	*verursacht einen Streit.*
The suspicious policeman…	*Der misstrauische Polizist…*
argues with the judge.	*streitet mit dem Richter.*
insults the secretary.	*beleidigt die Sekretärin.*
The leader of the society…	*Der Leiter der Gesellschaft…*
refutes the argument.	*widerlegt die Streitfrage.*

Swiss Cheese, Part V

He decided that he would take it to the farmer to see if he could change his mind. The farmer was very impressed when he saw the cheese, and even more impressed after he tasted it. Surely someone who could put so much effort into creating something so good was worthy of his daughter. He gave the two his blessing, and they lived happily ever after.

ACTIVITY 60

English *(cont.)*	German
admits her mistake.	*gibt seinen Fehler zu.*
pardons the secretary.	*entschuldigt die Sekretärin.*
The leader of the union of matadors…	*Der Leiter der Matadorengewerkschaft…*
provokes an argument.	*provoziert einen Streit.*
denies the accusation.	*verleugnet die Beschuldigung.*
disobeys the order.	*misachtet den Befehl.*
The lawyer…	*Der Rechtsanwalt…*
contests the decision.	*bestreitet die Entscheidung.*
presents the evidence.	*stellt die Beweise vor.*
The minister of finance…	*Der Finanzminister…*
believes the poet is guilty.	*glaubt, dass der Dichter schuldig ist.*
speaks with the chief by phone.	*spricht mit dem Chef per Telefon.*
The vice-president…	*Der Vizepräsident…*
makes the soup.	*kocht die Suppe.*
insists that the soup is good.	*besteht darauf, dass die Suppe gut ist.*

Performance Challenge

Individual   Write a poem in German about one of the things mentioned in this activity. Share your poem with a family member or friend. Rough out some ideas below.

....

....

....

....

....

....

....

....

....

....

....

....

....

....

....

....

....

....

....

....

....

....

....

....

....

....

Performance Challenge

Group   Divide the group into teams and appoint a judge. Choose a subject that can easily be debated. Have learners study as a team so that they can present their point of view. Try to keep the discussion completely in German.

The Mouse and the Lion

In this activity you will:

→ Increase reading, listening comprehension, and vocabulary usage.

Disc **4**   Track **7**

INSTRUCTIONS   Listen to and read the following story. Make a list of any new vocabulary words and their meaning. Practice using these words in sentences until you are familiar with them. Listen a second time in German only.

English	German
A little mouse was running back and forth in the jungle.	Eine kleine Maus rannte im Dschungel hin und her.
Suddenly it saw a big lion sleeping under a tree.	Plötzlich sah sie einen großen, schlafenden Löwen unter einem Baum.
The mouse went closer to have a look at the king of the jungle.	Die Maus kam näher, um den König des Dschungels zu sehen.
Suddenly the lion opened his eyes and saw the mouse.	Plötzlich öffnete der Löwe seine Augen und konnte die Maus sehen.
Like lightning his paw shot out and pinned the mouse down by its tail.	Wie ein Blitz holte er mit seiner Pfote aus und packte die Maus an ihrem Schwanz.
The little mouse pleaded:	Die kleine Maus flehte ihn an:
"I'm only an insignificant little mouse.	"Ich bin nur eine kleine, bedeutungslose Maus.
My daddy and mommy have died.	Mein Papa und meine Mama sind gestorben.
You're a thousand times greater than all of us.	Sie sind tausend mal größer, als wir alle.
And possibly someday I could help You."	Und es ist möglich, dass ich Ihnen eines Tages helfen könnte."
The lion began to laugh and said:	Der Löwe fing an zu lachen und sagte:
"How could such a little mouse as you help me?"	"Wie könnte solch eine kleine Maus, wie du, mir helfen?"

English (cont.)	German
The lion was so amused he let the mouse go.	Der Löwe war so amüsiert, dass er die Maus gehen ließ.
One day hunters came to the jungle.	Eines Tages kamen Jäger in den Dschungel.
They came to capture a lion for a zoo.	Sie kamen, um einen Löwen für einen Zoo zu fangen.
They set traps and snares and then waited.	Sie stellten Fallen und Schlingen auf und warteten dann.
The lion was caught in a net made of rope.	Der Löwe wurde in einem Netz aus Strikken gefangen.
He roared and struggled to get free, but to no avail.	Er brüllte und kämpfte, um frei zu kommen, aber nichts half.
The little mouse heard the roar of the lion and came quickly.	Die kleine Maus hörte das Brüllen des Löwen und kam schnell herbei.
"Your highness," he said, "don't roar.	"Ihre Hoheit," sagte sie, "hören Sie auf zu brüllen.
They will hear You.	Die werden Sie hören.
Lie still and be patient.	Liegen Sie still und seien Sie geduldig.
In just a few minutes You will be free."	In nur wenigen Minuten werden Sie frei sein."
Then the little mouse began to gnaw on the net.	Dann begann die kleine Maus am Netz zu nagen.
In a short time the lion was free.	In kurzer Zeit war der Löwe frei.
"You've saved my life.	"Du hast mein Leben gerettet.
How can I thank you?"	Wie kann ich dir danken?"
"Oh, don't thank me, Your highness.	"Sie haben mir nicht zu danken, Ihre Hoheit.
I was only paying You back for Your kindness to me."	Ich zahle Ihnen nur für Ihre Freundlichkeit mir gegenüber zurück."

Swiss Cheese, Part VI

Emmental is probably the best known valley in Switzerland, and the people who live there work hard. They are described as mild, but also energetic, and their cheese is said to have the same characteristics. It is aged for four months before it is ready to eat. The holes or "eyes" in Swiss cheese are caused by the bacteria that is introduced into the cheese.

Performance Challenge

Individual   Read this story again, then record yourself telling it in German from memory. Go back and compare your version to the one in the workbook. Repeat this several times, until you can retell the story completely from memory.

Performance Challenge

Group   Act the story out for a group of younger children. Do it first in English and then in German. See how many of the German words they are able to recognize.

Yugong Removes Mountains

INSTRUCTIONS Read through the following story. Learn more complex vocabulary.

English	German
It is said that in ancient times there lived an old man in North China named Yugong.	*Es wird gesagt, dass in alten Zeiten ein alter Mann in Nord-China namens Yugong lebte.*
In front of the door to his house there were two great mountains that blocked the way out most inconveniently.	*Vor der Tür seines Hauses standen zwei große Berge, die den Weg sehr unangenehm blockierten.*
One day Yugong called his family together and said:	*Eines Tages rief Yugong seine Familie zusammen und sagte:*
"With these two mountains facing our entrance, it is very inconvenient to get in and out.	*"Mit diesen zwei Bergen unserem Eingang gegenüber, ist es sehr beschwerlich herein und heraus zu kommen.*
Let's remove them.	*Lasst uns sie versetzen.*
What do you think about that?"	*Was haltet ihr davon?"*
Yugong's sons and grandsons all approved.	*Yugongs Söhne und Enkelsöhne willigten alle ein.*
Only his wife doubted.	*Nur seine Frau zweifelte.*
She said:	*Sie sagte:*
"You are almost ninety.	*"Du bist fast neunzig.*
You can't move even one rock away.	*Du kannst nicht einmal einen Stein fortbewegen.*
How then do you want to move away two big mountains?	*Wie willst du denn zwei große Berge versetzen?*
There are so many rocks on the mountain, and besides, where will you move them to?"	*Da gibt es so viele Steine auf dem Berg und außerdem, wohin willst du sie versetzen?"*

In this activity you will:

→ Follow a story and understand its meaning.

Do You Like Cheese?

A person who loves cheese, of any origin, is called a turophile.

English *(cont.)*	German
They all said:	*Sie sagten alle:*
"We can take the rocks and throw them into the lake."	*"Wir können die Steine nehmen und in den See werfen."*
The next day Yugong took his whole family to move the mountain.	*Am nächsten Tag nahm Yugong seine ganze Familie mit, um die Berge zu versetzen.*
The neighbors looked at Yugong, at such an advanced age, still wanting to move mountains, and came and helped him—even a seven- or eight-year-old child—all of them came.	*Die Nachbarn beobachteten ihn, wie er in seinem hohen Alter noch Berge versetzen wollte und kamen und halfen ihm—sogar ein sieben- oder achtjähriges Kind—alle von ihnen kamen.*
Yugong in high spirits said:	*Guten Mutes sagte Yugong:*
"Great!	*"Gut!*
If so many people work together they can surely move the mountains away."	*Wenn so viele Leute zusammen arbeiten, können sie die Berge sicher versetzen."*
They weren't afraid to work hard; they weren't afraid of hardship.	*Sie scheuten sich nicht hart zu arbeiten; sie scheuten keine Mühe.*
Day by day they dug the mountain without stopping.	*Tag für Tag gruben sie am Berg ohne aufzuhören.*
There was a man called Wise Old Man, who, seeing them digging the mountain, thought it was quite ridiculous.	*Da gab es einen alten Mann, welcher der Alte Weise Mann genannt wurde und als er sie am Berg graben sah, dachte er, dass es recht lächerlich war.*
He said to Yugong:	*Er sagte zu Yugong:*
"You're so old you can't even pull out the grass on the mountain.	*"Du bist so alt, du kannst nicht einmal das Gras von dem Berg herausziehen.*
How can you remove the two mountains?"	*Wie willst du dann die Berge versetzen?"*
Hearing this, Yugong said smiling:	*Als Yugong das hörte, sagte er lächelnd:*
"You're not even as smart as a child.	*"Du bist nicht einmal so klug, wie ein Kind.*
Though I will die, I have sons, and when they die, there will be grandsons.	*Obwohl ich sterben werde, habe ich Söhne und wenn die sterben, wird es Enkelsöhne geben.*
The more of us there are, the fewer rocks there will be.	*Je mehr es von uns gibt, desto weniger Felsen wird es geben.*

English (cont.)	German
Yet you fear we can't level the mountains."	Doch du befürchtest, wir können die Berge nicht abtragen."
When he heard this, Wise Old Man had no words to speak.	Als er das hörte, konnte der Alte Weise Mann keine Worte hervorbringen.
With Yugong and his family digging up the mountain, the gods were moved.	Die Götter waren gerührt, als er Yugong und seine Familie den Berg abtragen sah.
So they carried off the mountain on their backs.	Und sie tragen den Berg auf ihre Rücken ab.

★ **Performance Challenge**

Individual   Write about a time you went hiking in the mountains. Then pack a picnic lunch and go hiking with your family or friends. Share what you have written with them while on your hike.

....

....

....

....

....

....

....

....

....

....

★ **Performance Challenge**

Group   Have a "Pronunciation Competition" where students volunteer to read phrases from the story out loud in German. The teacher should be the judge and assign points for accent and fluency.

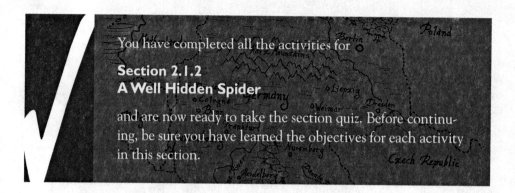

You have completed all the activities for

**Section 2.1.2
A Well Hidden Spider**

and are now ready to take the section quiz. Before continuing, be sure you have learned the objectives for each activity in this section.

Section 2.1.2 Quiz

INSTRUCTIONS Choose the most correct response. Check your answers in Appendix D, on page 402.

1. **Choose the grammatically correct sentence.**
   A. *Der König singt, wenn die Königin ist glücklich.*
   B. *Der König singt, wenn glücklich ist die Königin.*
   C. *Der König singt, wenn die Königin glücklich ist.*
   D. *Der König singt, wenn ist die Königin glücklich.*

2. **Choose the grammatically correct sentence.**
   A. *Die Königin singt, weil sie den König liebt.*
   B. *Die Königin singt, weil sie liebt den König.*
   C. *Die Königin singt, weil den König liebt sie.*
   D. *Die Königin singt, weil liebt sie den König.*

3. **Choose the grammatically correct sentence.**
   A. *Der Vizepräsident besteht darauf, dass ist die gute Suppe.*
   B. *Der Vizepräsident besteht darauf, dass gut ist die Suppe.*
   C. *Der Vizepräsident besteht darauf, dass die Suppe ist gut.*
   D. *Der Vizepräsident besteht darauf, dass die Suppe gut ist.*

4. **Choose the grammatically correct sentence.**
   A. *Der Detektiv den Schmuck in dem Badezimmer findet.*
   B. *Der Detektiv findet in dem Badezimmer den Schmuck.*
   C. *Der Detektiv findet den Schmuck in dem Badezimmer.*
   D. *Der Detektive findet Schmuck in dem Badezimmer den.*

5. **Was sah die kleine Maus im Dschungel?**

   A. eine andere Maus

   B. einen Affen

   C. einen Löwen

   D. einen Käse

6. **Wer hat gesagt, "Hören Sie auf zu brüllen?"**

   A. die Maus

   B. der Affe

   C. der Löwe

   D. der Käse

7. **Choose the grammatically correct sentence.**

   A. Wie kann ich du danken?

   B. Wie kann ich dir danken?

   C. Wie kann ich dich danken?

   D. Wie kann ich danken du?

8. **Was wollte Yugong versetzen?**

   A. den Himmel

   B. die Erde

   C. das Haus

   D. die Berge

9. **Wo wohnte Yugong?**

   A. in Europa

   B. in Afrika

   C. in Australien

   D. in Asien

10. **Choose the grammatically correct sentence.**

    A. Tag für Tag gruben sie am Berg ohne zu aufhören.

    B. Tag für Tag gruben sie am Berg ohne aufhören zu.

    C. Tag für Tag gruben sie am Berg ohne aufzuhören.

    D. Tag für Tag gruben sie am Berg zu ohne aufhören.

You have completed all the sections for

Module 2.1

and are now ready to take the module test. Before continuing, be sure you have learned the objectives for each activity in this module.

Module 2.1 Test

INSTRUCTIONS Choose the correct German translation of the English word, phrase, or sentence. Check your answers in Appendix D, on page 401.

1. **a spy**
   A. *ein Spy*
   B. *ein Spion*
   C. *der Spion*
   D. *der Doppelagent*

2. **a double agent**
   A. *ein Doppelagent*
   B. *der Doppelagent*
   C. *ein Doppelspion*
   D. *der Doppelspion*

3. **an imposter**
   A. *der Falsche*
   B. *der Schwindler*
   C. *ein Schwindler*
   D. *ein Imposter*

4. **a soccer player**
   A. *ein Fußballspieler*
   B. *ein Soccerspieler*
   C. *der Spieler*
   D. *ein Fußballer*

5. **so / then**

A. *dann*

B. *denn*

C. *wenn*

D. *also*

6. **perhaps**

A. *wahrscheinlich*

B. *zweifellos*

C. *genau*

D. *vielleicht*

7. **everything**

A. *jeder*

B. *alle*

C. *genau*

D. *alles*

8. **That is all.**

A. *Das ist es.*

B. *Das ist alles.*

C. *Es ist.*

D. *Alles.*

9. **in reality**

A. *in Wahrheit*

B. *in Recht*

C. *in Wirklichkeit*

D. *in Zweifel*

10. **probably**

A. *wahrscheinlich*

B. *wahrscheinlich*

C. *wirklich*

D. *merkwürdig*

11. **precisely**
    A. *zweifellos*
    B. *vielleicht*
    C. *wahrscheinlich*
    D. *genau*

12. **with**
    A. *in*
    B. *für*
    C. *mit*
    D. *durch*

13. **That is nothing.**
    A. *Das ist alles.*
    B. *Das ist zweifellos.*
    C. *Das ist jeder.*
    D. *Das ist nichts.*

14. **They are here.**
    A. *Sie seid hier.*
    B. *Sie sind hier.*
    C. *Sie ist hier.*
    D. *Ihr seid hier.*

15. **They are friends.**
    A. *Sie sind Freunde.*
    B. *Sie sind Freunds.*
    C. *Sind sie Freunde?*
    D. *Ihr sind Freunde.*

16. **strange**
    A. *alles*
    B. *wahrscheinlich*
    C. *merkwürdig*
    D. *vielleicht*

17. **without doubt**
    A. *zweifellos*
    B. *vielleicht*
    C. *wahrscheinlich*
    D. *genau*

18. **a man and a woman**
    A. *ein Mann und ein Frau*
    B. *ein Mann und seine Frau*
    C. *der Mann und eine Frau*
    D. *ein Mann und eine Frau*

19. **a dangerous woman**
    A. *ein freundlicher Frau*
    B. *eine gefährliche Frau*
    C. *ein gefärlicher Frau*
    D. *der Frau*

20. **the palace**
    A. *der Kastel*
    B. *die Palast*
    C. *der Palast*
    D. *das Schloss*

....

INSTRUCTIONS True or False. The following words and phrases are translated correctly.

21. **to dance = *tanzen***
    A. True
    B. False

22. **I know how = *dürfen***
    A. True
    B. False

23. **to joke = *yoken***
    A. True
    B. False

24. **I know.** = *Ich weiß.*

    A. True

    B. False

25. **in fact** = *eigentlich*

    A. True

    B. False

Module 2.2

Throughout this module we'll be learning about Vienna, Austria and the Eisriesenwelt Caves in Austria.

Keep these tips in mind as you progress through this module:

1. Read instructions carefully.

2. Repeat aloud all the German words you hear on the audio CDs.

3. Learn at your own pace.

4. Have fun with the activities and practice your new language skills with others.

5. Record yourself speaking German on tape so you can evaluate your own speaking progress.

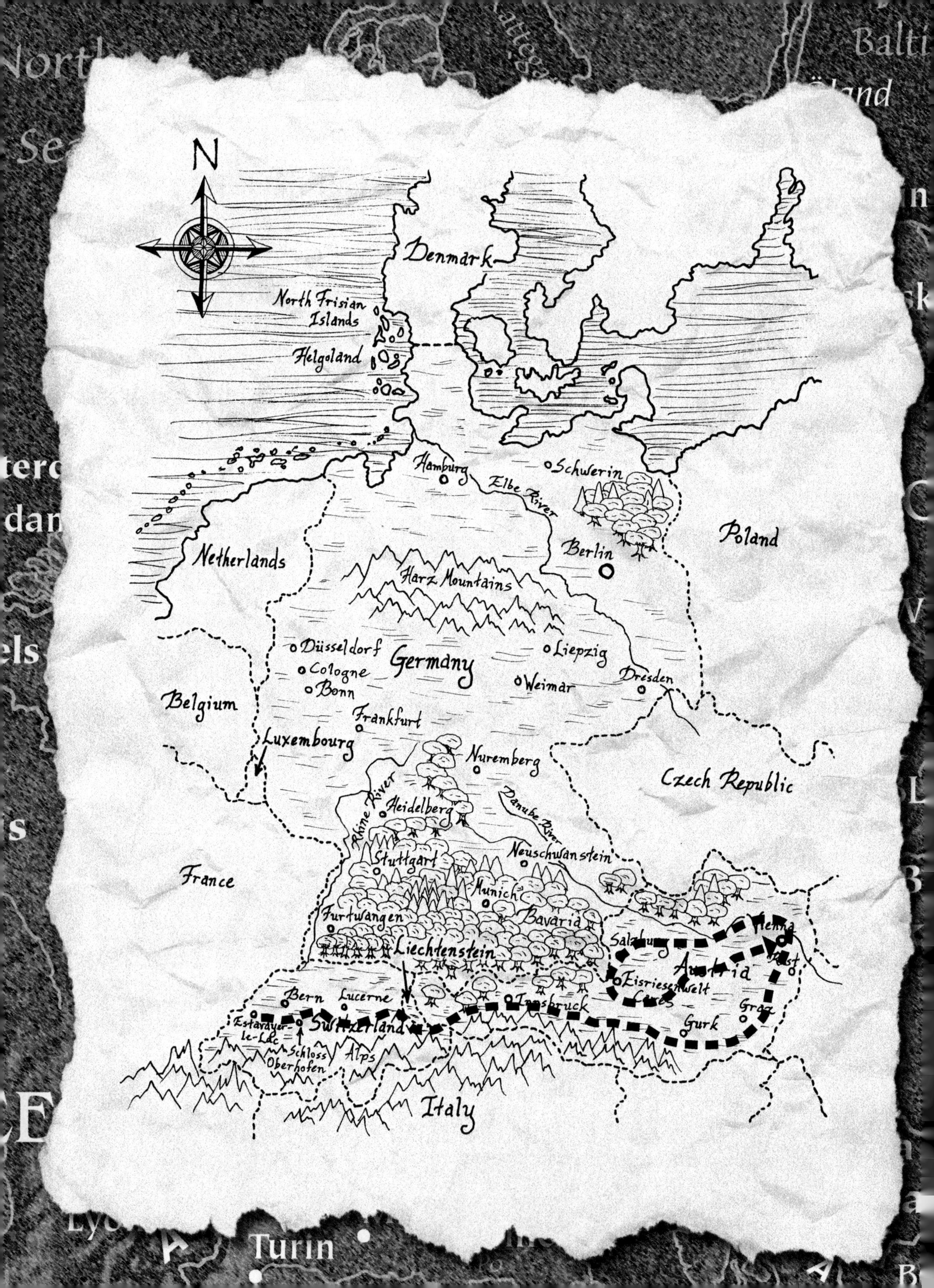

A Daring Rescue

Finally, you know what to do! You return to Spinne's cell and examine the lock again. The mouse figure appears to be on some sort of slide. You slide it over to the figure of the entangled lion. A small spring mechanism pops loose, and you're able to raise the metal wire mesh over the lion. You pause to remember the story. After *das Netz* was cut, *der Löwe* was free. Gingerly, you tug on the lion figure. It comes loose, and the lock opens. You open the door to find Spinne sitting on a dirty, straw-covered floor. He grins at you absently. "I wonder how many times they've changed the straw since this place was built," he comments.

You help him to his feet, feeling more concerned than ever. It's not like Spinne to linger in a place like this one second longer than he has to. "Come on, the trap door's this way," you tell him.

Just then, the trap door creaks slightly and begins to open. Quickly, you pull Spinne back behind the half-rotted crates and turn off your flashlight. Thanks to your extensive training, the would-be attacker who descends through the trap-door is knocked cold before he has a chance to shout an alarm to the others. You lock him in the cell Spinne just left. Hopefully, this will buy you a few hours' head start.

You climb out of the cellar and take a quick look around. The rest of the criminal group is still in the same room, deep in conversation. You help Spinne out of the cellar, and together, you sneak out the same window through which you entered.

The sun is rising over the housetops as you reach the main streets of Estavayer-le-Lac. Your first stop is the local police station. You don't know if the entire group is in the storehouse, but you are certain that having the members there arrested and thrown in jail would put a serious crimp in their plans. Spinne's account of his kidnapping is more than enough to send the town's police force racing toward the storehouse.

While all that is going down, though, you have another destination to reach. "Come on, Spinne, the Regional Museum should be open by now," you say.

As you learned from the bus driver, the Regional Museum in Estavayer-le-Lac is best known for its strangest exhibit—a collection of 19th century stuffed frogs, created by François Perrier, who also made tiny clothing for the stuffed frogs and posed them with props in parodies of human situations. You observe a frog tea party and a very proper frog social call, but the display that really catches your eye has two stuffed frogs in a miniature kitchen, with one bending over an old-fash-

✔ In this section you will:

→ Recognize your ability to understand German.

→ Listen to a German *Geschichte* and maintain comprehension without a text.

→ Use more small talk on a formal level.

→ Master new vocabulary.

Disc **4**   Track **8**

ioned hearth cooking what looks like soup. Closer inspection, though, reveals the pot is empty, except for a single small needle. This is it! Where could your clue be, though? You squint at the small display. There! On the kitchen table is spread a tiny map—tiny, but very detailed. Quickly getting the museum curator's permission to remove it, you lift the tiny map and examine it under a magnifying glass. It's a map of the Eisriesenwelt Caves in Austria. One point on the map is marked with a tiny red X.

"That must be it! We'll follow the map to where the ice key is hidden," you whisper excitedly.

"Great," Spinne replies. He tries to muster an enthusiastic smile, but you notice he's swaying unsteadily on his feet.

"Are you okay, Spinne?" you ask, helping him to one of the museum's benches. He feels feverish.

Spinne shakes his head. "While I was in there, they gave me a shot," he says in a quiet, frightened-sounding voice. "I thought it was a drug, to make me easier to interrogate. They never asked me anything, though. Now, I don't feel so great. I have this awful headache…" Spinne's voice trails off.

"You think you're infected," you finish grimly.

Spinne nods miserably. "I didn't figure it out until just now, so you've been exposed, too. *Tut mir Leid, Fliege.*"

"No worries," you say, forcing a cheerful smile. "This just means we'll need to finish the case faster."

Your mind races as you try to figure out what to do next. You need to get Spinne out of town before the Ungeschicklichkeit group realizes he's gone. There isn't much time, and you have to minimize the number of people exposed to Spinne, who might be contagious. There's an isolation unit at your organization's offices in Vienna, where Spinne could be comfortable and well-cared-for, and you need to go to Austria anyway for the Eisriesenwelt Caves.

You pull out your cell phone and dial a local tour agency that offers aerial tours of the surrounding mountains. Your German studies prove very useful, as no one at the agency speaks much English.

"Kann ich Ihnen helfen?" asks the employee who answers the phone.

"Ja, ich möchte eines Ihrer Flugzeuge kaufen," you reply.

"Kaufen? Wir veranstalten leider nur Rundflüge," the employee replies.

"Es handelt sich um eine sehr wichtige Angelegenheit. Ich bin Geheimagent, und ich brauche unbedingt ein Flugzeug," you explain.

The employee pauses, then offers to ask his boss. After a longer pause, he returns. *"Wir verkaufen Ihnen ein Flugzeug,"* he informs you.

SECTION 2.2.1 • A DARING RESCUE

"Dankeschön. Recht herzlichen Dank," you reply. *"Sie erhalten das Geld heute Abend."*

On your way to pick up the plane, you call your boss, explain the situation, and arrange for her to wire the money to pay for the plane directly to the tour agency.

Within an hour, you and Spinne are in a small plane, rising above the town of Estavayer-le-Lac and racing toward Vienna. When you arrive in Vienna, there's a team in biohazard suits waiting for Spinne, who is now running a high fever and murmuring deliriously.

"Finish the case, okay, Fliege?" he mumbles as the biohazard team eases him onto a stretcher.

You nod, then climb back into the plane. There's still enough fuel to get you to the Eisriesenwelt Caves and back. As you nose the plane back into the air, you review what you know about the caves. They're the largest accessible ice caves in the world. Regular tours through the safer and more stable parts of the caves still reveal elaborate ice formations and delicate frozen waterfalls.

You're not going to the parts on the tourist route, though. According to the map, you need to get into the most distant chamber of the caves. You just hope that, with the shifting of the ice, the chamber is still accessible.

You land the plane on a broad, level snow field above the caves. You take a few minutes to orient yourself on the map, then find an opening and rappel down into the caves.

The caves are lit with an eerie, pale blue light, as the sun filters through the thick ice. The ice groans as it shifts slowly downhill. You follow the map. Where the red X appears on the map, you find a small entrance to another cavern. You crawl through the entrance and find yourself in a cavern, no more than ten feet in diameter and barely high enough for you to stand up. In one corner is a small box. You pick it up and open it. Inside is another sheet of music and a key of something clear and smooth as ice, but it doesn't melt in your hand. You'll examine both more closely back at your plane. For now, you decide you'd better get out of here. The entrance to this cave is so small that even small shifts in the ice could trap you in here permanently.

You leave the cavern quickly and find your way back to your plane. You fly back to Vienna for refueling. While waiting in the airport for the fuel, you examine the key. It sparkles brightly in the sunlight, refracting rainbows all over the plane cabin. You grin. It might look like ice, but this key has been meticulously crafted of genuine Austrian crystal. You set the key with the others, then pull out the lighter your boss gave you and use it to read the clue on the new sheet of music. This one is longer and more difficult than the others you've seen: *suche nicht weit von dem, was das Milchmädchen pflanzt, nach der Stelle, an der Afanti sein Gold gepflanzt hat.* "Near what the milkmaid will plant, look where Afanti planted his gold," you translate aloud. You go back and review the original riddle: *Gold vom Tisch des Königs.* The king's table. You're probably headed for a castle, then.

Which one, though? This clue is going to require some serious studying. As the sun sinks toward the western horizon, you switch on the cabin light for some research and studying.

A Dairymaid's Dream

INSTRUCTIONS Listen to and read the story. Circle all of the nouns in German that you've heard before. Make a list of any new nouns and their meaning to help you expand your vocabulary base.

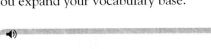

 In this activity you will:

→ Recognize your ability to understand German.

 Disc **4** Track **9**

English	German
A dairymaid was walking down the road carrying on her head a pot of milk that she had stolen.	*Ein Milchmädchen ging die Straße entlang und trug einen Krug Milch auf ihrem Kopf, den sie gestohlen hatte.*
She was going to the market to sell the milk.	*Sie war auf dem Weg zum Markt, um die Milch zu verkaufen.*
Walking along, she said to herself:	*Während sie so ging, sagte sie sich:*
"I'll sell this milk and buy some eggs.	*"Ich werde die Milch verkaufen und einige Eier kaufen.*
The eggs will give me chicks.	*Die Eier werden mir Küken geben.*
When the chicks have grown, I'll sell them and buy a little pig.	*Wenn die Küken herangewachsen sind, werde ich sie verkaufen und ein kleines Schwein kaufen.*
When the little pig is grown, it will give me lots of other little pigs.	*Wenn das kleine Schwein herangewachsen ist, wird es mir viele andere Schweine geben.*
In time, for sure I'll be rich."	*Mit der Zeit werde ich sicher reich werden."*
Just at that moment she tripped on a rock in the road, and the milk was all spilt on the street.	*Aber in diesem Augenblick stolperte sie über einen Stein und verschüttete die Milch auf der Straße.*
And with the milk her dreams of riches vanished.	*Und mit der Milch verschwanden ihre Träume vom Reichtum.*

The Eisriesenwelt Caves, Part I

Located near Salzburg, the Eisriesenwelt (or "World of the Ice Giants") are the largest ice caves in the world. The caves have been open to the public since 1920 and see nearly 200,000 tourists every summer.

Performance Challenge

Individual Write about your most embarrassing moment, in German.

....

....

....

....

....

....

....

....

....

....

....

....

....

....

....

Performance Challenge

Group Have the students take all of the nouns out of the story. Then, using the list of nouns, have them write a new story in German.

The Roman Alphabet

ACTIVITY 64

INSTRUCTIONS Listen to this exercise in German. Try to understand as much as you can. Don't worry if you don't understand the specifics. Aim for general comprehension.

Die Name der Konsonanten auf Deutsch

Konsonanten werden so ausgesprochen:

beh	tseh	deh	eff	geh	hah	yott	kah
b	c	d	f	g	h	j	k

ell	emm	enn	peh	kuh	err	ess	teh
l	m	n	p	q	r	s	t

fau	weh	ikks	üppßilon		tsett	ess-tsett	
v	w	x	y		z	ß	

Der erste Buchstabe des Alphabets ist kein Konsonant, sondern ein Vokal—der Vokal <A>. <A> ist kein Konsonant, weder auf Englisch noch auf Deutsch. <A> ist immer ein Vokal. Der letzte Buchstabe des Alphabets ist kein Vokal, sondern ein Konsonant— der Konsonant <Z>. <Z> ist kein Vokal, weder auf Englisch noch auf Deutsch. <Z> ist immer ein Konsonant. Anders gesagt, <A> ist der erste Buchstabe des römischen Alphabets und ist ein Vokal, und <Z> ist der letzte Buchstabe des römischen Alphabets und ist ein Konsonant.

Nach dem Buchstaben <A> kommt der Buchstabe <B>, und nach dem <B> kommt <C>. Vor dem Buchstaben <N> kommt der Buchstabe <M>, und vor dem <M> kommt <L>. Welcher Buchstabe kommt vor dem <L>? <K>. Welcher Buchstabe kommt zwischen <A> und <C>? Der Buchstabe <B> kommt zwischen <A> und <C>. Und <C> kommt zwischen <B> und <D>, nicht wahr?

In dem deutschen Alphabet kommt <M> bevor <N>. Diese Nasallaute sind die einzigen in dem Alphabet. Wieviele Nasallaute sind in dem Alphabet? Zwei. Und welche

In this activity you will:

→ Listen to a German *Geschichte* and maintain comprehension without a text.

  Disc **4** Track **10**

The Eisriesenwelt Caves, Part II

The Eisriesenwelt are a vast underground series of caves with nearly 26 miles of tunnels and chambers. The caverns near the entrance are lined with ice that is almost 65 feet thick. As you wind your way nearly 1 mile underground and 1 mile into the mountain, you are met by gigantic ice formations, columns, ice towers, ice waterfalls, stalactites, stalagmites, and glaciers.

sind sie? Das <M> und das <N>. Welcher kommt zuerst in dem Alphabet? Der Buchstabe <M> kommt zuerst. Das <O> kommt nach dem <N>, wie in dem englischen Alphabet. Aus den Buchstaben <M N O>, welcher ist ein Vokal?

Ist <Y> immer ein Konsonant? Nein, nicht immer. In dem deutschen Alphabet funktioniert <Y> gewöhnlich wie ein Vokal. In dem englischen Alphabet funktioniert <Y> gewöhnlich wie ein Konsonant. In den Wörtern "Dynamit," "Xylophon" und "System," ist <Y> ein Vokal. Alle Wörter, die mit einem <Y> anfangen, sind aus anderen Sprachen gekommen.

Der Buchstabe <C> steht im Deutschen gewöhnlich mit einem <H> zusammen. Wörter, die <C> anstatt <CH> haben, sind nicht ursprünglich deutsch. Zum Beispiel sind die

Wörter "Café" oder "Camping" nicht ursprünglich deutsch. Wo man den Buchstaben <C> auf englisch findet, findet man ein <K> im Deutschen. <CH> klingt wie in dem Wort NACH nach den Vokalen <A>, <O>, <U>, und <AU>. Nach allen anderen Vokalen klingt <CH> wie in dem Wort ICH.

<E> plus <I> plus <N> ergibt das Wort "EIN". Der erste Buchstabe ist <E>. <I> ist der zweite und <N> ist der dritte und der letzte Buchstabe.

In dem Alphabet kommt kein Buchstabe vor dem Buchstaben <A> und kein Buchstabe kommt nach dem Buchstaben <ß>. Es wird gesagt, dass <A> der erste Buchstabe ist, und dass <ß> der letzte Buchstabe des Alphabets ist.

Hier sehen Sie das Alphabet. Merken Sie, wie jeder Buchstabe zwei Formen hat: die großgeschriebene Form und die kleingeschriebene Form. Die großgeschriebenen Buchstaben sind größer als die kleingeschriebenen Buchstaben. Die großgeschriebenen Buchstaben beginnen alle als Substantive. Zum Beispiel, das Wort "Buchstabe" ist ein Substantiv. Das Wort "buchstabieren" ist ein Verb. Also wird "buchstabieren" kleingeschrieben. Merken Sie, dass nur der erste Buchstabe großgeschrieben wird. Alle anderen Buchstaben werden kleingeschrieben.

Performance Challenge

Individual Have fun with the ABCs this week. Find a recipe, a song, or an activity that starts with the letters A, B, and C and make the recipe, sing the song, or do the activity for a family member or friend.

Performance Challenge

Group Give each student a piece of paper with the letters of the alphabet written down the side. Have them come up with words in German for each of the letters.

Conversation Snatches 13

ACTIVITY 65

INSTRUCTIONS Listen to these dialogues. Create new dialogues of your own using these useful phrases!

✓ **In this activity you will:**

→ Use more small talk on a formal level.

 Disc **4** Track **11**

English	German
Let's watch a video tonight.	*Sehen wir uns doch ein Video heute abend an.*
Not a bad idea!	*Keine schlechte Idee!*
How much did you pay for these CDs?	*Wieviel hast du für diese CDs bezahlt?*
3.50 Marks each.	*DM 3.50 pro CD.*
Is life in Berlin costlier than in Antarctica?	*Ist das Leben in Berlin teurer als in der Antarktis?*
Much, much more expensive.	*Viel, viel teurer.*
But on the other hand the weather is milder.	*Aber dafür ist das Wetter milder.*
Of course.	*Natürlich.*
You should sleep less and work more.	*Du solltest weniger schlafen und mehr arbeiten.*
Or better, I should eat less and exercise more.	*Oder besser, ich sollte weniger essen und mich mehrbewegen.*
I'll pick you up at four o'clock.	*Ich hole dich um 4 Uhr ab.*
Perfect.	*Perfekt.*
You're late!	*Du bist spät dran!*
I know that.	*Das weiß ich.*
I've already waited for you a long time.	*Ich habe schon lange auf dich gewartet.*
Forgive me.	*Vergib mir.*

The Eisriesenwelt Caves, Part III

The caves were officially discovered in 1879 by Anton Posselt, but a huge ice wall blocked entry into them beyond the first chamber. His discovery went unnoticed by scientists and the public until in 1913, when Alexander von Mörk, a noted *speleologist* from Salzburg, climbed over the wall, diving through icy pools, to explore the caves. Von Mörk related his exploration to that of Thor from Norse mythology, and the rooms and structures in the caves bear names from the old Norse stories. With the addition of stairs and walkways, the caves opened to the public in 1920.

ACTIVITY 65

English (cont.)	German
But you are always late.	*Aber du kommst immer zu spät.*
You are right, Helga, I'm always late.	*Du hast recht, Helga, ich komme immer zu spät.*
Can't you come on time?	*Kannst du nicht pünktlich kommen?*
Tell me something!	*Erzähl mir etwas!*
What should I tell you?	*Was soll ich dir erzählen?*
Just tell why Nina didn't come with us.	*Sag einfach warum Nina nicht mitgekommen ist?*
I don't know.	*Das weiß ich nicht.*

Performance Challenge

Individual Research and write about the life of Johann Strauss. Listen to a musical composition by Strauss and in German, write your thoughts about it.

....

....

....

....

....

....

Performance Challenge

Group Come up with a list of famous people. Attach one name to the back of each student. Each student then asks the others "yes" or "no" questions in German about their identity until they discover who they are.

Afanti and the Beggar

INSTRUCTIONS Listen to and read the following story.

English	German
Once there was a poor man who had no food to eat.	*Es war einmal ein armer Mann, der nichts zu essen hatte.*
Hungry, he walked the streets of the city.	*Hungrig ging er durch die Straßen der Stadt.*
Passing a restaurant, he smelled the delicious food.	*Er kam an einem Restaurant vorbei und roch die köstlichen Speisen.*
He stopped and stood inhaling the smells.	*Er hielt an und inhalierte den Geruch.*
After a while the restaurant owner came out.	*Nach einer Weile kam der Besitzer des Restaurants heraus.*
"What are you doing here?" he asked the beggar.	*"Was machst du hier?" fragte er den Bettler.*
"Good sir, I haven't eaten in two days.	*"Guter Mann, ich habe zwei Tage lang nichts gegessen.*
I am dying of hunger.	*Ich sterbe vor Hunger.*
I thought perhaps by smelling your good food I could derive some sustenance."	*Ich dachte mir, dass wenn ich gute Speisen rieche, es mir vielleicht Nahrung zufügen könnte."*
"How long have you been here?"	*"Wie lange bist du schon hier?"*
"Only for a few minutes."	*"Nur seit ein paar Minuten."*
"Then you must pay me."	*"Dann musst du mich bezahlen."*
"Why should I pay you?	*"Warum soll ich dich bezahlen?*
I haven't consumed any food."	*Ich habe keine Speise gegessen."*

In this activity you will:

→ Recognize your ability to understand German.

Disc **4**   Track **12**

The Eisriesenwelt Caves, Part IV

Both Posselt and Von Mörk have chambers in the Eisriesenwelt named after them. Posselt Tower & Hall is located at the entrance of the caves, with a large stalagmite in the middle of the hall. Through the hall, at the top of a wooden stairway, rests the Posselt Cross, a wooden cross marking the furthest point reached by Posselt during his exploration in 1879. Von Mörk died in World War I, and his ashes were placed in an urn in Mörk's Cathedral, a chamber of ice that rises nearly 115 feet above the cave floor.

English (cont.)	German
"By smelling the food you consume the flavor.	"Beim Riechen der Speise konsumierst du das Aroma.
And if you do not pay me, I'll have you arrested and thrown into jail."	Und wenn du mich nicht bezahlst, werde ich dich verhaften und ins Gefängnis werfen lassen."
"But I am poor.	"Aber ich bin arm.
I have no money.	Ich habe kein Geld.
I can't pay you.	Ich kann dich nicht bezahlen.
Please let me go."	Bitte lass mich gehen."
Just then a policeman came by, and asked:	Gerade dann kam ein Polizist vorbei und fragte:
"What's going on here?"	"Was ist hier los?"
The restaurant owner answered:	Der Restaurantbesitzer sagte:
"This man has consumed my food but refuses to pay for it."	"Dieser Mann konsumierte meine Speise und will jetzt nicht dafür zahlen."
The policeman took the poor man to the police station and locked him in a cell.	Der Polizist nahm den armen Mann mit zur Polizeiwache und sperrte ihn in eine Zelle ein.
The poor man asked if his friend Afanti could come at once.	Der arme Mann fragte, ob sein Freund Afanti sofort kommen dürfte.
Afanti came and heard what had happened.	Afanti kam und hörte was geschehen war.
He told the judge that he himself would pay the restaurant owner.	Er sagte dem Richter, dass er selbst den Restaurantbesitzer selbst bezahlen würde.
Afanti and the beggar went to the restaurant together.	Afanti und der Bettler gingen zusammen zu dem Restaurant.
Afanti asked how much the man owed for the food.	Afanti fragte, wieviel der Mann ihm für die Speise schuldete.
"One kai five mao," said the owner.	"Einen Kai, fünf Mao," sagte der Besitzer.
Afanti reached into his pocket and pulled out a bag of coins.	Afanti griff in seine Taschen und zog einen Beutel mit Münzen heraus.
He held the bag up and shook it by the ear of the restaurant owner.	Er hielt den Beutel hoch und schüttelte es am Ohr des Restaurantbesitzers.

The Eisriesenwelt Caves, Part V

Even during the summer, the temperature in the caves doesn't raise much above 1 degree centigrade. So while a visit to this natural wonder is well worth it, be sure to dress warm so that you can enjoy it!

English *(cont.)*	German
The owner heard the coins jingle and reached up to take the money, but Afanti quickly withdrew it, smiling.	*Der Besitzer hörte die Münzen klimpern und griff nach dem Geld, aber Afanti zog es schnell zurück und lächelte.*
"My friend was able to smell your restaurant food," he said, "and now you were able to hear this money.	*"Mein Freund konnte die Speise in deinem Restaurant riechen," sagte er, "und du konntest das Geld hören.*
That satisfies completely his debt to you."	*Das gleicht seine Schulden komplett aus."*

Performance Challenge

Individual   Find a local, authentic German bakery or restaurant and practice ordering and paying for your order in German. Write a short summary of your experience in German, and whether or not you like the food you tried.

....

....

....

....

....

....

....

....

Performance Challenge

Group   Organize a German restaurant and get as many authentic German foods as you can find. Divide students into groups of servers and patrons. Have them order, eat, and pay for their food in German. Once complete, have the groups switch roles.

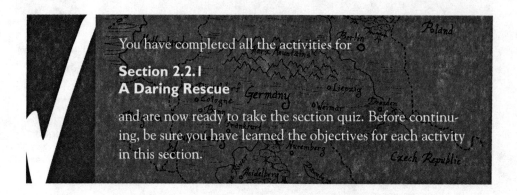

You have completed all the activities for

Section 2.2.1
A Daring Rescue

and are now ready to take the section quiz. Before continuing, be sure you have learned the objectives for each activity in this section.

Section 2.2.1 Quiz

INSTRUCTIONS Choose the most correct response. Check your answers in Appendix D, on page 402.

1. **Choose the grammatically correct sentence.**

   A. *Sie war auf dem Weg zum Markt, um die Milch zu verkaufen.*

   B. *Sie warst auf dem Weg zum Markt, um die Milch zu verkaufen.*

   C. *Sie war auf dem Weg zum Markt, um zu verkaufen die Milch.*

   D. *Sie auf dem Weg zum Markt war, um die Milch zu verkaufen.*

2. **Choose the grammatically correct sentence.**

   A. *Die Eier werden mir Küken geben.*

   B. *Die Eier werd mir Küken geben.*

   C. *Die Eier wird mir Küken geben.*

   D. *Die Eier worden mir Küken geben.*

3. **Was ist die richtige Reihenfolge (order) von der Geschichte "Der Traum eines Milchmädchens?"**

   A. *Schwein, Milch, Eier, Küken, Land, Weinstöcke, Trauben*

   B. *Eier, Schwein, Milch, Trauben, Küken, Land, Weinstöcke,*

   C. *Milch, Eier, Küken, Schwein, Land, Weinstöcke, Trauben*

   D. *Land, Weinstöcke, Trauben, Schwein, Eier, Küken, Milch.*

4. **Das Mädchen wurde reich.**

   A. *Richtig*

   B. *Falsch*

5. **Wie viele Nasallaute gibt es im deutschen Alphabet?**

   A. *zwei*

   B. *sechs*

   C. *zehn*

   D. *sechsundzwanzig*

6. **A, B, C, D, und E sind**

   A. *Zahlen*

   B. *Vokale*

   C. *Buchstaben*

   D. *Konstanten*

7. **Ich habe lange auf dich gewartet.**

   A. *Perfekt.*

   B. *Keine schlechte Idee.*

   C. *Vergib mir.*

   D. *Viel, viel teurer.*

8. **Choose the grammatically correct sentence.**

   A. *Es war einmal ein armer Mann, der nichts zu essen hatte.*

   B. *Es war einmal eine arme Mann, die nichts zu essen hatte.*

   C. *Es was einmal einer armer Mann, der nichts zu essen hatte.*

   D. *Es war einmal ein armer Mann, der zu essen hatte nichts.*

9. **Choose the grammatically correct sentence.**

   A. *Ich sterbe vor Hunger.*

   B. *Ich sterbe mit Hunger.*

   C. *Ich sterbe für Hunger.*

   D. *Ich sterbe von Hunger.*

10. **Choose the grammatically correct sentence.**

    A. *Mein Freund können die Speise riechen.*

    B. *Mein Freund könnt die Speise riechen.*

    C. *Mein Freund konnte die Speise reichen.*

    D. *Mein Freund konnte riechen die Speise.*

You have completed all the sections for

Module 2.2

and are now ready to take the module test. Before continuing, be sure you have learned the objectives for each activity in this module.

Module 2.2 Test

INSTRUCTIONS   True or False. The following sentences are translated correctly. Check your answers in Appendix D, on page 401.

1. *Ein Milchmädchen ging die Straße entlang.* = **A dairymaid was walking down the road.**

   A. True

   B. False

2. *Sie trug einen Krug Milch auf ihrem Kopf, den sie gestohlen hatte.* = **She was carrying a pot of milk in her arms that she had stolen.**

   A. True

   B. False

3. *Sie war auf dem Weg zum Markt, um die Milch zu verkaufen.* = **She was going to the market to buy the milk.**

   A. True

   B. False

4. *Während sie so ging, sagte sie sich:* = **Walking along, she said to herself:**

   A. True

   B. False

5. *Ich werde die Milch verkaufen und einige Eier kaufen.* = **I'll sell this milk and buy some eggs.**

   A. True

   B. False

6. **Wenn die Küken herangewachsen sind, werde ich sie verkaufen und ein kleines Schwein kaufen.** = When the chicks have grown, I'll sell them and buy a little pig.

   A. True

   B. False

7. **Wenn das kleine Schwein herangewachsen ist, wird es mir viele andere Schweine geben.** = When the little pig is grown, she will sell it at the market.

   A. True

   B. False

8. **Mit der Zeit werde ich sicher reich werden.** = In a week, I'll be rich.

   A. True

   B. False

9. **Aber in diesem Augenblick stolperte sie über einen Stein und verschüttete die Milch auf die Straße.** = Just at that moment she jumped on a rock in the road, and the milk was all spilt on the street.

   A. True

   B. False

10. **Und mit der Milch verschwanden ihre Träume vom Reichtum.** = And with the milk her dreams of riches vanished.

    A. True

    B. False

11. I'll pick you up at 4 o'clock. = *Ich hole dich um 16 Uhr ab.*

    A. True

    B. False

12. Perfect. = *Perfekt.*

    A. True

    B. False

13. You're late! = *Sind sind früh!*

    A. True

    B. False

14. I know that. = *Ich weiß nicht.*

    A. True

    B. False

15. **I've already waited for you a long time.** = *Ich habe schon lange auf dich gewartet.*

    A. True

    B. False

....

INSTRUCTIONS   Choose the correct English translation of the German word or phrase.

16. *die Trauben*

    A. pigeons

    B. grapes

    C. deafness

    D. trust

17. *kaufen*

    A. to sell

    B. to use

    C. to buy

    D. to trade

18. *der Buchstabe*

    A. the letter

    B. the animal

    C. the bookshelf

    D. the library

19. *teuer*

    A. cheap

    B. inexpensive

    C. expensive

    D. outrageous

20. *besser*

    A. well

    B. good

    C. better

    D. worse

21. *der Geruch*
    A. the smell
    B. the food
    C. the restaurant
    D. the street

22. *der Besitzer*
    A. the owner
    B. the manager
    C. the begger
    D. the smell

23. *das Geld*
    A. the gold
    B. the money
    C. the coins
    D. the charity

24. *die Münzen*
    A. the money
    B. the mouths
    C. the months
    D. the coins

25. *das Ohr*
    A. the eyes
    B. the place
    C. the oar
    D. the ear

Module 2.3

Throughout this module we'll be learning about Schloss Oberhofen, Switzerland, Bern, Switzerland, Neuschwanstein, Germany, and Helgoland, Germany.

Keep these tips in mind as you progress through this module:

1. Read instructions carefully.
2. Repeat aloud all the German words you hear on the audio CDs.
3. Learn at your own pace.
4. Have fun with the activities and practice your new language skills with others.
5. Record yourself speaking German on tape so you can evaluate your own speaking progress.

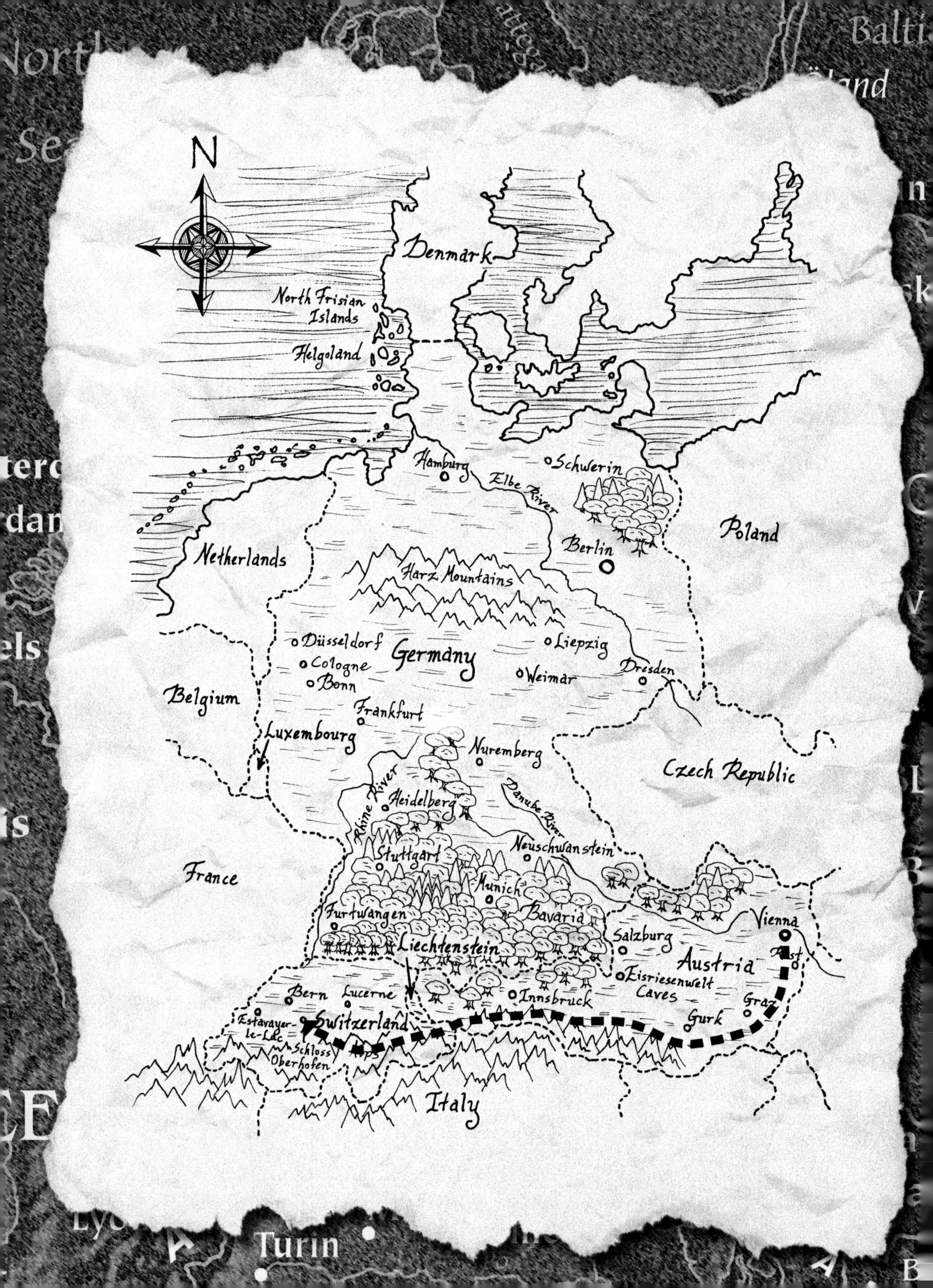

The Next Clue

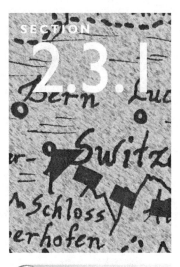

You wake up with a start. You must've fallen asleep while studying. You rub your stiff neck and look around the plane's cabin. Everything's undisturbed. Your cell phone rings. It's your boss.

"*Guten Morgen, Fliege,*" she greets you. "How are you doing with the case?"

You bring your boss up to speed, letting her know that you have the ice key and have just started work on the clues for the gold key. "How's Spinne?" you ask.

She's silent for a moment before answering. "Not good, Fliege. The doctors found it is the plague, and since he got it by direct injection, he has one of the worst cases they've seen. They can't get his fever down, and he's in a lot of pain. What about you? Any symptoms?"

"So far, so good," you reply.

"Good," she tells you. "Try to avoid close contact with people, just in case. We're counting on you, Fliege. Give me a call if you need any backup."

You thank your boss, then hang up. You look around the plane cabin again, trying to pick up last night's train of thought.

Then your eyes fall on the travel guide, still open, and you remember the last thing you studied before you dozed off. In Switzerland, just south of Bern, is Lake Thun. Several castles dot the area around the lake, including Schloss Oberhofen, which was once held by the powerful Habsburg family—one of the families you know was affected by the plague. On the grounds of that castle is a beautiful pavilion with grapevines twining up its pillars and roof. You haven't figured out the second part of the clue yet. However, you're sure that pavilion is where you need to go to find the gold key. Your plane is refueled and you're ready to go. You get permission for take off from airport authority and enter the air.

After a thankfully uneventful flight, you land in Bern and catch a cab to Schloss Oberhofen. While the driver speeds toward the castle, you take the opportunity to study more German. You hope these next activities will unlock the second part of the clue.

In this section you will:

→ Read and understand a *Geschichte auf deutsch.*

→ Read to increase all skill levels of language learning.

→ Recognize how much German you can comprehend, say, and read.

→ Expand your comprehension toward complete understanding.

→ Follow a conversation and understand its meaning.

 Disc **5**   Track **1**

The Shoemaker and the Elves

In this activity you will:

→ Read and understand a *Geschichte auf deutsch*.

Disc **5**   Track **2**

INSTRUCTIONS   Listen to and read the following story. Write down all the words you don't understand and familiarize yourself with them.

English	German
Long ago there was a shoemaker and his wife.	*Vor einer langen Zeit gab es einen Schuhmacher und seine Frau.*
Although they were very good people and worked very hard, they had little money.	*Obwohl sie sehr gute Menschen waren und hart arbeiteten, hatten sie wenig Geld.*
One winter day they realized they had no money left, and only enough leather left to make one pair of shoes.	*Eines Wintertages stellten sie fest, dass sie kein Geld mehr hatten und gerade noch genug Leder für ein Paar Schuhe hatten.*
That evening the shoemaker cut out the leather for the shoes.	*An diesem Abend schnitt der Schuhmacher das Leder für die Schuhe zu.*
He intended to make the shoes the next morning.	*Er hatte vor, die Schuhe am nächsten Morgen zu machen.*
He went to bed and slept soundly through the night.	*Er ging zu Bett und schlief ruhig die Nacht durch.*
When he woke up in the morning and set about to make the shoes, to his great surprise he found the pair of shoes already finished.	*Als er am Morgen aufwachte und bereit war, die Schuhe zu machen, stellte er mit großer Überraschung fest, dass das Paar Schuhe schon fertig war.*
He picked them up and examined them.	*Er nahm die Schuhe und überprüfte sie.*
Oh, they were perfectly made.	*Oh, sie waren perfekt gemacht.*
They were like the work of a master shoemaker.	*Sie waren wie die Arbeit eines Schuhmachermeisters.*

Bern, Switzerland, Part I

Built on a peninsula on the river Aare, Bern is the national capital of Switzerland with a population of approximately 130,000 people. It is also home to the Swiss parliament.

English *(cont.)*	German
That day a man came into the shop.	*An diesem Tag kam ein Mann in den Laden.*
He saw the shoes and liked them a lot.	*Er sah die Schuhe und sie gefielen ihm sehr.*
"These are the finest shoes I've ever seen," he said.	*"Dies sind die besten Schuhe, die ich je gesehen habe," sagte er.*
"I will buy this pair and pay you twice their value."	*"Ich werde sie kaufen und dir das Doppelte des Preises zahlen."*
With that money, the shoemaker was able to buy food to eat and had enough money left over to buy leather for two pairs of shoes.	*Mit diesem Geld war der Schuhmacher in der Lage Speise zum Essen zu kaufen und hatte außerdem genug Geld übrig, um Leder für die zwei Paar Schuhe zu kaufen.*
That evening he cut out the leather, then went to bed and slept soundly through the night.	*Am Abend schnitt er das Leder zu, ging zu Bett und schlief ruhig die Nacht durch.*
The next morning when he set about to finish the shoes, again to his surprise he saw that the shoes were already finished.	*Als er am nächsten Morgen erwachte und bereit war, die Schuhe fertigzustellen, war er wieder überrascht die fertigen Schuhe zu sehen.*
That day he sold both pairs of shoes.	*An diesem Tag verkaufte er beide Paare.*
He had enough money to buy food as well as leather for four pairs of shoes.	*Er hatte genug Geld, um Speise zu kaufen und auch Leder für vier Paar Schuhe zu besorgen.*
Again he cut the leather out at night.	*Wieder schnitt er das Leder am Abend zu.*
In the morning he found they were again already sewn and beautifully finished.	*Am Morgen fand er wieder alles genäht und wundervoll fertiggestellt.*
Soon his business was thriving once again.	*Sein Geschäft hatte bald wieder Erfolg.*
One evening in December after cutting out leather for his shoes, he said to his wife:	*Eines Abends im Dezember, nachdem er das Leder für seine Schuhe ausgeschnitten hatte, sagte er zu seiner Frau:*
"I wonder who it is who makes these shoes at night.	*"Ich frage mich, wer nachts die Schuhe macht.*
Let's stay up to watch and see."	*Lass uns aufbleiben und es beobachten."*

English (cont.)	German
They hid behind a curtain and watched.	Sie standen hinter den Gardinen und beobachteten.
In the middle of the night two little men appeared.	Mitternacht erschienen zwei kleine Männchen.
They sat down at the table.	Sie setzten sich an den Tisch.
With skilled hands they quickly shaped the shoes, sewed them and hammered them so perfectly that the shoemaker couldn't believe his eyes.	Mit geschickten Händen formten sie schnell die Schuhe, nähten und hämmerten sie so perfekt, dass der Schuhmacher seinen Augen nicht glaubte.
When the shoes were ready the two little men left.	Als die Schuhe fertig waren, verschwanden die zwei kleinen Männchen.
The wife said to the shoemaker:	Die Frau sagte zum Schuhmacher:
"These little men have helped us a lot.	"Diese kleinen Männchen haben uns so sehr geholfen.
We should show them our gratitude.	Wir sollten ihnen unsere Dankbarkeit zeigen.
I will make them some clothes.	Ich werde ihnen Kleidung machen.
Would you make them each a pair of shoes?"	Würdest Du für jeden ein Paar Schuhe machen?"
And so they did.	Und so machten sie es.
That evening they set out the presents on the table, and then hid themselves and watched to see what would happen.	Am Abend setzten sie die Geschenke auf den Tisch, versteckten sich und beobachteten, was geschehen würde.
At midnight the two little men again appeared.	Um Mitternacht erschienen die zwei kleinen Männchen wieder.
They were about to start working, but found no leather to make shoes with.	Sie waren bereit mit der Arbeit anzufangen, aber fanden kein Leder, um Schuhe zu machen.
Instead they found beautiful new clothes.	Statt dessen fanden sie wunderschöne neue Kleidung.
They put them on and then danced about for joy.	Sie zogen sie an und tanzten vor Freude.
After that they didn't return.	Danach kamen sie nicht wieder.

English *(cont.)*	German
The shoemaker and his wife lived long and happy lives, and their business prospered.	*Der Schuhmacher und seine Frau lebten ein langes und glückliches Leben und ihr Geschäft gedieh.*

Performance Challenge

Individual   Teach a small child how to say part of the story in German. Teach them simple nouns like shoes, shoemaker, wife, and elves. Then, have them recite the story back to you.

Performance Challenge

Group   Make a movie out of this story. Have each of the students play a different character and speak their parts in German.

ACTIVITY

68

ACTIVITY 68

Afanti Borrows His Landlord's Cooking Pots

In this activity you will:

➡ Read to increase all skill levels of language learning.

Disc **5** Track **3**

INSTRUCTIONS Listen to and read the following story. Recite the story out loud in German with the voice on the audio. Work toward fluency.

🔊

English	German
Once Afanti borrowed a cooking pot from a landlord.	Afanti lieh sich einmal einen Kochtopf von seinem Gutsherrn.
When he returned the pot to the landlord, he had placed a smaller cooking pot inside.	Als er den Topf zurückbrachte, stellte er einen kleinen Kochtopf hinein.
The landlord said:	Der Gutsherr sagte:
"Afanti, how is it there's an extra small pot?"	"Afanti, wie kommt es, dass da zusätzlich ein kleiner Topf ist?"
Afanti said:	Afanti sagte:
"When your cooking pot was in my house it gave birth to a little pot, so I brought the small pot to give to you."	"Als dein Kochtopf in meinem Haus war, brachte er einen kleinen Topf zur Welt und deshalb brachte ich den kleinen Topf, um ihn dir zu geben."
The landlord knew a cooking pot couldn't bear a child, but to get an extra cooking pot he immediately said with enthusiasm:	Der Gutsherr wusste, dass ein Topf keine Kinder zur Welt bringen kann, aber um einen zusätzlichen Topf zu bekommen, sagte er sofort enthusiastisch:
"Fine, fine!	"Gut, gut!
If you need a pot later on come to my house to borrow it."	Wenn du wieder einen Topf brauchst, dann komm zu meinem Haus und leih dir einen."

English (cont.)	German
Saying these words, he accepted the two pots.	Als er diese Worte sagte, nahm er die zwei Töpfe.
Some time later Afanti came again to borrow a pot.	Einige Zeit später kam Afanti wieder, um sich einen Topf auszuleihen.
He said:	Er sagte:
"A lot of friends have come to my house.	"Es sind viele Freunde zu meinem Haus gekommen.
I'd like to borrow the landlord's biggest cooking pot."	Ich würde mir gern den größten Topf des Gutsherrn ausleihen."
The landlord, expecting to get another extra pot, took the pot at once and gave it to Afanti.	In der Erwartung einen anderen zusätzlichen Topf zu bekommen, nahm der Gutsherr den Topf und gab ihn Afanti.
A week passed, and then another, but Afanti didn't come to return the pot.	Eine Woche verging und eine weitere, aber Afanti kam nicht um den Topf zurückzubringen.
The landlord was about to go get it when Afanti came.	Der Gutsherr war fast dabei hinzugehen um ihn zu holen als Afanti kam.
Very sadly he said to his landlord:	Sehr traurig sagte er zum Gutsherrn:
"I beg your forgiveness.	"Ich bitte um Vergebung.
After I took your pot to my house it got sick, and in a couple of days it died."	Nachdem ich den Topf zu meinem Haus mitgenommen hatte, wurde er krank und ist nach einigen Tagen gestorben."
"What?" the landlord cried in a loud voice.	"Was?" schrie der Gutsherr mit lauter Stimme.
"Can it die?"	"Kann er sterben?"
Afanti looked innocently at the landlord and said:	Afanti schaute den Gutsherrn unschuldig an und sagte:
"If a pot can bear a child, why can't it die?"	"Wenn ein Topf ein Kind zur Welt bringen kann, warum kann er dann nicht sterben?"

Bern, Switzerland, Part II

In Bern, locals and tourists alike enjoy an easy approach to life. The city's attraction is its ambience; traffic is kept out of the Old Town and you could spend days just wandering the streets and alleys, browsing through shops, sitting at cafés, and joining the locals for a plunge into the river if the weather is warm.

Performance Challenge

Individual   Find a German cookbook. Go through it and choose a recipe that you have not tried before. Make the recipe and share it with your family and friends. Explain the moral of the story to them as you eat, using as much German as possible.

Performance Challenge

Group   Split your group up into teams. Give each team a list of words in German that can be found at a restaurant or in a kitchen. Go on a scavenger hunt. The first team to find all of the words on their list wins.

Afanti Plants Gold

INSTRUCTIONS Listen to and read the following story. Do your best and try to understand as much as possible without looking at the English column.

In this activity you will:

→ Recognize how much German you can comprehend, say, and read.

 Disc **5**   Track **4**

English	German
One day when a king was hunting with some of his ministers, he came upon Afanti and saw he was covering some gold with sand.	*Eines Tages als ein König mit seinem Hofrat jagen ging, traf er auf Afanti und sah wie er Gold mit Sand bedeckte.*
The king asked him:	*Der König fragte ihn:*
"What on earth are you doing there?"	*"Was in aller Welt machst du da?"*
Afanti answered:	*Afanti antwortete:*
"Oh, Your Majesty, I am growing gold."	*"Oh, Eure Majestät, ich pflanze Gold an."*
"Do you mean you plant gold?" asked the king with surprise.	*"Du meinst, du kannst Gold anpflanzen?" fragte der König überrascht.*
"Oh yes, of course.	*"Oh ja, natürlich.*
I sow a little gold dust now, and in autumn I'll have a good crop of gold," Afanti answered.	*Ich streue jetzt ein wenig Goldstaub aus und im Herbst werde ich eine gute Menge Gold haben," antwortete Afanti.*
The king cleared his throat and said:	*Der König räusperte sich und sagte:*
"Say now, how would you like to cooperate in this thing?	*"Sag nun, wie du in dieser Sache mit mir zusammenarbeiten möchtest.*
I'll give you some gold dust, and you will plant gold for me, all right?"	*Ich werde dir Goldstaub geben und du pflanzt Gold für mich an, OK?"*
Afanti said:	*Afanti sagte:*
"Your Majesty, it will be my pleasure."	*"Es wird mir eine Freude sein, Eure Majestät."*

English (cont.)	German
On the following day he went to the king's palace and got a small amount of gold dust.	*Am folgenden Tag ging er zum Palast des Königs und bekam eine kleine Menge Goldstaub.*
He didn't go back to the king until fall.	*Bis zum Herbst ging er nicht zum König zurück.*
The king had been wondering when Afanti would harvest the gold, so when one day in October he brought a bag of gold dust, the king was delighted.	*Der König fragte sich, wann Afanti das Gold ernten würde und so war der König erfreut, als er an einem Tag im Oktober einen Sack Goldstaub brachte.*
"You have done well, Afanti.	*"Das hast du gut gemacht, Afanti.*
Next year let's sow a larger crop, all right?	*Lass uns nächstes Jahr eine größere Menge ausstreuen, OK?*
Go into my treasury and take as much gold as you like and sow it all."	*Geh in meine Schatzkammer und nimm soviel Gold, wie du möchtest und streu es alles aus."*
Of course Afanti was glad to hear these words.	*Natürlich war Afanti froh, diese Worte zu hören.*
He went to the king's treasury and filled a wheelbarrow with gold, which he then took home.	*Er ging zur Schatzkammer des Königs und füllte eine Schubkarre mit Gold, die er mit nach Hause nahm.*
Autumn came and the king was eagerly awaiting a rich harvest of gold.	*Der Herbst kam und der König wartete ungeduldig auf eine reiche Goldernte.*
October passed.	*Der Oktober ging vorbei.*
And November passed, but no gold was brought.	*Und der November ging vorbei, aber es wurde kein Gold gebracht.*
Finally in December Afanti came with a sad face.	*Im Dezember kam Afanti schließlich mit einem traurigen Gesicht.*
The king was overjoyed to see him.	*Der König war überglücklich ihn zu sehen.*
He said:	*Er sagte:*
"Well, Afanti, where are the carts of gold?	*"Gut, Afanti, wo ist die Fuhre Gold?*
Show me at once."	*Zeig es mir sofort."*
Afanti said with a sad voice:	*Afanti sagte mit trauriger Stimme:*
"Your majesty, forgive me.	*"Eure Majestät, vergib mir.*

Bern, Switzerland, Part III

In the eastern Old Town you will find the Bärengraben—bear pits. Two large, sunken bear dens house several brown bears, which have been the symbol of Bern since the early 16th century. The bears that live there now may look gentle, but tourists must still be careful. Heading left up the steep hill next to the Bärengraben, you will find the Rosengarten (Rose Garden), with an unparalleled collection of flowers and plants and a breathtaking view of the town.

English (cont.)	German
Our luck's been very bad.	*Unser Glück war nicht sehr gut.*
The weather's been cold.	*Das Wetter war kalt.*
There has been no rainfall.	*Es hat nicht geregnet.*
I did all I could, but the gold wilted and died."	*Ich habe alles getan was ich konnte, aber das Gold welkte dahin und starb."*
The king burst into a rage and said:	*Der König brach in Wut aus und sagte:*
"Nonsense, how can gold die from a drought?"	*"Das ist Schwachsinn, wie kann Gold wegen einer Dürre sterben?"*
Afanti answered:	*Afanti antwortete:*
"Well, Your Majesty, if You can believe gold can be grown, how is it You don't believe that it can die of drought?"	*"Gut, Eure Majestät, wenn Ihr* daran glaubt, dass Gold wachsen kann, warum glaubt Ihr dann nicht, dass es wegen einer Dürre sterben kann?"*

NOTE

Ihr is the archaic form of *Sie.* In this case, it refers to the king.

Performance Challenge

Individual 1   Afanti takes his gold to the King's castle in this story. Find out everything you can about Neuschwanstein Castle, the most famous castle in Germany. Write a one page report on your findings. Rough out some ideas below.

....

....

....

....

....

☆

Performance Challenge

Individual 2   The castle at Disneyland was modeled after Neuschwan-stein in Germany. Write about your favorite vacation in German and then share it with your family or friends. Rough out some ideas below.

....

....

....

....

....

....

....

☆

Performance Challenge

Group 1   Split students into two or three groups. Have each group rewrite the ending to Afanti Plants Gold. Once complete, ask the groups to act out their version of the story in German.

☆

Performance Challenge

Group 2   The castle at Disneyland was modeled after Neuschwanstein in Germany. Have the students write about their favorite vacation in German and then share it with the class.

Five Blind Men Describe an Elephant

INSTRUCTIONS Listen to and read this silly story.

✓ **In this activity you will:**
→ Expand your comprehension toward complete understanding.

 Disc **5** Track **5**

English	German
One day five blind men were chatting, and the subject turned to elephants.	*Eines Tages plauderten fünf blinde Männer miteinander und sie wechselten das Thema zu Elefanten.*
One of them said:	*Einer von ihnen sagte:*
"I've grown this old, and I still don't know what an elephant looks like."	*"Ich bin so alt geworden und weiß immer noch nicht, wie ein Elefant aussieht."*
"Neither do I."	*"Ich auch nicht."*
"I haven't seen one either."	*"Ich habe auch keinen gesehen."*
"Same here."	*"Das Gleiche hier."*
"What in fact does an elephant look like?"	*"Wie sieht ein Elefant wirklich aus?"*
All five wanted to see an elephant, so they decided to ask someone to take them to an elephant so they could feel it.	*Alle fünf wollten einen Elefanten sehen, so entschieden sie sich dazu, jemanden zu fragen, der sie zu einem Elefanten bringen kann, damit sie ihn fühlen konnten.*
At last the group of blind men finally got the chance to "see" what an elephant was.	*Endlich bekam die Gruppe blinder Männer die Gelegenheit einen Elefanten zu "sehen."*
With great delight they went up to the elephant and attentively began to feel it.	*Mit großem Vergnügen gingen sie zu dem Elefanten und begannen ihn aufmerksam zu fühlen.*

English (cont.)	German
"Aha!	"Aha!
Now I know, an elephant has the shape of a wall."	Nun weiß ich es, ein Elefant hat die Form einer Wand."
"No!	"Nein!
An elephant has the shape of a thick rope."	Ein Elefant hat die Form eines dicken Strickes."
"No!	"Nein!
No!	Nein!
An elephant looks like a big fan."	Ein Elefant sieht aus, wie ein großer Fächer."
"You are all wrong!	"Ihr seid alle im Unrecht.
An elephant looks like a pillar."	Ein Elefant sieht aus, wie eine Säule."
"All of you are wrong.	"Ihr alle seid im Unrecht.
An elephant looks like a snake."	Ein Elefant sieht wie eine Schlange aus."
Each thought only his own opinion was right.	Jeder dachte, dass nur seine Meinung richtig war.
Since each thought that the part that he touched constituted the whole elephant, they would not listen to one another or accept another's opinion.	Weil jeder dachte, dass ein Elefant aussieht wie der Teil, den er berührt hatte, wollte niemand auf den anderen hören oder die Meinung eines anderen akzeptieren.
And so it finally ended in a quarrel.	Und so endete es schließlich in einem Streit.

Bern, Switzerland, Part IV

Bern is also home to the Benisches Historisches Museum—a huge, turreted castle built in 1894 that has been turned into a museum. It has 7 floors, each of which houses a different exhibit. There are extraordinary porcelain and silver exhibits, but the highlight is the exhibit of paintings showing the "Dance of Death." These paintings are copies of the originals, which were painted on the wall of Bern's Dominican monastery in 1516. They are now lost. There are also original sandstone figures from The Last Judgment; an Islamic collection including daggers, a mounted Turkestan warrior in full armor, jewelry, ceramics and a reconstructed Persian sitting room; a scale model of Bern in the 1800s; and a display of Flemish tapestries.

Performance Challenge

Individual Visit the zoo. Write a one page report on the elephants using as much German as you can. If you aren't close to a zoo, use the Internet or the library for your research. Rough out some ideas below.

....

....

....

....

....

....

....

....

....

....

....

....

....

....

....

....

....

Performance Challenge

Group 1   Divide the group into teams. Blindfold each student and then pass around an object for them to describe in German. The first team to come to up with the correct answer wins.

Performance Challenge

Group 2   Divide the group into teams and appoint a judge. Choose a subject that can be debated easily. Have teams prepare a debate together and then debate the chosen subject. Try to keep the discussion completely in German.

Conversation Snatches 14

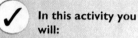

In this activity you will:

→ Follow a conversation and understand its meaning.

Disc **5**   Track **6**

INSTRUCTIONS   Listen to these dialogues and come up with a new dialogue of your own.

English	German
Now it's your turn.	*Jetzt bist du an der Reihe.*
Oh man, don't make me nervous!	*Ach Mensch, mach' mich nicht nervös!*
I'm furious. I'm so angry, I….	*Ich bin so wütend. Ich bin so böse, ich….*
Just a moment! First just count slowly from one to ten.	*Moment mal! Zähl erst mal langsam von eins bis zehn.*
You must study hard.	*Du musst hart lernen.*
Unfortunately I've no desire for studying.	*Leider habe ich keine Lust zu lernen.*
Are you coming with us then?	*Kommst du dann mit uns mit?*
Yes. Please wait for me. Right away.	*Ja. Bitte warten Sie auf mich. Sofort.*
All's well that ends well.	*Alles Gute endet gut.*
You mustn't say that.	*Das dürfen Sie nicht sagen!*
Will You have anything else?	*Wollen Sie sonst noch etwas haben?*
No. That's all.	*Nein. Das ist alles.*
By the way, I just got married.	*Übrigens, ich habe vor kurzem geheiratet.*
Oh, that's just great.	*Ach, das ist ja prima.*
Listen to me!	*Hören Sie mir zu!*
I am listening to You.	*Ich höre Ihnen zu.*
How do you plan to support yourself?	*Wie planst du dir deinen Lebensunterhalt zu verdienen?*

English (cont.)	German
I can earn money by babysitting and carwashing.	Ich kann mit Babysitting und Autoswaschen Geld verdienen.
That's easy to say.	Das ist leicht gesagt.
You were in the hospital. How are you doing?	Du warst im Krankenhaus. Wie geht es dir?
I'm as good as new.	Ich bin so gut wie neu.
As soon as I have enough money I'll buy a car.	Sobald ich genug Geld habe, werde ich mir ein Auto kaufen.
I'll sell you mine for just a thousand marks.	Ich werde dir meins für nur tausend Mark verkaufen.
You advised me to buy this car.	Sie haben mir geraten dieses Auto zu kaufen.
Oh well, a guy can make a mistake.	Nun, man kann sich irren.
If you will give me a dollar today, I'll give you back a dollar tomorrow.	Wenn du mir heute einen Dollar gibst, gebe ich dir morgen einen Dollar zurück.
Sure. Why not? Here you are.	Sicher. Warum nicht? Bitte.
I must go now.	Ich muss jetzt gehen.
We're going to miss You a lot.	Wir werden dich sehr vermissen.
What is Your profession?	Was sind Sie von Beruf?
I'm a carpenter.	Ich bin Zimmermann.
And Your wife?	Und Ihre Frau?
She's a teacher.	Sie ist Lehrerin.

Lake Thun, Part I

Located just south of Bern, Switzerland, is Lake Thun, which is often referred to as the "Riviera of the Bernese Oberland." With its mild climate that extends into the fall, Lake Thun is the perfect place for such outdoor sports as cross-country skiing, snowboarding, skydiving, hiking, sailing, diving, windsurfing, river rafting, repelling, and rock climbing.

Performance Challenge

Individual 1 The Autobahn is widely regarded as the world's first motorway. Write a one page paper in German about the Autobahn and then share your findings with your family or friends. Rough out some ideas below.

....

....

....

....

....

....

....

....

....

....

....

....

....

....

....

....

Performance Challenge

Individual 2   Ask your family and friends to empty out their pockets and purses and count the money in German.

Performance Challenge

Group   Ask the students to write about their first job in German. Have them include where they worked, their responsibilities, and what they spent their first paycheck on.

The Goose That Laid Golden Eggs

INSTRUCTIONS Read through this story. Read it out loud and aim for your best pronunciation of the German text.

 In this activity you will:

→ Follow a *Geschichte* with full comprehension.

English	German
Once upon a time there was a poor peasant couple in a small village.	*Es war einmal ein armes, bäuerliches Ehepaar in einem kleinen Dorf.*
From year to year they struggled to keep from starving.	*Sie kämpften von Jahr zu Jahr, um nicht zu verhungern.*
They were heavily in debt to their landlord, who allowed them only a tenth of an acre of land to toil.	*Sie hatten große Schulden bei ihrem Gutsbesitzer, der ihnen nur ein Zehntel eines Ackers zu bearbeiten erlaubte.*
They had to carry water in buckets from a distant river to water their crop of millet and rye.	*Sie mussten Wasser in Eimern von einem weit entfernten Fluss transportieren, um ihr Hirse- und Roggenfeld zu wässern.*
Early one morning as they went out to cultivate their field, they noticed a white goose in some bushes that was trying to hide itself.	*Eines frühen Morgens, als sie auf dem Weg waren ihr Feld zu bearbeiten, entdeckten sie eine weiße Gans, die sich in den Büschen zu verstecken versuchte.*
It was very thin and scarcely able to move.	*Sie war sehr dünn und konnte sich kaum bewegen.*
Its eyes already were wanting to close in death.	*Ihre Augen waren bereit sich zu schließen, um zu sterben.*
Thinking they could perhaps nurse it back to health and then sell it, they took it home and fed it some water and millet.	*Sie dachten sich, dass sie sie vielleicht gesund pflegen und verkaufen könnten und so nahmen sie sie mit nach Hause und gaben ihr Wasser und Hirse.*
The next day already it was stronger, and in a few days it was waddling around, eating happily.	*Am nächsten Tag war sie schon kräftiger und ein paar Tage später watschelte sie herum und fraß glücklich.*

Lake Thun, Part II

The lake is surrounded by medieval and baroque castles, churches, fortresses, and farmhouses. Many of the historical buildings now house museums. Classical music is performed in the castles and the churches, some of which are a thousand years old.

English (cont.)	German
On the day they were thinking to take it to the market to sell it, the goose suddenly started acting in a strange manner, honking excitedly.	An dem Tag, als sie darüber nachdachten zum Markt zu gehen um sie zu verkaufen, begann sie sich plötzlich auf einer komischen Art und Weise sich zu verhalten und begeistert zu quaken.
It had laid an egg.	Sie hatte ein Ei gelegt.
The peasants thought:	Die Bauern dachten:
"Maybe we shouldn't sell the goose right now.	"Vielleicht sollten wir die Gans nicht jetzt verkaufen.
As long as it can lay eggs, would it not be wise to keep it and sell the eggs?"	Würde es nicht weiser sein, sie zu behalten und die Eier zu verkaufen, solange sie Eier legen kann?"
Then they looked at the goose egg.	Dann schauten sie sich das Ei der Gans an.
"Look, it isn't white, it's yellow.	"Sieh, es ist nicht weiß, es ist gelb.
How strange!" the wife said.	Wie seltsam!" sagte die Frau.
"No, not yellow either.	"Nein, es ist auch kein Gelb.
It is gold," the man said.	Es ist Gold," sagte der Mann.
Picking it up, he noticed it was as heavy as lead.	Als er es aufhob, bemerkte er, dass es so schwer wie Blei war.
At first, thinking someone had played a trick on him, he was going to throw it away, but examining it closely, he saw it was pure gold.	Zuerst dachte er, dass ihm jemand einen Streich gespielt hatte und war dabei es wegzuschmeißen, aber nach genauerem prüfen, sah er, dass es pures Gold war.
"Martha, this egg is pure gold!	"Martha, das Ei ist aus purem Gold!
With this one egg we can pay off our debt.	Mit diesem einen Ei können wir unsere Schulden bezahlen.
Think of it!"	Stell dir das vor!"
They quickly hid their treasure, and of course told no one.	Sie versteckten schnell ihren Schatz und erzählten natürlich niemandem davon.
To make sure their goose wouldn't be stolen, they tied it to the bed.	Um sicher zu gehen, dass die Gans nicht gestohlen wurde, banden sie die Gans am Bett fest.
They fed it millet and rye, and even bought milk for it to drink.	Sie fütterten sie mit Hirse und Roggen und kauften sogar Milch für sie.

English (cont.)	German
Just as they hoped, the next day, the goose laid another gold egg.	*Genau wie sie es erhofften, legte die Gans am nächsten Tag wieder ein goldenes Ei.*
"Martha, we can do more than pay off our debt to the landlord.	*"Martha, wir können mehr als nur unsere Schulden an den Gutsbesitzer bezahlen.*
We are going to be rich.	*Wir werden reich sein.*
How shall we spend our money?"	*Wie werden wir all unser Geld anlegen?"*
"First we'll build us a mansion.	*"Zuerst werden wir uns eine Villa bauen.*
We can hire servants.	*Wir können Dienstboten anstellen.*
We can eat fine food and dress ourselves in fine clothes.	*Wir können feine Speisen essen und uns mit feinen Kleidern kleiden.*
We can even travel.	*Wir können sogar reisen.*
We will never have to work again.	*Wir werden nie wieder arbeiten müssen.*
Think of it: we can live like kings."	*Stell dir vor: wir können wie Könige leben."*
"But Martha, the villagers need help.	*"Aber Martha, die Dorfbewohner brauchen Hilfe.*
We could build a school for the children.	*Wir könnten eine Schule für die Kinder bauen.*
We could build roads and modernize our village, making it better for all the villagers.	*Wir könnten Straßen bauen und das Dorf modernisieren und es für alle Dorfbewohner verbessern.*
Let's not be greedy.	*Lass uns nicht habgierig sein.*
We didn't do anything to gain this good fortune.	*Wir haben nichts dafür getan, um dieses Glück zu verdienen.*
It is a gift from God.	*Es ist ein Geschenk Gottes.*
It's not ours to keep.	*Es ist nicht für uns, um es zu behalten.*
It's only ours to share."	*Es ist nur unser, um es zu teilen."*
Martha was red in the face.	*Martha wurde rot im Gesicht.*
Her voice was loud and shrill.	*Ihre Stimme war laut und schrill.*
"George, you are wrong.	*"Georg, das stimmt nicht.*
No one has ever helped us.	*Niemand hat uns jemals geholfen.*

Lake Thun, Part II

The lake is surrounded by medieval and baroque castles, churches, fortresses, and farmhouses. Many of the historical buildings now house museums. Classical music is performed in the castles and the churches, some of which are a thousand years old.

English (cont.)	German
While others have lived in comfort, they have let us struggle alone.	Während andere im Wohlstand gelebt haben, haben sie uns alleine kämpfen lassen.
Do you think our neighbors would share it with us?	Denkst du, dass unsere Nachbarn mit uns teilen würden?
Why should we help our neighbors?	Warum sollten wir unseren Nachbarn helfen?
We owe them nothing.	Wir schulden denen nichts.
If the fortune came to us from God, it is surely meant for us alone.	Wenn dieses Glück von Gott gekommen ist, ist es sicherlich für uns allein.
I say it is our turn to enjoy some blessings."	Ich sage dir, nun sind wir dran einige Segnungen zu geniessen."
Shocked by his wife's greed, the husband said:	Erschrocken über die Habgier seiner Frau sagte der Mann:
"I believe God is testing us.	"Ich glaube, dass Gott uns prüft.
If we do not share, the gift may be taken away."	Wenn wir nicht teilen, wird uns das Geschenk vielleicht wieder weggenommen werden."
Angered at her husband's "foolishness," the wife said:	Wütend über die "Dummheit" ihres Mannes, sagte die Frau:
"We can fool God.	"Wir können Gott täuschen.
We don't have to wait."	Wir müssen nicht warten."
"What do you mean?"	"Was meinst du?"
"We can get all the gold at once."	"Wir können das Gold mit einem Mal bekommen."
"How can we do that?"	"Wie können wir das machen?"
"We can kill the goose, open it up and take out the unlaid eggs."	"Wir können die Gans töten, sie öffnen und die ungelegten Eier herausnehmen."
Before her husband could object, the lady grabbed the goose twisted its neck, and then took a knife and cut open the goose's belly, expecting to find many gold eggs.	Bevor der Mann sich versah, griff die Frau nach der Gans, drehte ihr das Genick um, nahm ein Messer und öffnete ihren Bauch in der Erwartung viel Gold zu finden.
What do you think she found?	Was denkst du, was sie gefunden hat?
Right.	Richtig.

English (cont.)	German
There was not even one gold egg.	*Da war nicht einmal ein goldenes Ei.*
And furthermore, when they looked for the two eggs they had hidden away, they couldn't find them.	*Und außerdem konnten sie die andern zwei Eier, die sie versteckt hatten, nicht finden.*
They were gone.	*Sie waren verschwunden.*
So because of greed, the two remained as they were before.	*Wegen der Habgier, blieb ihnen nur, was sie zuvor hatten.*

☆
Performance Challenge

Individual   Find a German cookbook. Go through it and choose a recipe for an egg dish. Make the recipe and share it with your family and friends. Explain the moral of the story to them, as you eat, using as much German as possible.

☆
Performance Challenge

Group   Organize an activity where the students can go to a local shelter, nursing home, or hospital to volunteer their time. Have them write a one page paper, in German, about their experience.

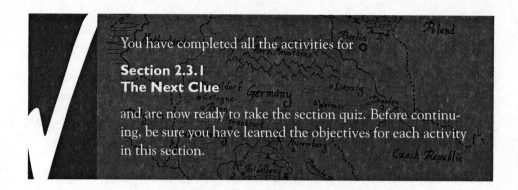

You have completed all the activities for

Section 2.3.1
The Next Clue

and are now ready to take the section quiz. Before continuing, be sure you have learned the objectives for each activity in this section.

Section 2.3.1 Quiz

INSTRUCTIONS   Choose the most correct response. Check your answers in Appendix D, on page 402.

1. **Was machte die Frau von dem Schuhmacher für die kleinen Männer, die Schuhe für sie gemacht haben?**

   A. *Essen*

   B. *Schuhe*

   C. *Leder*

   D. *Kleidung*

2. **Wann kamen die kleinen Männer zu dem Schuhmacher?**

   A. *Jeden Tag*

   B. *Mittags*

   C. *Um Mitternacht*

   D. *Abends*

3. **Was passierte (happened) zu dem Kochtopf am Ende der Geschichte?**

   A. *Er kocht.*

   B. *Er stirbt.*

   C. *Er singt.*

   D. *Er geht kaputt.*

4. **Was pflanzte Afanti an?**

   A. *Karotten*

   B. *Kleidung*

   C. *Gold*

   D. *Gurken*

5. **Für die blinden Männer ist der Elefant nicht wie**

   A. *eine Säule*

   B. *eine Schlange*

   C. *eine Wand*

   D. *eine Fliege*

6. **Choose the grammatically correct sentence.**

   A. *Alle fünf wollten einen Elefanten sehen.*

   B. *Alle fünf wollten sehen einen Elefanten.*

   C. *Alle fünf sehen wollten einen Elefanten.*

   D. *Alle wollten fünf sehen einen Elefanten.*

7. **Wollen Sie sonst noch etwas haben?**

   A. *Ach, das ist prima.*

   B. *Nun, man kann sich irren.*

   C. *Warum nicht.*

   D. *Nein, das ist alles.*

8. **Was sind Sie von Beruf?**

   A. *Ich bin glücklich.*

   B. *Ich bin Zimmermann.*

   C. *Ich bin ein großer Mann.*

   D. *Ich bin nicht reich.*

9. **Woher hat man die goldenen Eier?**

   A. *von der Gans*

   B. *von der Bank*

   C. *von dem Himmel*

   D. *aus der Erde*

10. **Warum hatte die arme Frau und der arme Mann kein Gold mehr?**

    A. *wegen Dieben*

    B. *wegen einem Einkauf*

    C. *wegen Habgier*

    D. *wegen Krankheit*

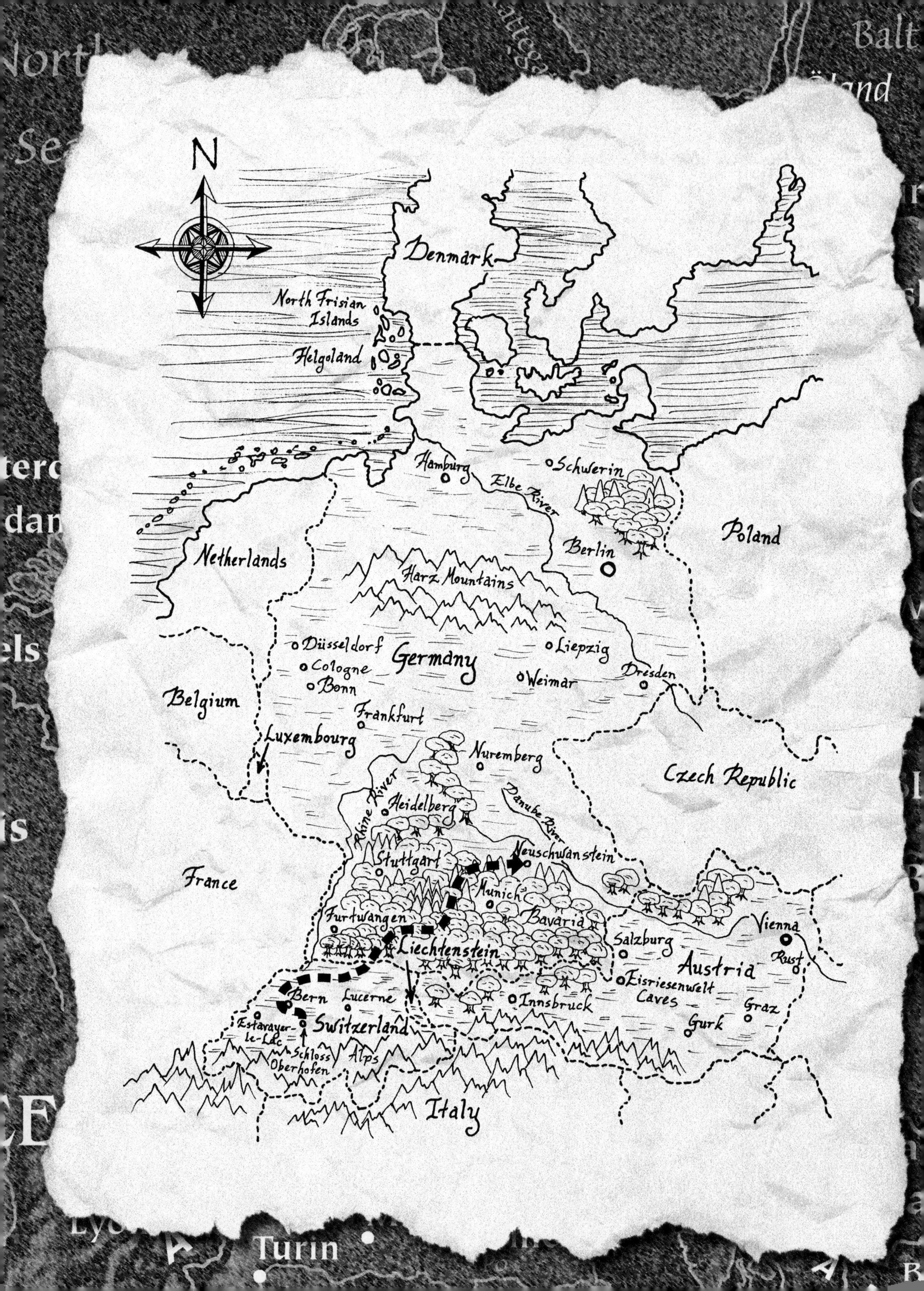

A Tale of Two Castles

You arrive at Schloss Oberhofen, purchase a map of the grounds and gardens, and hurry to the pavilion overgrown with grapevines. At the center of the pavilion is an ornate table, with matching chairs. *Der Tisch des Königs*, you guess, remembering the riddle. The last part of the clue still puzzles you, though. Afanti planted the gold in the dust, and you doubt you're going to find much dust on such well-kept grounds.

You take a closer look at the table. It has a very unusual centerpiece—a beautifully shaped bonsai tree, set in a miniature Japanese garden, complete with carefully combed patterns in the sand that surrounds the tree. This fine-grained sand is the closest thing this garden has to dust. You lean in for a closer look. Yes, there's a spot near one corner of the tray holding the miniature garden in which the sand looks rather lumpy. You carefully brush it aside and see a glimmer of gold. You brush the rest of the sand away. There is the gold key, and under it is another sheet of music. You remove both key and music, then carefully rearrange the sand. You look around. No one is in sight.

You sit down in one of the ornate chairs and examine the key. It's not made entirely of gold—that would be far too heavy and soft for a key. You think it's made of brass, but the elaborate handle is richly inlaid with faceted gold-brown topaz and with gold.

Then you take a closer look at the sheet music, once again using your boss's lighter to reveal the hidden clue. *Der Einsiedler trägt die Krone*, you read. *Der Einsiedler?* That's not a word you've encountered before. You look ahead in your book of German activities. *Der Einsiedler…der Einsiedler…* There it is! You find a story, *Der Einsiedler und die drei Räuber*—The Hermit and the Three Robbers.

You'll study the story in more detail later, but just understanding a clue has given you an idea. King Ludwig II of Bavaria, sometimes known as Mad King Ludwig and best known for his construction of elaborate castles like Neuschwanstein, was very reclusive. If any Bavarian monarch deserved to be called a hermit, it was Ludwig II. The best place to start looking for the crown in which you're supposed to find the final key would be the hermit king's favorite castle, Neuschwanstein. You jump up from your chair in excitement and experience a moment of light-

In this section you will:

- → Read and understand a *Geschichte auf deutsch*.
- → Follow a conversation and understand its meaning.
- → Read a *Geschichte* and retell it from memory.
- → Recognize how much German you can comprehend, say, and read.
- → Expand your comprehension toward complete understanding.

Disc **5**   Track **7**

SECTION **2.3.2**

headed dizziness. You shake your head. You must've just gotten up too quickly, that's all. You put the key and the music in your pack, then hurry back to the palace entrance, where you catch another cab back to Bern's airport.

It's mid-afternoon when you nose your plane back into the air and begin the flight back to Germany. You give your boss a quick call and let her know that you're on your way to Neuschwanstein for the final key.

"Excellent!" she congratulates you. "Be careful, though, Fliege. I just got word from the German government that the castle has been overrun, presumably by Herr Schuldig's forces."

You promise to be extra careful and ask if there's anything else.

"I've been doing what I can with the riddle, as well, while you and Spinne were tracking down the keys," your boss replies. "Give me a call when you have the last key. I think I know where the box to match them is hidden."

You speed the rest of the way to Germany, land in a small airport not far from the castle, and rent a motorbike. If the castle is indeed overrun, then you'll need to approach it with a lot more stealth than a typical car will allow.

A few miles before the castle, you turn the motorbike off the road and steer through the meadows and woods beside the road. You're glad you did—you spot several heavily armored vehicles lumbering down the road as you slip through the thick underbrush.

When you reach the castle, its gates and walls are heavily patrolled. There's no way you can sneak in while it's still light outside. You find a spot up a nearby tree where you can see inside but no one in the castle can see you. Then you settle down for a couple of hours of waiting and studying. You smile to yourself. This is actually a good thing. You'll have a chance to figure out exactly where you need to go for that last clue.

The Eagle Who Thought He Was a Chicken

ACTIVITY 73

In this activity you will:

→ Read and understand a *Geschichte auf deutsch*.

INSTRUCTIONS Listen to and read this story. The vocabulary is challenging so focus on overall comprehension in German.

 Disc **5** Track **8**

English	German
It was the wish of my father, God bless his memory, that his son should become a great statesman, a famous surgeon, or some other noble benefactor of mankind.	*Es war meines Vaters Wunsch, Gott segne sein Gedächtnis, dass sein Sohn ein großer Staatsmann werden sollte, ein berühmter Chirurg oder eine andere noble, wohltätige Persönlichkeit.*
But his son aspired only to earn fame and fortune as a football player, and he used this vain aspiration to excuse a nonchalant attitude toward his studies.	*Aber sein Sohn trachtete danach Ruhm und Ehre als Fußballspieler zu verdienen, und benutzte dieses eitle Streben als Entschuldigung für seine gleichgültige Einstellung seinem Studium gegenüber.*
"You are not just another boy," Father constantly told me.	*Du bist nicht wie jeder andere Junge," sagte Vater ständig zu mir.*
"You have the potential of greatness.	*"Du hast das Potential zur Größe in dir.*
But you must aspire high and set your mind to climb to the top.	*Aber du sollst nach Hohem trachten und deinen Verstand dazu einstellen, um an die Spitze zu klettern.*
Set your eyes on the stars, not on the ground."	*Sieh mit deinen Augen zu den Sternen und nicht auf den Boden."*
My resistance to his proddings and my attachment to more mundane goals gave him little comfort.	*Mein Widerstand gegen seine Vorstellungen und meine Neigung nach weltlichen Dingen gaben ihm wenig Hoffnung.*

Schloss Thun

One of the great historical museums is located inside the Schloss Thun, which was built in the 12th century. There are 5 floors of exhibits about the cultural development of the region over the last 4,000 years, which include a knight's hall, ceramics from Heimberg, majolica from Thun, military curios from the 19th century, and an archaeological section.

English (cont.)	German
One day as we were walking to church, after a long period of silence he started on the same subject:	Eines Tages, als wir zur Kirche gingen, nach einer langen Weile des Schweigens begann er mit dem gleichen Thema:
"Bobby," he said to me, "I don't think you know who you really are."	"Bobby," sagte er zu mir, "ich glaube nicht, dass du weißt, wer du wirklich bist."
"What do you mean?" I asked.	"Was meinst du?" fragte ich.
"I mean I don't think you understand your potential."	"Ich meine, dass ich denke, dass du dein Potential nicht erkennst."
"I don't understand what you're talking about, Dad," I said.	"Ich verstehe nicht, wovon du sprichst, Vater," sagte ich.
After another long pause, he said:	Nach einer langen Pause sagte er:
"Let me tell you a story my father told me when I was about your age."	"Lass mich dir eine Geschichte erzählen, die mir mein Vater erzählte, als ich in deinem Alter war."
Then he told me the following story.	Dann erzählte er mir die folgende Geschichte.
A baby eagle fell from its nest and was carried by the wind into a chicken yard.	Ein Adlerküken fiel aus dem Nest und wurde vom Wind in einen Hühnergarten geweht.
He was so stunned by the fall he couldn't remember how he got there or who he was.	Er wurde vom Fallen so betäubt, dass er sich nicht mehr daran erinnern konnte, wie er dorthin gekommen ist und wer er war.
At first the chickens were terrified and stayed far away quavering in fright, but one kindhearted old hen couldn't stand to hear the eaglet's hunger cries.	Zuerst fürchteten sich die Hühner und standen weit entfernt zitternd vor Angst, aber eine gutherzige, alte Henne konnte es nicht mehr aushalten die Hungerschreie des Adlers zu hören.
She boldly went out by the eaglet, scratched in some leaves with her claws, and found a nice big bug.	Mutig ging sie zu dem Adler, kratzte im Laub mit ihren Krallen und fand einen schönen großen Käfer.
She snatched up the bug with her beak and presented it to the baby eagle, who gulped it down and cried for more.	Sie schnappte mit ihrem Schnabel nach dem Käfer und gab ihn dem Adlerküken, welches ihn gierig hinunterschluckte und nach mehr schrie.

English (cont.)	German
Seeing this, the other chickens began to cluck nervously, but then decided that the only way to quiet the baby down would be for all of them to hustle food for the new chick.	Als die anderen Hühner das sahen, begannen sie nervös zu glucken, aber beschlossen dann, dass der einzigste Weg das Baby ruhig zu kriegen ist, dass jedes von ihnen nach Nahrung für das neue Küken sucht.
And so they did.	Und das taten sie.
Before long the eagle was pacified and, not remembering who he was, took up the life of a chicken.	Nach kurzer Zeit war der Adler zufriedengestellt und da er sich nicht erinnerte, wer er war, nahm er das Leben der Hühner an.
In fact, he quite enjoyed the easy life and all the attention he got.	Das heißt, er erfreute sich sehr an dem einfachen Leben und an all die Aufmerksamkeit, die er bekam.
Soon he grew so fat on the grubs fed him by the solicitous chickens that he began to look more like a turkey than an eagle.	Er wurde bald so fett vom Futter der besorgten Hühner, dass er anfing eher wie ein Truthahn auszusehen, als ein Adler.
Because he never tried to use his wings to fly, his wings remained quite undeveloped and as weak as those of a chicken.	Weil er niemals versuchte seine Flügel zum fliegen zu benutzen, blieben seine Flügel sehr unterentwickelt und waren genau so schwach, wie die der Hühner.
Then he learned to scratch in the dirt like a chicken, and his talons lost their sharpness.	Dann lernte er im Dreck zu scharren wie die Hühner, und seine Klauen verloren ihre Schärfe.
And from constantly focusing on the ground in search of grubs just beneath his feet, he became nearsighted.	Und vom ständigen auf den Boden Konzentrieren, um unter seinen Füßen nach Futter zu suchen, wurde er kurzsichtig.
A time or two, before his eyes grew dim, he noticed dark dots high in the sky.	Ein oder zweimal bevor seine Augen schwach wurden, bemerkte er dunkle Punkte hoch am Himmel.
They were his brothers soaring high among the clouds.	Es waren seine Brüder in den Wolken flogen.
But he didn't recognize them.	Aber er erkannte sie nicht.
How could he?	Wie konnte er das?
He had never looked at himself.	Er hatte sich nie selbst angeguckt.

Schloss Oberhofen

Schloss Oberhofen is located right on the lake and was once held by the Habsburgs. Its museum documents Bernese domestic life from the 16th to the 19th centuries. Other highlights include the castle's medieval chapel, a Turkish smoking room, historical landscaped gardens, and a children's chalet with a toy collection.

English (cont.)	German
And in fact there was not really much similarity now between him and his brothers.	Und in Wirklichkeit waren da nicht mehr viel Ähnlichkeiten zwischen ihm und seinen Brüdern.
This poor eagle, born to become master of the skies, convinced himself he was a chicken.	Der arme Adler, geboren als ein Meister des Himmels, war davon überzeugt, dass er ein Huhn war.
Though a voice deep down inside him told him it was his nature to fly as high as the clouds, he did not listen.	Doch eine Stimme tief in ihm sagte, dass es seine Natur war hoch in den Wolken zu fliegen, aber er hörte nicht hin.
Doubts silenced the voice of nature.	Zweifel brachte die Stimme der Natur zum Schweigen.
Impossible.	Unmöglich.
It is a foolish dream, he told himself.	Das ist ein dummer Traum, sagte er sich selbst.
A chicken can't fly.	Ein Huhn kann nicht fliegen.
A chicken can't be master of the skies.	Ein Huhn kann nicht Meister des Himmels sein.
And a chicken I must remain.	Und ich muss ein Huhn bleiben.
And so he did.	Und das tat er auch.
He lived the easy, unglorious life of a chicken, scratching in the dirt for grubs, while his brothers, masters of the sky, flew overhead.	Er lebte das einfache, unglorreiche Leben eines Huhnes, im Dreck nach Futter scharrend, während seine Brüder, die Meister des Himmels, über ihm herflogen.
Putting his arm around my shoulder, my father said to me:	Als die Geschichte zu Ende war, legte mein Vater seinen Arm um meine Schulter und sagte zu mir:
"Son, you must understand that you're an eagle.	"Sohn, du musst verstehen, dass du ein Adler bist.
You were born to fly high above the ground.	Du bist dazu geboren hoch über dem Erdboden zu fliegen.
But if you want to achieve your potential, you will have to begin to see it."	Aber wenn du dein Potential erreichen willst, musst du anfangen es zu sehen."
I didn't reply.	Ich antwortete nicht.
He must have thought his teaching fell on deaf ears.	Er muss gedacht haben, dass seine Belehrung auf taube Ohren stieß.

English (cont.)	German
Many years have come and gone since then, but I have never forgotten.	*Viele Jahre sind seitdem vergangen, aber ich habe es nie vergessen.*
Just the other day I heard my own son express his aspiration to earn fame and fortune as a soccer player.	*Erst vor einigen Tagen hörte ich meinen eigenen Sohn den Wunsch äußern Ruhm und Ehre als Fußballspieler zu verdienen.*
Perceiving that he has in him the potential of greatness, I decided I'd better take a walk with him.	*Ich hatte das Gefühl, dass er das Potential zu Großen in sich hat und entschied mich besser einen Spaziergang mit ihm zu machen.*
I put my arm around his shoulder as we walked, and told him the story of the eagle who thought he was a chicken.	*Ich legte meinen Arm um seine Schulter während wir spazieren gingen und erzählte ihm die Geschichte von dem Adler, der dachte, dass er ein Huhn sei.*
I'm not sure he was listening, but I suspect so.	*Ich war mir nicht sicher ob er zuhörte, aber ich vermute es.*

Performance Challenge

Individual It is important to set goals so that you know what you want to achieve. In German, write five goals that you want to accomplish this year, then explain why they are important to you.

1. ....

2. ....

3. ....

4. ....

5. ....

Performance Challenge

Group Ask the students to write about a piece of helpful advice given to them by their fathers. Have them use as much German as possible.

Questions of a Small Child 11

In this activity you will:

→ Follow a conversation and understand its meaning.

  Disc **5** Track **9**

INSTRUCTIONS Listen to this fun conversation.

English	German
Mama, who do I look like?	*Mama, wem sehe ich ähnlich?*
Like Daddy.	*Dem Vati.*
And you, who do you look like?	*Und du, wem siehst du ähnlich?*
A bit like my mother, your grandmother.	*Ein bisschen meiner Mutter, deiner Großmutter.*
And my brother Hans, who does he look like?	*Und mein Bruder Hans, wem sieht er ähnlich?*
A little like my father-in-law, your dad's dad.	*Ein bisschen meinem Schwiegervater, dem Vater deines Vaters.*
And my brother Mark?	*Und mein Bruder Mark?*
Like my brother, your Uncle Wilhelm.	*Meinem Bruder, deinem Onkel Wilhelm.*
Interesting!	*Interessant!*

Performance Challenge

Individual Research your ancestry. Find out as much as you can about your family using written histories, memories, and pictures. Write a brief history, in German, about your family, going back at least three generations. Rough out some ideas below.

....

....

....

....

....

....

....

....

....

....

....

....

....

....

....

....

....

....

....

....

....

....

Performance Challenge

Group   Have students bring a picture of themselves when they were
small. Number and arrange the pictures on a chalkboard. Have students
guess the identity of each of the pictures, then have the students tell
about themselves as a child, in German.

Cat in Boots

In this activity you will:

→ Read and comprehend *Geschichte* that are longer.

INSTRUCTIONS Read through this familiar tale.

English	German
A miller bequeathed to his three sons everything he possessed: a mill, a donkey, and an old cat.	*Ein Müller vermachte seinen drei Söhnen alles, was er besaß: eine Mühle, einen Esel und einen alten Kater.*
The first son got the mill, the second son got the donkey, but the third son got only the cat.	*Der erste Sohn bekam die Mühle, der zweite Sohn bekam den Esel, aber der dritte Sohn bekam nur den Kater.*
The youngest son was perplexed because he got such a small share of the inheritance.	*Der jüngste Sohn war verwirrt, weil er nur solch einen kleinen Teil der Erbschaft bekommen hatte.*
He said:	*Er sagte:*
"My older brothers will be able to earn a livelihood, but I, after I eat my cat and make a muff of his skin, will surely die."	*"Meine älteren Brüder werden in der Lage sein sich ihren Unterhalt zu verdienen, aber ich werde sicher sterben, nachdem ich den Kater esse und Pulswärmer aus ihrem Fell mache."*
Hearing the youth talk this way, the cat said to him:	*Als der Kater den Jungen so reden hörte, sagte er zu ihm:*
"Don't worry. Just give me a pair of boots to wear and a big paper bag to carry.	*"Sei nicht beunruhigt. Gib mir nur ein Paar Stiefel zum anziehen und einen großen Papiersack zum tragen.*
I'll go into the woods and you shall see that you are not that badly off."	*Ich werde in den Wald gehen und du wirst sehen, dass du nicht so schlecht dran bist."*
The poor young man got a small pair of boots and a big paper bag and gave these to the cat.	*Der arme junge Mann beschaffte ein kleines Paar Stiefel und einen großen Papiersack und gab dies dem Kater.*
The cat pulled on the boots and, taking the paper sack, set off into the woods.	*Der Kater zog die Stiefel an, nahm den Papiersack und ging in den Wald.*
He knew there were many rabbits there.	*Er wusste, dass es dort viele Kaninchen gab.*

English *(cont.)*	German
In the woods, he put some thistles in the bag and then, hiding in some bushes nearby, he waited for some young rabbits to come to see what was inside the sack.	*Als er in dem Wald war, steckte er einige Disteln in den Sack, versteckte sich und wartete bis einige junge Kaninchen kommen würden, um zu sehen, was in dem Sack ist.*
He did not wait long before a young rabbit got into the bag.	*Er wartete nicht lange bis ein junges Kaninchen in den Sack ging.*
At this, the cat quickly pounced on the bag and closed it.	*Der Kater sprang sofort auf den Sack und machte ihn zu.*
The rabbit struggled inside the bag, but soon suffocated and died.	*Das Kaninchen kämpfte in dem Sack, aber erstickte schnell und starb.*
Then the cat went to the palace and asked to speak to the king.	*Dann ging der Kater zum Palast und verlangte mit dem König sprechen zu dürfen.*
Making a low bow before the king, the cat said:	*Der Kater machte eine tiefe Verbeugung und sagte:*
"Your Majesty, inside this bag is a wild rabbit which my Lord the Marquis of Carabas has ordered me to present to you."	*"Eure Majestät, in diesem Sack ist ein wildes Kaninchen, welches der Marquis von Karabas mir befohlen hat, dir zu präsentieren."*
The cat had hit upon this title for his master.	*Der Kater erfand diesen Namen für seinen Meister.*
The king replied graciously:	*Der König antwortete freundlich:*
"Tell your master that I thank him and am very pleased with his gift."	*"Sag deinem Meister, dass ich ihm danke und, dass ich mit seinem Geschenk sehr zufrieden ist."*
For the next two or three months, the cat continued in this manner.	*Für die nächsten zwei oder drei Monate machte sie in dieser Art und Weise weiter.*
Every two or three days he would present a gift to the king in the name of his master the Marquis of Carabas.	*Jeden zweiten oder dritten Tag präsentierte er dem König ein Geschenk im Namen seines Meisters, dem Marquis von Karabas.*
One day, he learned that the king was going to take his daughter for a drive in his carriage along the bank of the river.	*Eines Tages fand er heraus, dass der König seine Tochter zu einer Fahrt in seiner Kutsche entlang am Ufer des Flusses mitnehmen würde.*
The king's daughter was the most beautiful princess in the world.	*Die Tochter des Königs war die schönste Prinzessin in der Welt.*

Sites to See Near Schloss Oberhofen

Walking around town you will find open air markets with flowers and fresh produce, handicrafts, antiques and flea markets. There are also annual festivals such as the Barrel Organ Festival and several Swiss folk music concerts to attend. If you're interested in sightseeing, then add the Museum of Timekeepers and Mechanical Musical Instruments and the St. Beatus caves to your list.

English *(cont.)*	German
So the cat said to his master:	*So sagte der Kater zu seinem Meister:*
"If you follow my advice your fortune will be secure.	*"Wenn du meinen Anweisungen folgst, wird dir dein Glück sicher sein.*
Will you do as I tell you?"	*Wirst du tun, was ich dir sage?"*
"Yes, I will do as you tell me."	*"Ja, ich werde tun, was du mir sagst."*
"Just go and bathe in the river at the place that I'll show you.	*"Geh einfach an der Stelle im Fluss baden, die ich dir zeigen werde.*
I will take care of the rest."	*Ich werde mich um den Rest kümmern."*
Though he didn't know what good would come of it, the poor young man went and did as the cat advised him.	*Der arme junge Mann ging und tat, was die Katze ihm angewiesen hatte, aber wusste nicht, was Gutes auf ihn zukommen würde.*
While he was bathing, the king's carriage approached.	*Während er badete, näherte sich die Kutsche des Königs.*
As it passed by, the cat cried out at the top of his voice:	*Als er vorbeikam, schrie der Kater mit voller Stimme:*
"Help!	*"Hilfe!*
Help!	*Hilfe!*
My Lord the Marquis of Carabas is drowning."	*Mein Herr der Marquis von Karabas ist am ertrinken."*
Hearing the cry, the king looked out the coach window.	*Als der König das Schreien hörte, schaute er aus dem Fenster der Kutsche.*
He at once recognized the cat who had so often brought him presents, and he ordered the driver of the carriage to stop.	*Er erkannte sofort den Kater, der ihm so oft Geschenke gebracht hatte und befahl dem Kutscher anzuhalten.*
His servants flew to rescue the Marquis from the river.	*Seine Diener stürzten los, um den Marquis aus dem Fluss zu retten.*
As they dragged the poor Marquis out of the river, the cat went up to the carriage and said:	*Als sie den armen Marquis aus dem Fluss zerrten, ging der Kater zur Kutsche und sagte:*
"Your Majesty, you are very kind.	*"Eure Majestät, du bist sehr freundlich.*
My master has suffered misfortune.	*Mein Meister muss unglücklicherweise leiden.*

English *(cont.)*	German
While he was bathing, thieves came and carried off his clothes."	*Während er badete, kamen Diebe und stahlen seine Kleider.*"
(Actually the cat had hidden the tattered clothes under a rock.)	*(In Wirklichkeit hatte der Kater die zerlumpte Kleidung unter einem Stein versteckt.)*
The king immediately ordered his servants to go and fetch one of his most beautiful suits for the Marquis of Carabas.	*Der König befahl sofort seinen Dienern einen seiner besten Anzüge für den Marquis von Karabas zu holen.*
Then the king embraced him and invited him to join them for a drive.	*Dann umarmte ihn der König und lud ihn ein, sie bei ihrer Fahrt zu begleiten.*
And the princess then and there fell in love with him.	*Und die Prinzessin verliebte sich dann dort in ihn.*
The cat was delighted to see his plans begin to succeed.	*Der Kater war begeistert zu sehen, dass sein Plan begann erfolgreich zu sein.*
He ran on ahead of the carriage and came to some peasants who were working in a field.	*Er rannte der Kutsche voraus und kam zu einigen Bauern, die auf dem Feld arbeiteten.*
He asked them:	*Er fragte sie:*
"For whom do you work?"	*"Für wen arbeitet ihr?"*
They answered:	*Sie antworteten:*
"For a cruel ogre who will kill us if we don't work."	*"Für das grausame Ungeheuer, das uns töten wird, wenn wir nicht arbeiten."*
He said to them:	*Er sagte zu ihnen:*
"Listen, good people, the king is coming this way in his carriage.	*"Hört, gute Leute, der König kommt auf diesem Weg in seiner Kutsche entlang.*
If you tell him that this field belongs to the Marquis of Carabas, I'll destroy the ogre and set you free."	*Wenn ihr dem König sagt, dass das Feld dem Marquis von Karabas gehört, werde ich das Ungeheuer vernichten und euch befreien."*
When the king passed by, he stopped and asked the peasants whose field it was they were harvesting.	*Als der König vorbeikam, hielte er an und fragte die Bauern, wem das Feld gehört, welches sie ernteten.*
"It belongs to the Marquis of Carabas," they responded.	*"Es gehört dem Marquis von Karabas," antworteten sie.*

English *(cont.)*	German
The king said to the Marquis of Carabas:	*Der König sagte zum Marquis von Karabas:*
"You have a fine field there.	*"Du hast ein gutes Feld hier.*
Every year it must yield an abundant crop."	*Das muss jedes Jahr eine reiche Ernte einbringen."*
The cat continued running on ahead of the carriage and came to some corn-pickers and asked them:	*Der Kater rannte der Kutsche weiter voraus und kam zu einigen Leuten die Mais ernteten und fragte sie:*
"For whom do you work?"	*"Für wen arbeitet ihr?"*
"For an evil ogre," they said, "a tyrant.	*"Für ein böse Ungeheuer," sagten sie, "ein Tyrann.*
We have to work for him or he'll kill us."	*Wir müssen für ihn arbeiten oder er wird uns töten."*
He said to them:	*Er sagte zu ihnen:*
"Listen, good people, the king is coming this way in his carriage.	*"Hört, gute Leute, der König kommt auf diesem Weg in seiner Kutsche entlang.*
If you tell him that these cornfields belong to the Marquis of Carabas, I'll get rid of the ogre and set you free."	*Wenn ihr ihm sagt, dass das Maisfeld dem Marquis von Karabas gehört, werde ich das Ungeheuer vernichten und euch befreien."*
When the king passed by, he stopped and asked the peasants whose cornfields these were.	*Als der König vorbeikam, hielt er die Kutsche an und fragte die Bauern, wem die Maisfelder gehören.*
"They all belong to the Marquis of Carabas," they responded.	*"Sie gehören alle dem Marquis von Karabas," antworteten sie.*
So again the king congratulated the Marquis of Carabas on his property.	*Wieder gratulierte der König dem Marquis von Karabas zu seinem Eigentum.*
Still the cat ran on ahead of the carriage.	*Der Kater lief immer noch der Kutsche vorraus.*
At length he came to a fine castle.	*Mit einem Vorsprung kam er zu einem herrlichen Schloss.*
The castle belonged to an ogre.	*Das Schloss gehörte einem Ungeheuer.*
Actually, all the lands the king had passed through belonged to this ogre.	*In Wirklichkeit gehörte das ganze Land, an dem der König vorbeikam, diesem Ungeheuer.*

Neuschwanstein Castle

Neuschwanstein Castle, built by King Ludwig II as an escape from reality, is often called "The Castle of the Fairy Tale King." It opened to the public in 1886, after being lived in for only 100 days by the king and just seven weeks after his mysterious death. Neuschwanstein is said to be the inspiration for the castle at Disneyland.

English (cont.)	German
The ogre was not only very rich but he possessed marvelous powers.	Das Ungeheuer war nicht nur reich, sondern besaß auch erstaunliche Macht.
The cat asked to speak to the ogre.	Der Kater bat darum, mit dem Ungeheuer zu sprechen.
The ogre received him politely enough and asked him to sit down.	Das Ungeheuer empfing ihn freundlich genug und bat ihn, sich zu setzen.
The cat said to him:	Der Kater sagte zu ihm:
"I'm told you have the power to change yourself into any kind of animal."	"Mir wurde gesagt, dass du in der Lage bist, dich in jedes Tier zu verwandeln."
"That is true," answered the ogre.	"Das ist wahr," antwortete das Ungeheuer.
The cat asked:	Der Kater fragte:
"Can you, for example, turn yourself into a lion or an elephant?"	"Kannst du dich zum Beispiel in einen Löwen oder Elefanten verwandeln?"
"Yes I can," he answered, and to prove it he turned himself into a lion.	"Ja, das kann ich," antwortete er und um es zu beweisen, verwandelte er sich in einen Löwen.
The cat was so frightened by the lion that he quickly climbed a tree.	Der Kater war so erschrocken über den Löwen, dass er schnell auf einen Baum kletterte.
When the ogre assumed his natural form again, the cat climbed down and confessed that he had been terribly frightened.	Als das Ungeheuer sich wieder in seine natürliche Form umwandelte, kletterte der Kater herunter und gab zu, dass er sich sehr erschrocken hat.
Then he said:	Dann sagte er:
"That is a marvelous power you have, to turn yourself into a huge animal.	"Das ist eine erstaunliche Macht die du hast, dich in ein großes Tier zu verwandeln.
But you can't turn yourself into a small animal—like a rat or a mouse.	Aber du kannst dich nicht in ein kleines Tier verwandeln—wie eine Ratte oder eine Maus.
That would be impossible, wouldn't it?"	Das ist unmöglich, oder?"
"Not at all," said the ogre.	"Überhaupt nicht," sagte das Ungeheuer.
"Watch!"	"Sieh!"

English *(cont.)*	German
At that moment he transformed himself into a mouse and began running about the floor.	*In diesem Augenblick verwandelte er sich in eine Maus und begann auf dem Boden herumzulaufen.*
As soon as he saw the mouse, the cat pounced on it, killed it, and ate it.	*Als der Kater die Maus sah, schnappte sie nach ihr, tötete sie und fraß sie.*
Just at that time the king's carriage arrived at the castle.	*Gerade zu dieser Zeit erreichte der König das Schloss mit seiner Kutsche.*
Upon hearing the noise of the coach, the cat ran out to meet it and said:	*Als der Kater das Geräusch der Kutsche hörte, rannte er hinaus um sie zu treffen und sagte:*
"Your Majesty, welcome to the castle of my Lord the Marquis of Carabas."	*"Eure Majestät, willkommen in dem Schloss meines Herrn dem Marquis von Karabas."*
"Oh my!" said the king.	*"Ooooooh!" sagte der König.*
"Does this great castle also belong to You?	*"Gehört Ihnen auch dieses große Schloss?*
Let's go in and see what it is like inside."	*Lasst uns hinein gehen und sehen, wie es von innen aussieht."*
You can guess what happened after this.	*Du kannst dir vorstellen, was danach passierte.*
The princess fell more and more in love with the Marquis.	*Die Prinzessin verliebte sich mehr und mehr in den Marquisen.*
Seeing this, the king was so pleased that he said:	*Als der König das sah, war er so erfreut, dass er sagte:*
"It depends entirely on yourself, my dear Marquis, whether or not you become my son-in-law."	*"Es hängt ganz allein von dir ab, mein lieber Marquis, ob du mein Schwiegersohn wirst oder nicht."*
The Marquis made several low bows.	*Der Marquis machte einige tiefe Verbeugungen.*
That same week he was married to the princess.	*In der gleichen Woche war er mit der Prinzessin verheiratet.*
The cat became a great lord and never again had to eat mice.	*Der Kater wurde ein großer Herr und musste nie wieder Mäuse fressen.*

Performance Challenge

Individual   Write a brief report on German fashion. Use as many German words as you can. Draw your own version of a modern German fashion design.

....

....

....

....

....

....

....

....

....

....

....

....

....

....

....

Performance Challenge

Group   Have your students study German fashion from a specific time period. Create a fashion show using items from that period. Describe all the clothing in as much German as possible.

A Clever Judge

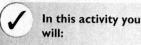

In this activity you will:

→ Read a *Geschichte* and retell it from memory.

Disc **5** Track **10**

INSTRUCTIONS Listen to and read the following story. Retell it in your own words.

English	German
An old man came to a judge one day and told him his money had been stolen while he and some of his friends were having a party.	*Ein alter Mann ging eines Tages zu einem Richter und erzählte ihm, dass sein Geld gestohlen wurde, während er und einige seiner Freunde eine Party hatten.*
"That's easy," said the judge.	*"Das ist einfach," sagte der Richter.*
"Bring in all of them tomorrow."	*"Bringen Sie alle morgen hierher."*
The next day all the guests were gathered in the court before the judge.	*Am nächsten Tag versammelten sich alle Gäste im Gericht vor dem Richter.*
"One of You is a thief.	*"Einer von Ihnen ist ein Dieb.*
I'll give each of You a stick.	*Ich werde jedem von Ihnen ein Stück Holz geben.*
These are magic sticks.	*Das sind magische Holzstücke.*
The one which the thief takes will grow five centimeters tonight.	*Das Stück, welches der Dieb nimmt, wird über Nacht fünf Zentimeter wachsen.*
Then we'll find out who the thief is."	*Dann werden wir herausfinden, wer der Dieb ist."*
Having said this, the judge left them.	*Nachdem er das gesagt hatte, verließ sie der Richter.*
In the night the thief felt very worried, but at last he got an idea and thought himself quite clever.	*Der Dieb war sehr beunruhigt in der Nacht, aber er hatte schließlich eine Idee und dachte, dass er sehr klug war.*
The next day the men gathered again before the judge.	*Am nächsten Tag versammelten sich die Männer wieder vor dem Richter.*
They each showed their sticks.	*Jeder von ihnen zeigte sein Holzstück.*
Except for the thief's they were all the same length.	*Sie waren alle gleich lang, außer dem des Diebes.*

English *(cont.)*	German
He had cut five centimeters of it off.	*Er hatte fünf Zentimeter davon abgeschnitten.*
"Ha!	*"Ha!*
So You are the thief!" exclaimed the judge.	*So sind Sie der Dieb!" stellte der Richter fest.*
As his hands were being tied, the thief was at a loss.	*Als seine Hände gefesselt wurden, war der Dieb verwirrt.*
He said:	*Er sagte:*
"That's strange.	*"Das ist seltsam.*
I don't think mine is five centimeters longer.	*Ich denke nicht, dass meins fünf Zentimeter länger ist.*
I cut it off."	*Ich habe es abgeschnitten."*

Performance Challenge

Individual Write about a time when you tried to be clever, and it didn't work. Use as many German words from the dialogue as you can.

....

....

....

....

....

....

Performance Challenge

Group Set up a mock courtroom and act out this story in German.

The Hermit and the Three Robbers

✓ **In this activity you will:**

→ Recognize how much German you can comprehend, say, and read.

INSTRUCTIONS   Read this story. Circle all the words you already know.

Eine mittelalterliche Geschichte aus Italien

◀))

English	German
There was once a hermit who lived in the mountains.	*Es war einmal ein Einsiedler, der in den Bergen lebte.*
One day as he was walking through the forest, a storm came up.	*Eines Tages als er durch den Wald ging, kam ein Sturm auf.*
Seeing a space between two large boulders, he sought shelter there.	*Er sah einen Platz zwischen zwei großen Felsen und suchte dort Schutz.*
Once under the shelter of the rocks, he noticed a narrow opening in the side of the mountain.	*Unter dem Obdach der Felsen bemerkte er eine schmale Öffnung in dem Berg.*
Curious, he crawled into the opening and discovered a large cave.	*Neugierig kroch er durch die Öffnung und entdeckte eine große Höhle.*
As his eyes grew accustomed to the dark inside the cave, he noticed something shining at the back.	*Als seine Augen sich an die Dunkelheit in der Höhle gewöhnt hatten, bemerkte er etwas Leuchtendes im Hintergrund.*
It turned out to be a heap of gold.	*Es stellte sich heraus, dass es ein Haufen Gold war.*
Quickly he turned and crawled out and fled in terror through the forest in spite of the rain.	*Er drehte sich schnell um, kroch hinaus und flüchtete durch den Wald ungeachtet des Regens.*

English *(cont.)*	German
As he was running, he came upon three robbers.	*Als er rannte, traf er auf drei Räuber.*
Wondering what he was running from, they stopped him and asked:	*Sie wunderten sich, warum er davon rannte, und hielten ihn an und fragten:*
"Why are you running through the rain?"	*"Warum rennst du durch den Regen?"*
"I am running from evil."	*"Ich renne dem Bösen davon."*
"What evil inspires you to run like this through the rain?"	*"Welches Böse bewegt dich dazu, durch den Regen zu laufen?"*
"Don't ask to know.	*"Fragt mich nicht.*
It would destroy any man.	*Es würde jeden Mann vernichten.*
It would destroy you."	*Es würde euch vernichten."*
Hearing this, the robbers became very curious.	*Als die Räuber das hörten, wurden sie sehr neugierig.*
"Tell us," they said, "what is the nature of the evil that threatens you?"	*"Erzähl uns," sagten sie, "was gibt es in der Natur so schlimmes, das dich ängstigt."*
"I dare not even speak of it," said the hermit.	*"Ich wage es nicht einmal auszusprechen," sagte der Einsiedler.*
"You must tell us.	*"Du musst es uns erzählen.*
We're not afraid."	*Wir haben keine Angst."*
"No, I cannot.	*"Nein, ich kann nicht.*
I must not."	*Ich darf nicht."*
"You will tell us or we will kill you!	*"Du wirst es uns erzählen oder wir werden dich umbringen!*
Come, lead us to it."	*Komm, führ uns dorthin."*
"I am running from Death.	*"Ich laufe dem Tod davon.*
He is close behind.	*Er ist dicht hinter mir.*
Flee with me, I beg you."	*Flüchtet mit mir, ich bitte euch."*
"You are insane.	*"Du bist wahnsinnig.*
No one is pursuing you.	*Niemand jagt dich.*
Come, lead us to Death.	*Komm, führ uns zum Tod.*
Show us what it is you fear."	*Zeig uns, was dich ängstigt."*

English *(cont.)*	German
The poor hermit was terrified.	Der arme Einsiedler fürchtete sich sehr.
He took them to the mouth of the cave, but warned them, saying:	Er nahm sie zum Eingang der Höhle, aber warnte sie und sagte:
"I warn you, do not enter this dangerous place.	"Ich warne euch, betretet diesen gefährlichen Ort nicht.
Flee before it is too late.	Flüchtet, bevor es zu spät ist.
Your lives are in danger."	Euer Leben ist in Gefahr."
Dragging him by the hand, the robbers crawled through the narrow opening into the cave, and there they found the gold.	Die Räuber zerrten ihn am Arm und krochen durch die schmale Öffnung in die Höhle und dort fanden sie das Gold.
"Here is Death," said the hermit.	"Hier ist der Tod," sagte der Einsiedler.
"If you give in to his temptations, he will kill you."	"Wenn ihr seinen Versuchungen nachgebt wird er euch umbringen."
Laughing greedily, the robbers began to assess their treasure.	Die Räuber lachten habgierig und begannen den Schatz abzuschätzen.
"It is too heavy to carry.	"Es ist zu schwer zu tragen.
One of us must go to the village and get a cart."	Einer von uns muss ins Dorf gehen und einen Wagen holen."
"Yes, and bring meat and juice so we can celebrate our good fortune."	"Ja, und bring Fleisch und Saft mit, so dass wir unser Glück feiern können."
Laughing at the hermit's absurd fear, they sent him on his way, warning him never to come back, lest death overtake him.	Sie lachten über des Einsiedlers absurde Angst, schickten ihn auf seinen Weg und warnten ihn nie zurück zu kommen, sonst würde der Tod über ihn kommen.
Furthermore, they told him, if he ever spoke a word about this, for sure they would kill him.	Außerdem sagten sie ihm, dass wenn er jemals ein Wort darüber sagen würde, sie ihn sicherlich töten werden.
Then the two older ones sent the younger one off to the village with a gold coin to bring a cart and some meat and juice.	Dann schickten die beiden älteren den jüngeren zum Dorf mit einer Goldmünze, um einen Frachtwagen zu mieten, und Fleisch und Saft zu kaufen.
As he was walking to the village, he thought up a plan.	Als er zu dem Dorf lief, dachte er sich einen Plan aus.

English (cont.)	German
"Even dividing the fortune three ways the three of us are enormously rich.	"Selbst wenn wir den Schatz gleichmäßig durch drei teilen, werden drei von uns enorm reich sein.
But if it were not divided, if it all fell to me, I would be the richest man in Italy.	Aber wenn wir es nicht teilen und ich alles bekomme, wäre ich der reichste Mann von Italien.
My companions have not always dealt fairly with me.	Meine Kameraden waren nicht immer fair zu mir.
Now I'll get even with them.	Nun werde ich mit ihnen abrechnen.
I will pay them back what they deserve, then I'll be the sole master of the treasure."	Ich werde ihnen das zurückzahlen, was sie verdienen und dann werde ich der alleinige Besitzer des Schatzes sein."
In the village he quickly found what he was seeking.	Im Dorf fand er schnell, was er suchte.
With the gold, he rented a cart and bought a good supply of meat and juice, and also a small vial of poison.	Mit dem Gold mietete er einen Wagen, kaufte eine gute Portion Fleisch und Saft und auch ein kleines Fläschchen Gift.
He poured the poison into the juice.	Er schüttete das Gift in den Saft.
"Ha!" he said to himself.	"Ha!" dachte er sich.
"When my companions drink the juice, they'll die, and the treasure will belong to me alone."	"Wenn meine Kameraden den Saft trinken, werden sie sterben und der ganze Schatz wird alleine mir gehören."
The two robbers waiting in the cave, gloating over their new-found treasure while their companion was absent, thought up a scheme of their own.	Die zwei Räuber warteten in der Höhle, starrten auf ihren neugefundenen Schatz und während ihr Kamerad abwesend war, dachten sie selbst über eine Intrige nach.
"A sharing of the treasure by two persons would yield to each considerably more than among three.	"Der Schatz durch zweigeteilt würde für jeden beträchtlich mehr hergeben als durch drei geteilt.
We have only to do away with our companion and we each gain very much for ourselves."	Wir müssen nur unseren Kameraden aus dem Weg schaffen und jeder von uns bekommt sehr viel mehr dazu."
So when their companion arrived with the cart and the food and juice, these two fell upon him with knives.	Als der Kamerad mit dem Wagen, dem Essen und dem Saft die Höhle erreichte, überfielen sie ihn mit Messern.

English (cont.)	German
Then they feasted upon the provisions he had brought.	Dann taten sie sich gütlich an den Provisionen, die er mitgebracht hatte.
Before long, they were seized with violent pangs, and as they lay dying, they thought of the hermit's dire warning:	Nach kurzer Zeit überkam sie ein stechender Schmerz und als sie so im Sterben lagen, erinnerten sie sich an die schreckliche Warnung des Einsiedlers:
"I tell you, do not enter this cursed place.	"Ich sage euch, betretet diesen verfluchten Ort nicht.
Flee before it is too late.	Flüchtet, bevor es zu spät ist.
Your lives are in jeopardy."	Euer Leben ist in Gefahr."
To this day, no one has taken the gold from the cave.	Bis zum heutigen Tag hat niemand das Gold aus der Höhle geholt.

The Wolf and the Lamb

INSTRUCTIONS Read through this story. Don't look at the English column unless you need to.

English	German
There was once a wolf who was drinking at a spring on the slope of a hill.	*Es war einmal ein Wolf, der Wasser aus dem Brunnen an einem Berghang trank.*
Raising his eyes, he noticed a lamb drinking a little below him.	*Als er mit seinen Augen aufblickte, bemerkte er ein trinkendes Lamm ein wenig abwärts.*
He thought to himself:	*Er dachte zu sich selbst:*
"If only I could find an excuse to seize this lamb, I would have a tasty dinner."	*"Wenn mir bloß eine Entschuldigung dafür einfallen würde, dieses Lamm zu ergreifen, würde ich bestimmt ein leckeres Abendessen haben."*
He yelled at the lamb brutally:	*Er schrie das Lamm brutal an:*
"You old sissy, how dare you sully the water that I drink?"	*"Du Weichling, wie kannst du dich wagen, das Wasser zu beschmutzen, das ich trinke?"*
The little lamb said humbly:	*Das kleine Lamm sagte demütig:*
"That can't be my fault, for I am below the stream in respect to you.	*"Das kann nicht meine Schuld sein. Im Verhältnis zu dir bin ich bachabwärts.*
The water runs from you to me."	*Das Wasser läuft von dir zu mir."*
"Well then," said the wolf, "why did you insult me last year?"	*"Nun," sagte der Wolf, "warum hast du mich letztes Jahr beleidigt?"*
The lamb said:	*Das Lamm sagte:*
"Sir, it couldn't have been me.	*"Das kann ich nicht gewesen sein.*
I am only three months old."	*Ich bin erst drei Monate alt."*

In this activity you will:

→ Expand your comprehension toward complete understanding.

King Ludwig II, Part I

According to his mother, Ludwig grew up "dressing up, play acting…" and was not ready to take over the throne at age 18, having no experience in life or politics. He had a vision of a country that was based on music and art, not war and spent his time on those things that he loved. In 1866, Prussia conquered Austria and Bavaria in the German War. From then on, Bavaria's foreign policy was dictated by Prussia and the King was only a servant of his Prussian uncle.

English *(cont.)*	German
The wolf answered in a belligerent tone:	*Der Wolf antwortete in kriegerischem Ton:*
"OK, if it wasn't you, it must've been your father."	*"OK, wenn du es nicht gewesen bist, dann muss es dein Vater gewesen sein."*
And with that the wolf pounced on the defenseless lamb, killed it, and set about to eat it.	*Und so fiel er über das wehrlose Lamm her, tötete es und fing es zu fressen an.*
The wolf was not at all bothered by the birds that scolded:	*Es ärgerte den Wolf überhaupt nicht, dass die Vögel ihn schalten:*
"A tyrant needs no pretexts to carry out his evil designs."	*"Ein Tyrann braucht keinen Vorwand, um seine schlechten Vorhaben auszuführen."*

Performance Challenge

Individual   Talk to your parents about what you were able to do when you were three months old. Ask about other milestones such as walking, talking, smiling, etc. Write a paragraph in German on what you find out about your life at that age.

....

....

....

....

....

....

....

Performance Challenge

Group   Set up a fishing pond. Write the words from the story in German on the fish. Have each student take turns fishing out words. If they can pronounce the word, award them a point. The student with the most points at the end of the game wins.

SECTION 2.3.2 • A TALE OF TWO CASTLES

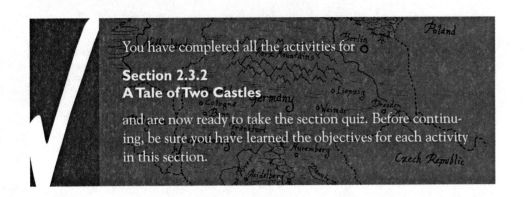

You have completed all the activities for

**Section 2.3.2
A Tale of Two Castles**

and are now ready to take the section quiz. Before continuing, be sure you have learned the objectives for each activity in this section.

Section 2.3.2 Quiz

INSTRUCTIONS   Choose the most correct response. Check your answers in Appendix D, on page 402.

1. **Choose the grammatically correct sentence.**

   A. *Du musst verstehen, dass du ein Adler bist.*

   B. *Du bist Adler, verstehen muss du.*

   C. *Du musst bist ein Adler, verstehen.*

   D. *Du musst verstehen, dass du bist ein Adler.*

2. **Wem sehe ich ähnlich?**

   A. *der Vater*

   B. *den Vater*

   C. *dem Vater*

   D. *des Vaters*

3. **Wem siehst du ähnlich, Mutter?**

   A. *die Großmutter*

   B. *der Großmutter*

   C. *dem Großmutter*

   D. *die Oma*

4. **Was hatte der Müller nicht?**

   A. *eine Mühle*

   B. *ein Haus*

   C. *einen Kater*

   D. *einen Esel*

5. **Was musste der Kater nie wieder fressen?**

   A. *Fisch*

   B. *Käse*

   C. *Milch*

   D. *Mäuse*

6. **Was machte der Dieb?**

   A. *schnitt fünf Zentimeter ab*

   B. *stahl Holzstücke*

   C. *brachten in ein Haus ein*

7. **Welches Böse bewegt dich dazu,**

   A. *zu laufen durch den Regen*

   B. *durch den Regen laufen*

   C. *durch den Regen zu laufen*

8. **Was passierten den drei Räubern am Ende der Geschichte?**

   A. *sie starben*

   B. *sie waren reich*

   C. *sie gingen ins Gefängnis*

9. **Wer ist der Tyrann?**

   A. *das Lamm*

   B. *der Mann*

   C. *der Wolf*

   D. *der Löwe*

10. **Wie wußte der Richter, wer der Dieb war?**

   A. *Der Dieb war sehr glücklich.*

   B. *Das Stück, welches der Dieb nahm, ist über Nacht fünf Zentimeter gewachsen.*

   C. *Das Stück, welches der Dieb nahm, war fünf Zentimeter kurzer.*

N
Denmark
North Frisian Islands
Helgoland
Hamburg
Schwerin
Elbe River
Berlin
Poland
Netherlands
Harz Mountains
Düsseldorf
Cologne
Bonn
Germany
Liepzig
Weimar
Dresden
Belgium
Frankfurt
Luxembourg
Nuremberg
Czech Republic
Rhine River
Heidelberg
Stuttgart
France
Munich
Furtwangen
Bavaria
Liechtenstein
Salzburg
Vienna
Austria
Rust
Eisriesenwelt Caves
Innsbruck
Bern
Lucerne
Estavayer-le-Lac
Switzerland
Schloss Oberhofen
Alps
Gurk
Graz
Italy
North
Turin

Finding the Cure

Disc **5**   Track **11**

After studying German, you spend an hour mapping the patrol patterns of the guards on the castle wall. You find your opening. Just after dark, you scale the castle wall and silently let yourself down the other side. You huddle behind some shrubbery waiting for the guards to march to the other side of the grounds. Then you rush to the unused servants' entrance on the side of the building, pick the lock, and let yourself in. To your relief, no alarms sound. The interior of the building is dimly lit, with most of the castle closing down for the night. You know from your earlier research that King Ludwig had a stage built in Neuschwanstein for performances of his friend Wagner's works. Looking around, you notice that this stage is just to your left. This is as good a place as any to start your search.

Carefully, you creep among the ornately carved benches leading up to the stage. The stage itself is empty and obviously hasn't been used for some time. You struggle not to cough on the dust you stir up walking across it. The area behind the curtains is dark and deserted enough that you risk a little light, and immediately you are glad you did. The backstage area is piled high with a tremendous assortment of props, costumes, and set pieces. You carefully make your way among the piles. The costumes look like a good place to start. Each one has a label on the hanger telling you which operatic role corresponds to which costume.

After searching through several racks of costumes, you find a very plain, shabby one. The tag reads *der Einsiedler*. A shiver of excitement runs up your spine. *Der Einsiedler trägt die Krone.* You feel the costume, carefully checking for pockets or bags that might conceal a crown. Nothing. You push the costume aside. Directly behind it is a small chest, precariously balanced on the corner of an old shelf. You open the chest. Inside, wrapped in yellowed old silk, is a crown. This clearly isn't something that belongs with the royal jewels—it is old, dented, and tarnished to the point that it is almost black. It is also a lot heavier than a costume crown should be. You turn it upside-down. The lining is loose. You pull it free. Jammed into a small compartment inside is a blackened wrought iron key. You pull it free, then carefully replace the crown in the chest and pull the costume back over it.

Despite your caution, though, the costume knocks the chest off the shelf. The crown tumbles out of the chest and rolls noisily across the floor. You cringe. It's too late, though. Alarms sound through the castle. You look around the stage area. There's nothing useful here, but you remember seeing some windows in the area across from the stage.

You race past the benches and across the hall, then dive out of the nearest window. Lights are coming on behind you, and you hear shouting voices. You race to the wall and clamber up and over it as swiftly as you can, narrowly avoiding several spotlights that are now sweeping the grounds. You let yourself down the other side and are breathing hard and sweating profusely by the time you get back to the motorbike hidden outside. You pull on your helmet, double-check your pack to make sure all keys and music sheets are safe, then steer the motorbike through the woods and underbrush, back toward the town where you left your plane. The night breeze is chilly, and you are shivering by the time you get back to the plane. To your surprise, you can't seem to stop shivering.

As you wait for takeoff clearance, you place a quick call to your boss.

"I have all the keys," you inform her.

"*Wunderbar,*" she tells you. "Your next destination is Helgoland. It's one of the North Frisian Islands. It was once used as a submarine base, and until very recently offered tours of its bunkers and underground tunnels. We now have reason to believe Herr Schuldig is using it as his security headquarters. I'm sending a map of the old base layout to your cell phone. I've marked the bunker in which we believe the box is hidden."

"*Perfekt. Vielen Dank,*" you reply.

You receive clearance for takeoff and steer the plane swiftly upward into the night sky. You crank the cabin's heat up as high as it will go and finally stop shivering. Now, though, you can't seem to cool off. You're getting an awful headache and are starting to feel light-headed again. You hope you're not coming down with the plague. You have to finish this mission.

In the wee hours of the morning, you land the plane on the island next to Helgoland and take a single-man submarine beneath the water separating you from Helgoland. The underwater entrance your boss marked is still there and is, to your great relief, unguarded. Evidently, it was too small to merit Herr Schuldig's attention. Shivering again, with the edges of your vision swimming, you make your way down a series of empty corridors to the bunker your boss marked on the map. Its door has another old-fashioned story lock, this one with rotating discs that line up to show the order of events in the story "Puss in Boots." Thankfully, this is one of the stories you've studied, so you open the lock in mere seconds.

Silently, you close the door behind you. There, in one corner of the room, is an elaborate box with seven keyholes. In order, you insert each key into its proper hole and turn it. As the last key turns, musical notes emerge from the box. You recognize the melody of "Flight of the Valkyries." The locks click open, and you open the box. Inside is a single sheet of paper, a final sheet of music. You hold it up to your boss's lighter, and a final message in delicate, spidery writing appears. It's a chemical formula. This is it! You've found the cure! Feeling giddy, you call your boss and read her the exact formula.

"Perfect, Fliege! We'll get it into production at once," she tells you. "Now that we have the cure, we're sending in teams to take down Herr Schuldig and his forces. You have one hour to get out of Helgoland. After that, I can't guarantee your safety. If you can, take the employee who's helped us so much with you."

"Roger that," you reply. "I'll meet you back in Berlin."

Behind you, the door opens softly. You whirl around. You feel as though your head keeps whirling for several seconds longer than your body, but you manage to stay on your feet. In the doorway stands a man in his mid-twenties, who pushes thick glasses up on his nose and smiles shyly. "You figured it out," he tells you. "I was hoping someone would."

"So, what happens now?" you ask, trying not to sound too suspicious or uneasy.

The man shrugs. "I was hoping you had a good way out of here," he replies. "Now that the secret is out, I doubt it will be safe here for long, especially not for me."

You nod. "Right on both counts, though I don't know if coming with me is any safer."

"I'll take my chances," he replies with a grin. He picks up the music box and closes it gently. "My grandfather made it," he explains. "He was a master crafts-man. I thought it was appropriate to put it to good use."

You lead him back to the underwater entrance and your single-man submarine. You slip on gloves and a mask to minimize the risk of spreading the infection. It's a tight squeeze, but you both make it back to the island where your plane is wait-ing. Strange colors are swimming on your peripheral vision, but you know you have to make it back to Berlin. You steer the plane back into the sky and head south at top speed. Herr Schuldig's former employee, sensing something isn't right, sits in his seat with hands clenched and face pale.

After what feels like forever, you finally see the lights of Berlin below, and you circle the plane down to a rough but adequate landing. Once the plane is shut down, your temporary travel companion opens the hatch, and you both disem-bark. Your boss is there to greet you. Feeling dizzy and sick, though, you keep your distance.

"Are you all right, Fliege?" she asks.

You open your mouth to answer, but darkness closes in.

It's light outside when you wake up. Looking around, you discover you're in an isolation room, with an IV dripping steadily into your arm. You're feeling much better. The door to your room opens, and your boss comes in.

"Don't worry, Fliege, you're not contagious anymore," she tells you. "Congratula-tions on saving the world, by the way. Herr Schuldig and his forces are in custody. Plague victims around the world, including yourself and Spinne, are recovering nicely, and upwards of a dozen governments around the world are beating down my door wanting to thank you in person."

You're not sure how to respond to all this. "You're welcome?" you say tentatively.

Your boss grins, then laughs out loud. "Starting tomorrow, you'll be well enough for them to come beat down your door instead," she replies. "And starting next week, you and Spinne are both due for a nice, long vacation for your excellent work. After that... who knows? If you're lucky, I might have another case lined up for you."

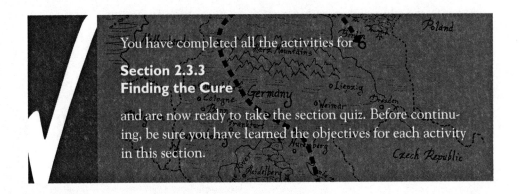

You have completed all the activities for

**Section 2.3.3
Finding the Cure**

and are now ready to take the section quiz. Before continuing, be sure you have learned the objectives for each activity in this section.

Section 2.3.3 Quiz

INSTRUCTIONS   Complete this quiz over the cultural material presented in this course. Feel free to consult Appendix C and the information in the course as needed. Check your answers in Appendix D, on page 402.

1. **The family name, Habsburg, is derived from the German name of which castle?**
   A. Hawk Castle in Switzerland
   B. Hofburg Castle in Vienna
   C. Heart Castle in Salzburg
   D. Hohenwerfen Castle in Werfen

2. **How are the holes in Swiss cheese created?**
   A. Each hole is carved into the cheese by hand.
   B. A cheese punch is used to make the holes.
   C. Holes are made by introducing bacteria into the cheese.
   D. The holes are a natural result of the aging process.

3. **A chocolate company in Pennsylvania bears the name of which Swiss city?**
   A. Bern
   B. Zurich
   C. Neuchâtel
   D. Lausanne

4. **The Habsburg family was split into two groups. What were they called?**
   A. The Royal Habsburgs and the Common Habsburgs
   B. The Austrian Habsburgs and the Spanish Habsburgs
   C. The French Habsburgs and the German Habsburgs
   D. The Old Habsburgs and the New Habsburgs

5. **What is the Neuschwanstein Castle sometimes called?**
   A. The Knight's Castle
   B. The Sleeping Beauty Castle
   C. The Castle on the Lake
   D. The Castle of the Fairy Tale King

6. **In what year did the Ausleich unite Austria and Hungary?**
   A. 1867
   B. 1883
   C. 1910
   D. 1918

7. **Large collections of what are on display in both Estavayer-le-Lac and Múnchenstein?**
   A. Old coins
   B. Frogs
   C. Clocks
   D. Stuffed birds

8. **How many languages were spoken in the Austro-Hungarian Empire?**
   A. Four languages
   B. Seven languages
   C. Twelve languages
   D. Fifteen languages

9. **What was used to differentiate families during tournaments and battle?**
   A. Specially designed swords
   B. Personalized armor
   C. Coats of Arms
   D. Flags

10. **The first clocks manufactured in the Black Forest made the sound of what animal every hour and half hour?**
    A. A rooster
    B. A cow
    C. A cat
    D. A donkey

11. **What draws 200,000 tourists to The Eisriesenwelt every summer?**

    A. Numerous tourist attractions

    B. Excellent weather during the summer months

    C. The largest ice caves in the world

    D. The Annual International Music Festival

12. **The Habsburg Empire was divided into what two states?**

    A. Cisleithania and Transleithania

    B. Furtwangen and Innsbruck

    C. Salzburg and Bern

    D. Germany and Austria

13. **How thick is the ice near the entrance of the ice caves?**

    A. 26 inches thick

    B. 10 yards thick

    C. 65 feet thick

    D. A mile thick

14. **What well-known American movie was filmed in the city of Salzburg?**

    A. Singing in the Rain

    B. The Sound of Music

    C. Amadeus

    D. Anne of Green Gables

15. **Emmental is another name for what?**

    A. A milk cow

    B. German chocolate

    C. The train station in Bern

    D. Swiss cheese

16. **What is one of the annual festivals held near Schloss Oberhofen?**

    A. Wurstfest

    B. The Barrel Organ Festival

    C. The Opera Festival

    D. Cider and Wassail Fest

SECTION 2.3.3

17. **What has been the symbol of Bern since the 16th century?**

    A. A red and blue striped flag

    B. Blacksmiths

    C. The brown bear

    D. Wooden coins

18. **What is the city of Furtwangen known for?**

    A. Clocks

    B. Cherries

    C. Trains

    D. Spoons

19. **According to his mother, what did King Ludwig spend most of his time doing as a child?**

    A. Fencing and horseback riding

    B. Dining and dancing

    C. Building and inventing

    D. Dressing up and play acting

20. **How long does Swiss cheese have to age before it is ready to be eaten?**

    A. A week

    B. A year

    C. Four months

    D. Eight weeks

21. **What famous musician was born in Salzburg?**

    A. Johann Sebastian Bach

    B. Ludwig van Beethoven

    C. Wolfgang Amadeus Mozart

    D. Frederic Chopin

22. **What has made the city of Neuchâtel, Switzerland well-known?**

    A. Cuckoo clocks were first manufactured there.

    B. It produces high-quality chocolate.

    C. It is home to the best ski resorts in the world.

    D. Numerous diamond mines are located on the outskirts of the city.

SECTION 2.3.3

23. **How long did King Ludwig II live in Neuschwanstein Castle?**
    A. One hundred days
    B. Five weeks
    C. Ten months
    D. Twelve years

24. **On two occasions, Innsbruck hosted a large event. What event was it?**
    A. The International Jazz Festival
    B. The Winter Olympics
    C. The Annual Bach Festival
    D. The European Music Showcase

25. **To commemorate the sacrifice and bravery of a group of Swiss soldiers, what was created?**
    A. The Lion Monument
    B. The Statue of the Soldier
    C. The Flying Eagle
    D. The Swiss Obelisk

You have completed all the sections for

Module 2.3

and are now ready to take the module test. Before continuing, be sure you have learned the objectives for each activity in this module.

Module 2.3 Test

INSTRUCTIONS   True or False. The following sentences are translated correctly. Check your answers in Appendix D, on page 401.

1. **Now it's your turn. = *Jetzt bist du an der Reihe.***
    A. True
    B. False

2. **Oh man, don't make me nervous. = *Ach Mensch, mach mich nicht nervös.***
    A. True
    B. False

3. **I'm furious. = *Ich bin traurig.***
    A. True
    B. False

4. **Just a moment. = *Moment mal.***
    A. True
    B. False

5. **First just count slowly from one to ten. = *Zähl erst mal langsam von eins bis zwanzig.***
    A. True
    B. False

6. **You must study hard. = *Du musst genug schlafen.***
    A. True
    B. False

7. Unfortunately, I've no desire for studying. = *Leider habe ich keine Lust zu studieren.*
   A. True
   B. False

8. Are you coming with us then? = *Kommst du denn mit uns?*
   A. True
   B. False

9. Yes. Please wait for me. Right away. = *Ja, bitte warten Sie auf mich. Sofort!*
   A. True
   B. False

10. All's well that ends well. = *Alles gut endet gut.*
   A. True
   B. False

11. *Was meinst du?* = What do you mean?
   A. True
   B. False

12. *Wir können das Gold mit einem Mal bekommen.* = We cannot get all the gold at one time.
   A. True
   B. False

13. *Wie können wir das machen?* = How can you do that?
   A. True
   B. False

14. *Wir können die Gans töten, sie öffnen und die ungelegten Eier herausnehmen.* = We can kill the goose, open it up and take out the unlaid eggs.
   A. True
   B. False

15. *Was denkst du, was sie gefunden hat?* = What do you think that they found?
   A. True
   B. False

16. **Da war nicht einmal ein goldenes Ei.** = There was not even a single golden egg.

    A. True

    B. False

17. **Sie war verschwunden.** = They were gone.

    A. True

    B. False

18. **Wegen ihrer Habgier, blieb ihnen nur, was sie zuvor hatten.** = Because of their charity, they were left with more than they had before.

    A. True

    B. False

19. **Dann erzählte er mir eine Geschichte.** = Then he read me a poem.

    A. True

    B. False

20. **Ich verstehe nicht, was du sagst.** = I don't understand what you are saying.

    A. True

    B. False

....

INSTRUCTIONS   Read the following story in German. In the questions that follow, choose the correct word choice.

Es war einmal ein Wolf, der Wasser aus dem Brunnen an einem Berghang trank. Als er mit seinen Augen aufblickte, bemerkte er ein trinkendes Lamm ein wenig bachabwärts. "Wenn mir bloß eine Entschuldigung dafür einfallen würde, dieses Lamm zu ergreifen, würde ich bestimmt ein leckeres Abendessen haben." Er schrie das Lamm brutal an: "Du großer Weichling, wie kannst du dich wagen, das Wasser zu beschmutzen, das ich trinke?" Das kleine Lamm sagte demütig: "Das kann nicht meine Schuld sein. Im Verhältnis zu dir bin ich bachabwärts. Das Wasser läuft von dir zu mir."

21. **Brunnen**

    A. bridge

    B. whale

    C. spring

    D. river

22. *Berghang*

   A. slope of a hill

   B. cliff

   C. mountain peak

   D. meadow

23. *Lamm*

   A. sheep

   B. lamb

   C. goat

   D. calf

24. *Entschuldigung*

   A. reason

   B. lie

   C. excuse

   D. plan

25. *leckeres*

   A. low-calorie

   B. tasty

   C. light

   D. free

You have completed all the modules for

Semester 2

Congratulations on completing this language course. Use German everyday and become a lifelong learner.

Appendix A
Student Answer Keys

Answers to activity questions and exercises are provided for checking the student's own work. Answers to module tests and section quizzes are found in Appendix D and are provided for grading purposes.

Activity Answers

Activity 3: Commentary

1. to buy
2. to write
3. to work
4. to play
5. to understand
6. to read
7. to think
8. to learn
9. to speak
10. to see
11. to hear

Activity 3: Self Quiz

1. *Ich will Deutsch lernen.*
2. *Wir wollen gut Deutsch sprechen.*
3. *Wollen Sie heute Deutsch lernen?*
4. *Warum müssen wir lauter sprechen?*
5. *Können sie uns nicht hören?*
6. *Willst du arbeiten oder spielen?*
7. *Können Sie Chinesisch verstehen?*
8. *Sollst du ein Auto kaufen?*

9. *Man muss hart lernen und denken.*
10. *Sie wollen jetzt mit uns spielen.*

Activity 4: Self Quiz

1. *Ich muss besser lernen.*
2. *Sie wollen mit uns Deutsch lernen.*
3. *Hans, du solltest dieses Buch lesen.*
4. *Herr und Frau Schultz, ihr solltet ein neues Auto kaufen.*
5. *Können wir ein Boot kaufen?*
6. *Wir können ein bisschen schneller sprechen. Ist das besser?*
7. *Hans, du musst ein bisschen lauter sprechen.*
8. *Wo wollen Sie arbeiten?*
9. *Können Sie heute mit uns arbeiten?*
10. *Kannst du mich jetzt hören?*
11. *Wer kann Chinesisch schreiben?*
12. *Ich kann Chinesisch lesen, aber ich kann es nicht schreiben.*

Activity 10: Self Quiz

1. *Wem*
2. *der*
3. *ihm*
4. *ihr*
5. *dir*
6. *dieser*
7. *diesem*
8. *euch*

9. *ihm, ihr*

10. *dir*

11. *mir*

Activity 11: Self Quiz

1. *Er gab einem Mann einen Mantel.*

2. *Er gab dem Mann den Mantel.*

3. *Er gab ihm auch einen Hut.*

4. *Er gab dem Kind eine Katze.*

5. *Er gab ihr auch einen Hut.*

6. *Er gab der Dame ein Buch.*

7. *Er gab dir und mir Geld.*

8. *Er gab meinem Vater eine Krawatte und meiner Mutter einen Ring.*

9. *Er gab deiner Tochter eine Bluse and deinem Sohn eine Krawatte.*

10. *Wer gab euch Geld?*

11. *Hans, gab Albert dir das Geld? or Hans, hat Albert dir das Geld gegeben?*

Activity 14: Self Quiz

1. *Wo*

2. *hinter der Dame*

3. *vor dir*

4. *vor mir, meiner Tochter*

5. *auf dem Sofa, euch*

6. *mit dem Mann, auf der Plattform*

Activity 15: Self Quiz

1. *Ich saß neben dem Mann, der dir das Buch gab.*

2. *Wer saß neben der Dame?*

3. *Hans saß neben euch.*

4. *Er saß auf dem Sofa, auf der Plattform.*

5. *Ich saß neben dem Kind, zwischen dem Hund und der Katze.*

6. *Wer stand hinter euch?*

7. *Vor mir saß ein kleines Kind mit einem großen Buch.*

8. *Die Dame, die neben mir saß, gab dir und ihm eine Krawatte.*

Activity 19: Observations

1. to believe

2. to follow

3. to help

4. to serve

5. to answer

6. to guess

Activity 19: Self Quiz

1. *Wer glaubt mir?*

2. *Ich glaube Ihnen.*

3. *Ich will dir helfen, Hans.*

4. *Kannst du uns helfen?*

5. *Wer kann euch helfen?*

6. *Wer soll mir folgen?*

7. *Wem soll ich folgen?*

8. *Du musst diesem Mann folgen, Hans.*

9. *Man muss seinem Vater und seiner Mutter dienen.*

10. *Glaubt Hans mir nicht?*

Activity 20: Self Quiz

1. *Man muss dem König dienen.*

2. *Hans, du solltest diesem Man helfen.*

3. *Ich soll Ihnen folgen.*

4. *Wer soll mir folgen?*

5. *Wie kann ich Ihnen helfen?*

6. *Hans, kannst du mir helfen?*

7. *Ich will dir nicht antworten, Marie.*

8. *Ich glaube euch nicht.*

9. *Glaubt Hans mir nicht?*

10. *Warum sollte er Ihnen glauben?*

Activity 25: Self Quiz

1. *dort*

2. *dorthin*

3. *dem*

4. *dahinter*

5. *davor*

6. *darauf*

Activity 31: Self Quiz 1

1. *des Hundes*
2. *der Katze*
3. *meines Sohnes*
4. *meiner Tochter*
5. *unserer Freunde*
6. *unserer Großmutter*
7. *Ihrer Freunde*
8. *meiner Freunde*
9. *seines Autos*
10. *der Soldaten*
11. *der Kinder*
12. *Mozarts Genie*
13. *dieses Tagebuchs*

Activity 31: Self Quiz 2

1. *Das Tagebuch meines Bruders (Vaters, Sohnes, Onkels, Freundes)*
2. *Das Tagebuch deiner Schwester (Mutter, Tochter, Tante, Freundin)*
3. *Das Tagebuch dieses Kindes (Mädchens, Fräuleins)*
4. *Das Tagebuch des Königs (Präsidenten, Doktors, Senators)*
5. *Das Tagebuch der Königin (Prinzessin, Studentin)*

Activity 32: Self Quiz

1. *Der Name des Kindes ist Marie.*
2. *Der Name meiner Katze ist Smokey.*
3. *Der Preis dieses Buches ist fünf Mark.*
4. *Der Preis dieser zwei Bücher ist nur zehn Mark.*
5. *Der Preis dieser Vase ist zehn Mark.*
6. *Heute ist der Geburtstag meiner Schwester.*
7. *Gestern war der Geburtstag meines Bruders.*
8. *Wir lesen das Tagebuch unseres Großvaters.*
9. *Haben Sie das Tagebuch Ihres Großvaters gelesen?*
10. *Wie lautet die Adresse Ihres Onkels in Berlin?*

11. *"Wir müssen schlafen," sagte einer der Männer.*
12. *"Nein," flüsterte eines der Kinder.*
13. *Hier sind Maries Buch und Richards Tagebuch.*
14. *Hier sind das Haus meines Vaters und das Auto meiner Mutter.*

Activity 38: Self Quiz

1. *Mein Schlüssel ist rot.*
2. *Dieser rote Schlüssel ist meiner.*
3. *Karls Schlüssel ist blau.*
4. *Mutters Schlüssel ist grün.*
5. *Dieses Buch ist nicht unseres; es ist Ihres.*
6. *Unser Buch ist grün; Ihr Buch ist blau.*
7. *Ja, Ihres ist das blaue; unseres ist das grüne.*
8. *Ihr Glas ist das rote; seins ist das grüne.*
9. *Diese Vase ist nicht meine; sie ist Vaters.*
10. *Diese Vase ist nicht unsere; sie ist ihre.*
11. *Wessen Armbanduhr ist das? Meine. Sie gehört mir.*
12. *Gehört dieser Ring Ihnen?*
13. *Ja, er ist meiner.*
14. *Und dieser gehört meiner Schwester.*
15. *Wem gehört dieses Ding? Uns.*

Activity 41: Challenge

Wenn du einen Bruder hättest und er eine Frau hätte, würde sie auch deine Schwägerin sein. So, eine Schwägerin ist die Frau deines Bruders.

Activity 43: Self Quiz

1. *Warme Milch*
2. *Kalter Tee*
3. *Kaltes Wasser*
4. *guter Milch, guten Tees*
5. *guter Leute*
6. *gutes Wasser, gute Milch*
7. *dem guten Wasser, der guten Milch*
8. *gutem Wasser, guter Milch*
9. *der guten Milch, des guten Tees*

10. *guter Milch, guten Tees*

Activity 44: Self Quiz

1. *Warme Milch ist gut.*
2. *Die warme Milch ist gut.*
3. *Kaltes Wasser ist gut.*
4. *Das kalte Wasser ist gut.*
5. *Kalter Tee ist nicht gut.*
6. *Der kalte Tee ist nicht gut.*
7. *Sie leben ohne gutes Wasser.*
8. *Er trinkt die gute Milch nicht.*
9. *Sie machen es mit kalter Milch.*
10. *Sie machen es mit der kalten Milch.*
11. *Der Preis des kleinen, roten Buches*
12. *Hier ist ein kleines, rotes Buch.*
13. *Wir lesen das kleine, rote Buch.*
14. *Wir leben ohne das kleine, rote Buch.*

Activity 53: Translation Exercise

1. *Geben Sie ihm die lange, weiße Linie.*
2. *Nehmen Sie alle Linien und legen Sie sie hierher.*
3. *Sind diese schwarzen Linien nicht kurz?*
4. *Diese schwarzen Linien sind auch nicht lang.*
5. *Diese weißen Linien liegen nicht; sie stehen.*
6. *Geben Sie mir nicht die schwarze Linie; geben Sie mir die weiße.*
7. *Nehmen Sie auch nicht diese schwarze Linie.*
8. *Hier ist die kurze, weiße Linie. Nehmen Sie sie, aber legen Sie sie nicht auf die schwarzen Linien.*
9. *Nehmen Sie die anderen zwei kurzen, weißen Linien.*
10. *Geben Sie ihm nicht diese Linien.*

Activity 54: Rapid Oral Translation 1

1. *Wer ist der Spion? Wer weiß? Ich weiß nicht.*
2. *Es ist sicher, dass es hier einen Schwindler gibt, einen Doppelagenten.*
3. *Der Fußballspieler, ist er ein Schwindler?*
4. *Ich glaube, er ist der Fußballspieler.*
5. *Nein, er ist nicht der Fußballspieler, aber er ist wahrscheinlich ein Doppelagent.*
6. *Die Prinzessin von Monaco, ist sie eine Freundin des Spions?*
7. *Wahrscheinlich, aber das bedeutet überhaupt nichts. Sie ist auch eine Freundin des Prinzen.*

Activity 54: Rapid Oral Translation 2

1. *Da ist ein Spion in dem Garten.*
2. *Ja, und wahrscheinlich ist eine Frau bei ihm.*
3. *Wirklich? Wissen Sie wer sie ist?*
4. *Ich weiß es nicht, aber sie könnte die Doppelagentin sein, die eine Freundin des Prinzen ist.*
5. *Robert, der Freund des Prinzen ist zweifellos ein Schwindler und ein gefährlicher Mann. Er könnte ein Spion sein.*
6. *Oh, das ist ziemlich merkwürdig.*
7. *Warum? Warum merkwürdig?*
8. *Weil…weil…Oh, ich weiß es nicht, aber es könnte sein, dass…*
9. *Die Situation ist schwerwiegend, nicht wahr?*
10. *Ich stimme Ihnen zu, sie ist sehr schwerwiegend.*

Appendix B
Scope and Sequence

Semester I Module I

Includes the following grammar and content:

Grammar	Content
Infinitive verb forms	Simple questions and answers
Modal auxiliary verbs	Telling a joke
Genders	Simple storytelling
The dative case	Grammar tests
Prepositions	Pronunciation practice
Personal pronouns: nominative, accusative, dative	Basic phone skills
Past, present, and future tenses	Oral translation exercises
Verb conjugations	Translation tests
Verbs that require a direct object	Listening and reading comprehension
	Pictographs
	Application of verbs and vocabulary
	Store-related vocabulary
	Some family vocabulary
	Short conversations
	Question words and related vocabulary
	Grammar tests
	Self quizzes
	Cultural information
	Section quizzes
	Module test

Semester I Module 2

Includes previous module plus the following:

Grammar	Content
Genitive—the preposition "of"	Vocabulary-building stories
Future tense and future progressive tense	Doctor-related vocabulary
Past tense verbs	Numbers with age and time
The dative and accusative cases	"Who" questions
Verbs of motion	Vocabulary relating to fishing and weather
Past tense verbs to present tense verbs (gerund form)	Reading, comprehending, and listening to only German
Subjunctive form	Some family-related vocabulary
Possession and belonging	Telling time
Additional prepositions	Small talk
Possessive pronouns	Grammar tests
	Self quizzes
	Cultural information
	Section quizzes
	Module test

Semester I Module 3

Includes previous two modules plus the following:

Grammar	Content
Adjectives—strong form	Vocabulary of family members
Imperative tense of verbs	Geometry-related vocabulary (basic shapes)
How to use possessives	Feelings and emotions
Possessional case	Introductions and farewells
Proper use of adjectives	Doctor-related vocabulary
	Grammar tests
	Self quizzes
	Cultural information

Grammar (cont.)	Content
	Section quizzes
	Module test

Semester 2 Module 1

Includes previous semester plus the following:

Grammar	Content
Review of there is / there are	Words and patterns
Dependent clauses	Vocabulary related to German food
Imperative tense verbs	Words and patterns
Expressing ownership	Vocabulary related to a university and to work
Additional past tense verbs	Listening and reading comprehension
Subjunctive tense verbs	Written and oral translation exercises
Attestation prefaces	Conversation practice
Manner	Generating sentences
Modifiers	Additional questions
Conjunctions	Additional animal vocabulary
Additional present tense verbs	Grammar tests
Reflexive verbs	Self quizzes
Gerund phrases	Cultural information
Present perfect tense verbs	Section quizzes
	Module test

Semester 2 Module 2

Includes previous module plus the following:

Grammar	Content
Future tense	Farm-related vocabulary
Additional past tense	Consonant names
Additional imperative	Creating dialogues
Past perfect tense	Grammar tests
Additional dependent clauses	Self quizzes

Grammar (cont.)	Content
Additional prepositional phrases	Cultural information
Additional present perfect tense	Section quizzes
	Module test

Semester 2 Module 3

Includes previous two modules plus the following:

Grammar	Content
Additional dependent clauses	Listening and reading comprehension
Additional past tense	Descriptions
Additional future tense	Pronunciation practice
Additional prepositional phrases	Grammar tests
Additional present perfect tense	Self quizzes
Additional past perfect tense	Cultural information
Additional gerund phrases	Section quizzes
Expressing similarities	Module test
Additional imperative tense	
Conditional tense verbs	

Semester 1 Objectives

Activity 1
→ Comprehend the meaning of a story.

Activity 2
→ Understand new vocabulary in a conversation or story.

Activity 3
→ Master object pronouns with finite and infinite verbs.

Activity 4
→ Test your knowledge of finite and infinite verbs.

Activity 5
→ Understand the story of "The Three Little Pigs" in German.

Activity 6
→ Understand new vocabulary in a conversation or story.

Activity 7
→ Understand and use small talk.

Activity 8
→ Expand grammar skills.

Activity 9
→ Identify and describe objects.

Activity 10
→ Build fluency for dative case.

Activity 11
→ Recognize how much German you can comprehend, say, read, and write.

Activity 12
→ Comprehend the meaning of a story and use that knowledge to write your own story.

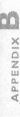

Activity 13
→ Understand the story of "The Three Billy Goats" in German.

Activity 14
→ Expand preposition skills.

Activity 15
→ Test your knowledge of prepositions.

Activity 16
→ Learn family relationships.

Activity 17
→ Expand your comprehension toward complete understanding.

Activity 18
→ Expand comprehension, fluency, and use of past and present tense.

Activity 19
→ Build fluency for dative case.

Activity 20
→ Test your knowledge of the dative case.

Activity 21
→ Use more small talk on a formal level.

Activity 22
→ Recognize how much German you can comprehend, say, read, and write.

Activity 23
→ Understand new vocabulary in a conversation or story.

Activity 24
→ Learn how to use the accusative case, dative case, and motion verbs.

Activity 25
→ Practice the use of prepositional compounds.

Activity 26
→ Practice the use of motion verbs.

Activity 27
→ Master new vocabulary.

Activity 28
→ Follow a *Geschichte* with full comprehension.

Activity 29
→ Follow a conversation and understand its meaning.

Activity 30
→ Use repetition to gain full comprehension.

Activity 31
→ Learn the rules of the genitive case.

Activity 32
→ Test your knowledge of the genitive case.

Activity 33
→ Comprehend the meaning of a story.

Activity 34
→ Use more small talk on a formal level.

Activity 35
→ Expand your comprehension toward complete understanding.

Activity 36
→ Comprehend the meaning of a story.

Activity 37
→ Learn how to use possessives.

Activity 38
→ Test your knowledge of possessional case.

Activity 39
→ Follow a *Geschichte* with full comprehension.

Activity 40
→ Comprehend the meaning of a story.

Activity 41
→ Read a dialogue for comprehension and then repeat it.

Activity 42
→ Understand vocabulary in the areas of geometry.

Activity 43
→ Learn proper adjective use.

Activity 44
→ Test your knowledge of adjective use.

Activity 45
→ Use more small talk on a formal level.

Activity 46
→ Master new vocabulary.

Activity 47
→ Follow a conversation and understand its meaning.

Activity 48
→ Master new vocabulary.

Activity 49
→ Read a dialogue for comprehension and then repeat it.

Activity 50
→ Increase reading, listening comprehension, and vocabulary usage.

Activity 51
→ Recognize your ability to understand German.

Activity 52
→ Recognize your ability to understand German.

Activity 53
→ Increase reading comprehension, and vocabulary usage.

Semester 2 Objectives

Activity 54
→ Master new vocabulary.

Activity 55
→ Recognize your ability to understand German.

Activity 56
→ Read and understand a *Geschichte auf deutsch.*

Activity 57
→ Read and listen to a *Geschichte* and understand new vocabulary from context.

Activity 58
→ Read to increase all skill levels of language learning.

Activity 59
→ Read a *Geschichte auf deutsch* and recognize and understand new vocabulary from context.

Activity 60
→ Learn and use important phrases.

Activity 61
→ Increase reading, listening comprehension, and vocabulary usage.

Activity 62
→ Follow a story and understand its meaning.

Activity 63
→ Recognize your ability to understand German.

Activity 64
→ Listen to a German *Geschichte* and maintain comprehension without a text.

Activity 65
→ Use more small talk on a formal level.

Activity 66
→ Recognize your ability to understand German.

Activity 67
→ Read and understand a *Geschichte auf deutsch.*

Activity 68
→ Read to increase all skill levels of language learning.

Activity 69
→ Recognize how much German you can comprehend, say, and read.

Activity 70
→ Expand your comprehension toward complete understanding.

Activity 71
→ Follow a conversation and understand its meaning.

Activity 72
→ Follow a *Geschichte* with full comprehension.

Activity 73
→ Read and understand a *Geschichte auf deutsch.*

Activity 74
→ Follow a conversation and understand its meaning.

Activity 75
→ Read and comprehend *Geschichte* that are longer.

Activity 76
→ Read a *Geschichte* and retell it from memory.

Activity 77
→ Recognize how much German you can comprehend, say, and read.

Activity 78
→ Expand your comprehension toward complete understanding.

Appendix C
Index of Marginalia

Introduction

Culture facts and other interesting information can be found in the margins throughout the course. While not part of your course curriculum, these marginalia provide a fun and educational view into the many exciting facets of German-speaking regions.

Index

Culture Notes

As you've worked through the course, you may have been interested in certain countries or interesting facts and histories. Write any notes about people, places, or things that you would like do more research on.

Appendix D
Grading Answer Keys

Module Test Answers

1.1	1.2	1.3	2.1	2.2	2.3
1. A	1. D	1. A	1. B	1. A	1. A
2. C	2. A	2. A	2. A	2. B	2. A
3. D	3. C	3. B	3. C	3. B	3. B
4. D	4. C	4. A	4. A	4. A	4. A
5. A	5. D	5. A	5. A	5. A	5. B
6. B	6. B	6. B	6. D	6. A	6. B
7. D	7. B	7. A	7. D	7. B	7. A
8. C	8. C	8. D	8. B	8. B	8. A
9. A	9. B	9. D	9. C	9. B	9. A
10. B	10. D	10. B	10. A	10. A	10. A
11. D	11. C	11. A	11. D	11. A	11. A
12. A	12. D	12. C	12. C	12. A	12. B
13. D	13. B	13. D	13. D	13. B	13. B
14. C	14. C	14. A	14. B	14. B	14. A
15. B	15. B	15. A	15. A	15. A	15. A
16. B	16. B	16. C	16. C	16. B	16. A
17. A	17. B	17. B	17. A	17. C	17. B
18. A	18. C	18. D	18. D	18. A	18. B
19. B	19. A	19. B	19. B	19. C	19. B
20. A	20. C	20. A	20. D	20. C	20. A
21. B	21. D	21. D	21. A	21. A	21. C
22. B	22. C	22. C	22. B	22. A	22. A
23. B	23. A	23. D	23. B	23. B	23. B
24. A	24. D	24. B	24. A	24. D	24. C
25. B	25. C	25. A	25. A	25. D	25. B

Section Quiz Answers

1.1.1	1.1.2	1.1.3	1.2.1	1.2.2	1.2.3	1.3.1	1.3.2	2.1.1	2.1.2	2.2.1	2.3.1	2.3.2	2.3.3
1. C	1. A	1. C	1. C	1. A	1. B	1. C	1. D	1. B	1. C	1. A	1. D	1. A	1. A
2. D	2. C	2. D	2. D	2. B	2. A	2. D	2. C	2. D	2. A	2. A	2. C	2. C	2. C
3. B	3. D	3. B	3. A	3. B	3. A	3. C	3. B	3. D	3. D	3. C	3. B	3. B	3. C
4. A	4. A	4. C	4. D	4. A	4. C	4. B	4. D	4. C	4. C	4. B	4. C	4. B	4. B
5. C	5. D	5. A	5. B	5. C	5. D	5. D	5. A	5. D	5. C	5. A	5. D	5. D	5. D
6. D	6. B	6. C	6. B	6. C	6. D	6. B	6. C	6. A	6. A	6. C	6. A	6. A	6. A
7. C	7. A	7. D	7. C	7. D	7. D	7. A	7. D	7. C	7. B	7. C	7. D	7. C	7. B
8. A	8. D	8. A	8. B	8. D	8. A	8. C	8. D	8. A	8. D	8. A	8. B	8. A	8. D
9. D	9. C	9. D	9. A	9. A	9. B	9. D	9. B	9. C	9. D	9. A	9. A	9. C	9. C
10. B	10. D	10. C	10. D	10. B	10. C	10. A	10. A	10. D	10. C	10. C	10. C	10. C	10. A
													11. C
													12. A
													13. C
													14. B
													15. D
													16. B
													17. C
													18. A
													19. D
													20. C
													21. C
													22. B
													23. A
													24. B
													25. A